ENTITY RESOLUTION AND INFORMATION QUALITY

ENTITY RESOLUTION AND INFORMATION QUALITY

JOHN R. TALBURT

AMSTERDAM • BOSTON • HEIDELBERG • LONDON
NEW YORK • OXFORD • PARIS • SAN DIEGO
SAN FRANCISCO • SINGAPORE • SYDNEY • TOKYO

Morgan Kaufmann Publishers is an imprint of Elsevier

ELSEVIER

Morgan Kaufmann Publishers is an imprint of Elsevier.
30 Corporate Drive, Suite 400, Burlington, MA 01803, USA

This book is printed on acid-free paper.

Notices
Knowledge and best practice in this field are constantly changing. As new research and experience
broaden our understanding, changes in research methods, professional practices, or medical
treatment may become necessary.

Practitioners and researchers must always rely on their own experience and knowledge in
evaluating and using any information, methods, compounds, or experiments described herein.
In using such information or methods they should be mindful of their own safety and the safety
of others, including parties for whom they have a professional responsibility.

To the fullest extent of the law, neither the Publisher nor the authors, contributors, or editors,
assume any liability for any injury and/or damage to persons or property as a matter of products
liability, negligence or otherwise, or from any use or operation of any methods, products,
instructions, or ideas contained in the material herein.

Library of Congress Cataloging-in-Publication Data
Application submitted

British Library Cataloguing-in-Publication Data
A catalogue record for this book is available from the British Library.

ISBN: 978-0-12-381972-7

For information on all Morgan Kaufmann publications,
visit our Web site at www.mkp.com or www.elsevierdirect.com

Printed and bound by CPI Group (UK) Ltd, Croydon, CR0 4YY

Dedication

To Rebeca and Geneva for their patience and understanding during the writing of this book

CONTENTS

FOREWORD

Entity resolution is the process of probabilistically identifying some real thing based upon a set of possibly ambiguous clues. Humans have been performing entity resolution throughout history. Early humans looked at footprints and tried to match that clue to the animals that made the tracks. Later, people with special domain knowledge looked at the shape of a whale's spout to determine if the particular whale belonged to the right class of whale to hunt. During World War II, English analysts learned to identify individual German radio operators solely based upon that operator's "fist," the timing and style the operator used to key Morse code.

In the middle of the twentieth century, people began applying the power of computers to the problem of entity resolution. For example, entity resolution techniques were used to process and analyze U.S. Census records and the early direct marketing industry developed "merge-purge" systems to help identify and resolve individuals and households. The speed of the computer allows analysis of far more data than possible by a human expert, but requires that the heuristics and expertise we often take for granted in humans to be codified into algorithms the computer can execute.

One industry that is particularly interested in effective entity resolution is the direct marketing industry. Acxiom Corporation provides many entity resolution services to the direct marketing industry and has developed many tools and algorithms to address the entity resolution problem. I met John Talburt in 1996 when we both began work at Acxiom. At that time, much of the knowledge about how to effectively apply computers to the problem of entity resolution was fragmented and dispersed. For example, the criteria for what made two entities similar or distinct was often defined differently across teams, as was the assessment of the quality of the results. Similarly, from a technical perspective, the strategies and techniques for extracting clues from digital data, including possible transformations to correct or enhance the extracted clues, were often based directly upon the experience of the particular people involved. This was also true of the matching algorithms used for resolution. While some papers had been published about the techniques, much of the knowledge was held in the heads of practitioners. That knowledge was carefully guarded and often considered as trade secrets or as competitive advantages, particularly in the commercial sector.

In 1997, John and I, along with several others at Acxiom, set out to create a single entity resolution system that combined all the experience and knowledge about entity resolution for names and postal addresses. The product resulting from this effort is called AbiliTec™. At the start of the AbiliTec™ project, most of the people working on the project had either no previous background in entity resolution or hard won trial-and-error knowledge from implementing previous entity resolution systems. I was one of the ones with no previous knowledge and looking back, I realize, not for the first time, how valuable a comprehensive introductory book would have been to our efforts.

I am very happy that John has written this book to help fill that need. In this book, John has brought organization to the topic and provides definitions and clarifications to terminology that has been overlapping and confusing. This book continues the transformation of entity resolution into a discipline rather than merely a toolbox of techniques. John is uniquely qualified to write this book. He not only has practical experience building important real-world entity resolution systems (e.g., AbiliTec™), but also the academic background to explain and unify the theory of entity resolution. John also brings his expertise in information quality to this book. Information quality and entity resolution are closely related and John, along with Rich Wang from MIT, were the driving forces behind the creation of the Information Quality program at the University of Arkansas at Little Rock (UALR). This was the first program of its kind in the world and is at the center of the information quality field.

I am writing this forward on September 11, 2010, the anniversary of the terrorist attacks on Washington and New York. This gives me a perspective on how entity resolution continues to expand and evolve since the early "merge-purge" days. Following the terrorist attacks, the United States government investigated how entity resolution techniques could help prevent such attacks. The government looked at entity resolution techniques not only already employed by the security agencies, but also commercial systems such as those used in the gambling industry and the direct marketing industry. John was engaged, and is still engaged, in some of the work with the government on these problems. Much of the entity resolution work up to that time was focused on analyzing direct attributes of an individual (e.g., name, address, date of birth, etc.), but these efforts brought much more focus on the links between people and how those links can help in identifying and resolving not only at the individual level, but also at the group level.

Resolution through linkage has become critical not only for security and law enforcement work, but also in analysis of social networks. Indeed, the explosion of applications on the Internet has generated many new challenges for entity resolution. The early direct marketing industry dealt with people with known names at postal addresses. Today, in the Internet world, people are increasingly known by multiple artificial names or personas and are contacted through virtual addresses. This requires new techniques for entity resolution. For example, resolving anonymous entities (e.g., visitors at a web site) based upon browsing "fingerprints" (e.g., IP address of the client machine, operating system of that machine, the browser used, etc.) is an interesting challenge and an active area of work. Examples such as this also bring questions of privacy into the discussion of entity resolution. Similarly, efforts supporting selective exposure of private data on the Internet (e.g., information cards) and distributed authentication (e.g., OpenID) also complicate and expand the discussion of entity resolution from both a technical and policy perspective. This book will not only help provide the background for these efforts, but also help organize and frame the discussions as entity resolution continues to evolve.

Terry Talley
September 11, 2010

PREFACE

Motivation for the Book

Entity resolution (ER) and information quality (IQ) are both emerging disciplines in the field of information science. It is my hope that this book will make some contribution to the growing bodies of knowledge in these areas. I find it very rewarding to be a part of starting something new. The opportunity to help organize the first graduate degree programs in IQ has been an exciting journey. One of the struggles has been to find appropriate books and resources for the students. Not many college-level textbooks have been written on these topics. With the notable exceptions of *Introduction to Information Quality* by Craig Fisher, Eitel Lauria, Shobha Chengalur-Smith, and Richard Wang, and *Journey to Data Quality* by Yang Lee, Leo Pipino, James Funk, and Richard Wang, most of the titles in the area of IQ have been written by practitioners for primarily for other practitioners. However, I must say that this is not necessarily a bad thing. Very practical and detailed books like *Data Quality Assessment* by Arkady Madanchik and *Executing Data Quality Projects: Ten Steps to Quality Data and Trusted Information* have served well as texts for some of our classes and have been well-received by both instructors and students. As more schools begin to teach courses in these areas I have no doubt that more textbooks will be produced to meet the demand.

As you read this book, especially Chapter 2, you will see that I take a very broad view of IQ. I think that the six-domain framework of IQ knowledge and skills developed by the International Association for Information and Data Quality (IAIDQ) that also appears in Chapter 2 is an excellent outline of the scope of the new discipline. It confirms that many of the currently popular information technology and information management themes such as master data management and data governance properly fall within the discipline of IQ, and that many others such as entity and identity resolution and information architecture to have very strong bonds with IQ.

This book has emerged from the material developed for a graduate course titled Entity Resolution and Information Quality that has been offered as an elective in the Information Quality Graduate Program at the University of Arkansas at Little Rock since the fall of 2009. In these offerings, the book *Data Quality and Record Linkage Techniques* by Thomas Herzog, Fritz Scheuren, and William Winkler has been an important resource for the students. Although I highly recommend this book for its excellent coverage of value imputation, the Fellegi-Sunter record linkage model, and a number of well-written case studies, it does not cover the breadth of topics that in my view comprise the whole of entity resolution. As with IQ, I also take a very broad view of entity resolution, and one of my goals for writing this book was to encourage both ER and IQ researchers and practitioners to take a more holistic view of both of these topics.

My observation has been that there are many highly-qualified practitioners and researchers publishing in these areas. For example, it is not hard to find papers that plumb the depths of almost any given topic in entity resolution. My hope is that this book will help place these more narrowly defined topics into the larger framework of ER, and that by doing so, it will promote the cross-fertilization of ideas and techniques among them. I am sure that not everyone will entirely agree with my definitions or categorizations, but this is the view I offer for the reader's consideration. Knowledge grows by examining and contrasting ideas, and building step-by-step on the work of others.

Audience

Although written in textbook format, I believe that IT professionals, as well as students, will find it helpful. Even for experts in this area, I think it can be useful if for no other reason than to provide an organized perspective at the very broad range of topics that comprise entity resolution. My hope is that the designers of ER systems may be inspired to create even more robust applications by integrating some of the techniques and methods presented here that they had not previously considered. I also think that the material in this book will be useful to both technical and non-technical managers who want to be conversant in the basic terminology and concepts related to this important area of information systems technology.

Because IQ is very interdisciplinary, the UALR Information Quality program was positioned as a graduate program to accommodate students coming from a variety of undergraduate disciplines. Even though the course that motivated the writing of this book is taught at the graduate level, most of the material is accessible to upper-division undergraduate students and could support either an undergraduate or a dual-listed graduate/undergraduate course.

Organization of the Material

The first two chapters of the book cover the principles of ER and the principles of IQ, respectively. They cover the basic terminology and concepts that are used throughout the remainder of the book including the definition of ER, the unique reference assumption, and the fundamental law of ER. The main thrust of Chapter 1 is the ER is much more than just record matching, that it is about determining the equivalence of references. It discusses the five ER activities of entity reference extraction, entity reference preparation, entity reference resolution, entity identity management, and entity association analysis. Chapter 1 also introduces the four ER architectures of merge-purge or record linkage, heterogeneous database join, identity resolution, and identity capture, and the four methods for determining the equivalence of references including direct matching, transitive equivalence, association analysis, and asserted equivalence.

Chapter 2 outlines the emerging discipline of IQ. Here the primary emphasis is that IQ must always be connected to business value, that IQ is more than just cleaning data, it is about viewing information as a non-fungible asset of the organization and that its quality is directly related to the value produced by its application. It also discusses the information product model of IQ and the application of TQM principles to IQ management. Both Chapter 1 and 2 speak to the close relationship between ER and IQ.

Chapter 3 describes the major theoretical models that underpin the basic aspects of ER starting with the Fellegi-Sunter theory of record linkage. This is followed by the Stanford Entity Resolution Framework and the Algebraic Model for Entity Resolution with a brief description of the ENRES meta-model.

Chapter 4 is a brief excursion into the realm of entity-based data integration (EBDI). It describes a model for EBDI that is an extension of the algebraic model for entity resolution. The algebraic EBDI model provides a framework for formally describing integration contexts and operators independently of their actual implementation. It also discusses some of the more commonly defined integration selection operators and how they are evaluated.

As a balance to the theoretical discussions in Chapters 3 and 4, the material in Chapter 5 describes the operation of three commercial ER systems. It also includes step-by-step details on how two of these tools are setup to execute actual ER scenarios.

Chapter 6 extends Chapter 5 by describing a non-commercial, open-source system called OYSTER. Although used in this book as an instructional tool, OYSTER has the demonstrated capability of supporting real applications in business and government. OYSTER is the only open-source ER system with a resolution engine that can be configured to perform merge-purge (record linkage), identity resolution, or identity capture operations. An appendix to the book provides the reader with example OYSTER XML scripts that can be used to operate each of these configurations and guidance for those who want to download and experiment with OYSTER.

Chapter 7 discusses some of the trends in ER research and practice. These include the growing use of identity resolution to support information hubs, the impact high-performance computing on entity resolution, research in the application of graph theory and network analysis to improve resolution results, and the use of machine learning techniques, such as genetic programming, to optimize the accuracy of entity-based data integration.

In addition to OYSTER, another important resource for the material in this book is the use of synthetic data. Synthetic data solves one of the more difficult problems in teaching ER and IQ when the entities are persons. Privacy and legal concerns make it very difficult to obtain and use personally identifiable information. Even though using trivial examples such as, John Doe on Elm Street, can illustrate many of the basic ER concepts, they fail to exhibit the many complexities, nuances, and data quality issues that make real entity references difficult to resolve. In order to give students more realistic ER exercises, synthetic data is used. The synthetic data used in the Chapter 5 scenarios are available to the reader through the Center for Advanced Research in Entity Resolution and Information Quality (ERIQ, ualr.edu/eriq). The data was generated in previous research projects as a way to simulate a population of synthetically generated identities of different ages moving through a set of real US addresses over a period of time.

ACKNOWLEDGEMENTS

There are many people and organizations whose support for the UALR Information Quality Graduate Program and the Center for Advanced Research in Entity Resolution and Information Quality (ERIQ) have made it possible for me to write this book and to whom I owe a great debt of gratitude. First and foremost I want to thank my friend and mentor Dr. Richard Wang, Director of the MIT IQ Program and currently serving as the Chief Data Quality Officer and Deputy Chief Data Officer of the U.S. Army. Without his vision, encouragement, and tireless efforts to establish information quality as an academic discipline none of my work would have been possible. I am also grateful to Acxiom Corporation and its leadership team for its willingness to underwrite and support these programs during their formation especially former Acxiom executives Charles Morgan, Rodger Kline, Alex Dietz, Jerry Adams, Don Hinman, Zack Wilhoit, Jim Womble, and Wally Anderson, as well as, the current CEO, John Meyer, and executives Jennifer Barrett, Jerry Jones, Chad Fitz, Todd Greer, and Catherine Hughes. I would also like to thank Dr. Mary Good, the Founding Dean of the UALR Donaghey College of Engineering and Information Technology for her support and willingness to embark into uncharted academic waters.

Special thanks to Mike Shultz, CEO of Infoglide Software, who provided the academic license for their Identity Resolution Engine (IRE); and Bob Barker of 2020 Outlook who helped to arrange the collaboration. Also Dr. Jim Goodnight, President of SAS who provided the academic license for dfPowerStudio; and Lisa Dodson, Product Manager for DataFlux; who helped us learn how to use it.

Others who have provided support include Jim Boardman, Dr. Neal Gibson, and Dr. Greg Holland, Arkansas Department of Education; Rick McGraw, Managing Partner for Black Oak Partners; Alba Alemán and Raymond Roberts, Citizant; Frank Ponzio, Symbolic Systems; Larry English, Information Impact International; Michael Boggs, Analytix Data Services; Ken Kotansky and Steven Meister, AMB New Generation Empowerment; Terry Talley, Southwest Power Pool; Chuck Backus, Lexis-Nexis (who suggested the student data challenge exercise); Rob Williams and Brian Tsou, US Air Force Research Laboratory (AFRL) at Wright Patterson Air Force Base, as well as Qbase and the Wright Brothers Institute in Dayton, Ohio.

I would also like to acknowledge Dr. Ali Kooshesh, Sonoma State University, for his work on the genetic programming approach to entity-based data integration, and Dr. Ray Hashemi, Armstrong Atlantic State University, who assisted me on several ER-related projects. I also owe a great debt to the many students who have contributed to the development of this material especially Eric Nelson his for help in the development of OYSTER; Yinle Zhou, my teaching assistant in the ER course and co-developer with Sabitha Shiviah of the synthetic data generator (SOG); Isaac Osesina for providing input on entity reference extraction and named-entity recognition (NER); and Fumiko Kobayashi for her work in testing and documenting OYSTER. Finally I would like to thank my Department Chair, Dr. Elizabeth Pierce, and my support staff including Natalie Rego, Administrative Assistant for the Information Quality Graduate Program, Brenda Barnhill, the ERIQ Center Program Manager, and Gregg Webster, the ERIQ Center Technical Manager.

1

PRINCIPLES OF ENTITY RESOLUTION

Entity Resolution

Entity resolution (ER) is the process of determining whether two references to real-world objects are referring to the same object or to different objects. The term *entity* describes the real-world object, a person, place, or thing, and the term *resolution* is used because ER is fundamentally a decision process to answer (resolve) the question, Are the references to the same or to different entities? Although the ER process is defined between pairs of references, it can be systematically and successively applied to a larger set of references so as to aggregate all the references to same object into subsets or clusters. Viewed in this larger context, ER is also defined as "the process of identifying and merging records judged to represent the same real-world entity" (Benjelloun, Garcia-Molina, Menestrina, et al., 2009).

Entities are described in terms of their characteristics, called *attributes*. The values of these attributes provide information about a specific entity. *Identity attributes* are those that when taken together distinguish one entity from another. Identity attributes for people are things such as name, address, date of birth, and fingerprint—the kinds of things often asked for to identify the person requesting a driver's license or hospital admission. For a product identity, attributes might be model number, size, manufacturer, or universal product code (UPC).

A *reference* is a collection of attributes values for a specific entity. When two references are to the same entity, they are sometimes said to *co-refer* (Chen, Kalashnikov, Mehtra, 2009) or to be *matching references* (Benjelloun, et al., 2009). However, for reasons that will be clear later, the term *equivalent references* will be used throughout this text to describe references to the same entity.

An important assumption throughout the following discuss of ER is the *unique reference assumption*. The unique reference assumption simply states that a reference is always created to refer to one, and only one, entity. The reason for this assumption is that in real-world situations a reference may appear to be ambiguous—that is, it could refer to more than one entity or possibly no entity. For example, a salesperson could write a product description on a sales order, but because the description is incomplete, the person processing the order might not be clear about which product is to be ordered. Despite this problem, it was the intent of the salesperson to reference a specific product. The degree of completeness, accuracy, timeliness, believability, consistency, accessibility, and other aspects of reference data can affect the operation of ER processes and produce better or worse outcomes. This is one of the reasons that ER is so closely related to the field of information quality (IQ).

Background

The concepts of entity and attribute are foundational to the *entity-relation model* (ERM) that is at the very core of modern data modeling and database schema design. The entity-relation diagram (ERD) is the graphical representation of an ERM and has long been considered a necessary artifact for any database development project. The relational model, first described by E. F. Codd (1970), was later refined into what we now know as the ERM by Peter Chen (1976). In the ERM, information systems are conceptualized as a collection of entities, each having a set of descriptive attributes and also having well-defined relationships with other entities.

Figure 1.1 shows a simple ERD illustrating a data model with three entity types: Instructor, Course, and Student. The line connecting the Instructor and Course entity types indicates that there is a relation between them. Similarly, the diagram shows that Course and Student entity types are related. Furthermore, in the ERD style used here, the adornments on the relation line give more detail about these relationships. For example, the triangular configuration of short lines, sometimes called a crow's

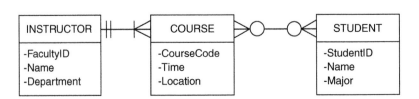

Figure 1.1: Example of a Simple ERD

foot, at the junction of the relation line with an entity indicates a *many-to-one relationship*. In this example it indicates that one Instructor entity may be related to (be the instructor for) more than one Course entity. The additional adornment of a single bar with the crow's foot further constrains the relation by indicating that each Instructor entity must be related to (assigned to) at least one Course entity. The double bar at the junction of this same relation and the Instructor entity is used to indicate an *exactly-one relationship*. Here it represents the constraint that each Course entity must be related to (has assigned to it) one, and only one, Instructor entity. The crow's foot symbol with a circle that appears at both ends of the relation between the Course and Student entities indicates a *zero-to-many relation*. This means that any given Student entity may be related to (enrolled in) several Course entities, or in none. Conversely, any given Course entity may be related to (have in it) several Student entities, or none.

Each entity type also has a set of attributes that describes the entity. For example, the Instructor entity type has the three attributes FacultyID, Name, and Department. Assigning values to these attributes defines a particular instructor, called an *instance* of the Instructor entity. By the previous definition, an instance of an entity is also an entity reference. A fundamental rule of ERM is that every instance of an entity should have a unique identifier. Codd (1970) called this the Entity Identity Rule. A *primary key* is an identity attribute or group of identity attributes selected by the data modeler because the combination of values taken on by these attributes will be unique for each entity instance. However, at the design stage, it is not always clear that a particular combination of descriptive attributes will have this property, or it if does, that the combination will continue to be unique as more instances of the entity are acquired. For this reason data modelers often play it safe by adding another attribute to an entity type that does not describe any intrinsic characteristic of the entity but is simply there to guarantee that each instance of the entity has a primary key. For example, in Figure 1.1, with only name and department as the identity attributes for the Instructor entity, it is conceivable that a department could have two instructors with the same name. If this were to happen, the combination of name and department would no longer meet the requirements to form a primary key. By adding a FacultyID attribute as a third attribute and by controlling the values assigned to FacultyID, it is possible to guarantee that each instance of the Instructor entity has a unique primary key value. Called *surrogate keys,* the values for these artificial keys have no intrinsic meaning, such as a FacultyID value of "T1234" or an Employee_Number of "387."

In theory, ER should never be a problem in a well-designed database because two entity instances should be equivalent if, and only if, they have the same primary key. When this is true, it allows information about the same entity in different tables of the database to be brought together by simply matching instances with the same primary key value through what is called a *table join operation*.

The problem is that these artificial primary keys must be assigned when the instance is entered into the database and maintained throughout the life cycle of the entity, and there is no guarantee that this will always be done correctly. An even greater problem is that the same entity may be represented in different databases or even different tables within the same database, using a different primary key. In other situations the references may lack key values because they came from a nondatabase source or were extracted from a database without including the key. ER in a database context is sometimes referred to as the problem of *heterogeneous database join* (Thuraisingham, 2003; Sidló, 2009).

ER systems that provide heterogeneous database join functionality are often employed by law enforcement and intelligence agencies, where each agency maintains a separate database of entities of interest, with each using a different scheme for primary keys. In this setting, the ER system acts as a "hub" that connects to each of the databases. When an entity reference from an investigation is entered, the system reformats the reference information as a query appropriate to each database and returns the matching results to the user. The Identity Resolution Engine® by Infoglide Software®, discussed in Chapter 5, is an example of a commercial system that provides this type of functionality. Chapter 7 discusses the growing trend to use ER hub architectures as a solution to the problem of bringing together information about a common set of entities held in independently maintained systems.

Entity versus Entity Reference

Although instances of an entity type are often called entities by data modelers, it is important to understand that in the context of ER, instances of an ERM entity type are not entities. An instance of an entity type, such as the Student entity type in Figure 1.1, is just a row in the Student database table inside the computer. The instance is only a reference to a real student walking around campus and attending classes. In an ER context, entities do not exist in the information system—they exist in the real world. More than a nuance in terminology, the distinction between an entity and an entity reference is fundamental to understanding ER.

ER Principle #1: Information systems store and manipulate references to entities, not the entities.

Figure 1.2 illustrates how many combinations and variations of identity attributes such as name, size, quantity, manufacturer, and product code can lead to multiple references to the same item. The same situation can occur with place entities that have attributes such as postal address, global positioning system (GPS) coordinates, or landmark references, and event entities that have attributes such as name, date, time, attendees, and location.

As a business example, suppose that the entity type is a customer of a business—a person. The same customer may be referenced by many different records in the company's information system or, in some cases, multiple systems. There are many reasons that a company might create multiple references to the same customer. It may be the result of the customer having purchased items through different branches, departments, or sales channels of the company. Each sales channel often has its own database, and that database may not be properly integrated with other databases in the company. Databases that do not share information across the company with other systems are sometimes called *data silos*. Recognition that information about critical business entity types such as customer and product should be synchronized across the entire enterprise has given rise to the practice of *master data management* (MDM) (Loshin, 2008).

Another reason for the proliferation of customer references in a business is that customer characteristics, especially contact information, change over time. If changes to customer contact information such as name, mailing address, telephone, or email

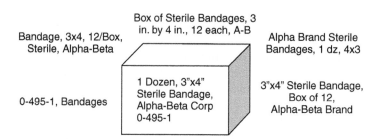

Bandage, 3x4, 12/Box, Sterile, Alpha-Beta

Box of Sterile Bandages, 3 in. by 4 in., 12 each, A-B

Alpha Brand Sterile Bandages, 1 dz, 4x3

1 Dozen, 3"x4" Sterile Bandage, Alpha-Beta Corp 0-495-1

0-495-1, Bandages

3"x4" Sterile Bandage, Box of 12, Alpha-Beta Brand

Figure 1.2: Entity versus Entity References

address are not captured and managed properly, the system may assume that transactions using the unrecorded contact information represent a new customer rather than one the system already recognizes. Recognizing that these records are actually references to the same customer is the essence of ER.

In other cases the problem may simply be the lack of proper information quality controls on manual data entry that allow errors or variations in data values to enter the system. Maydanchik (2007) describes a number of ways in which data quality errors can be introduced into an information system, including bringing data from outside, by processes changing data within the system, and through data decay.

ER in the context of customers, whether the customers are consumers (individuals) or other businesses, is called *customer data integration* (CDI). CDI is an essential component of *customer relationship management* (CRM). CRM is an enterprisewide process intended to give a company a competitive advantage by improving each customer's experience with the business. Dyché and Levy (2006) describe CRM as implying "that a company is thinking about and acting toward its customers individually ..." An obvious first step in accomplishing this objective is to have a complete picture of a customer's interactions with the company through effective CDI.

CRM is one of several widely adopted IT movements that have brought focus on ER. Others have been the adoption of data warehousing for business intelligence in the early 1990s and, most recently, the needs of law enforcement and national intelligence agencies in collecting information for persons and organizations of interest.

Entity Resolution Activities

The notion of entity resolution first emerged in the context of removing equivalent references between two lists, where each list was assumed to not contain equivalent references. Fellegi and Sunter (1969), who worked at the Bureau of Statistics in Canada, dealt with this problem frequently. They described the process as *record linking* or record linkage. Later, in the context of relational database systems, where the focus is on the problem of finding and merging multiple instances of the same entity type (Hernández & Stolfo, 1995), it was called the *merge-purge* process. Describing this process as *entity resolution* (ER) began to appear around 2004 in articles and presentations by researchers at the Stanford InfoLab, led by Hector Garcia-Molina (2006).

The merge-purge process represents the most basic form of ER and begins by collecting all the references to be resolved into a single dataset. In a process that systematically compares pairs of references, those references that are deemed to be equivalent are collected into groups or clusters. Often, but not always, the goal of the process is to reduce (purge) the set of references by collapsing each group of equivalent references into a single representative reference. This is usually done by keeping the best *exemplar record* from the group or by combining the attribute values of all the records in the group to create a single *merge record*; hence the term *merge-purge*.

In other cases the goal is to simply identify the groups of equivalent records without collapsing them. This is done by assigning each reference in the same group a common identifier called a *link,* with different groups having different link values. *Linking* is a method for representing resolution decisions about entity references—that is, giving two reference instances (records) the same link value represents the decision that they are equivalent references. Whether the equivalent records are actually merged (merge-purge) or assigned link values (record linking), the net effect is the same.

Because record linking is just a way of representing a resolution decision, entity resolution (ER) will be the preferred term used in this text for describing the overall decision process rather than the term *record linking*. Although its roots are in the merge-purge and record-linking processes, ER has grown in both practice and theory and now describes a much broader set of activities. ER in this larger context encompasses five major activities:

- *ERA1: Entity reference extraction.* Locating and collecting entity references from unstructured information.
- *ERA2: Entity reference preparation.* The application of profiling, standardization, data cleansing, and other data quality techniques to structured entity references prior to the start of the resolution process.
- *ERA3: Entity reference resolution.* Resolving (deciding) whether two references are to the same or different entities.
- *ERA4: Entity Identity management.* Building and maintaining a persistent record of entity identity information over time.
- *ERA5: Entity relationship analysis.* Exploring the network of associations among different but related entities.

Just as the term information technology (IT) is used in both the broad sense of "Big IT" as meaning anything to do with computers and the narrower sense of "Little IT," which signifies a defined program of technical study, the same can be said of ER. Taken together, the five activities shown in Figure 1.3 comprise "Big ER."

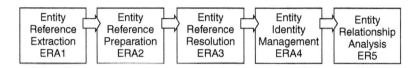

Figure 1.3 The Five Major ER Activities, in Order

Many people use the term ER in the "Little ER" sense of comprising only ERA3 or as ERA2 followed by ERA3. For example, merge-purge, which represents the extent of ER for many organizations, is primarily an ERA3 activity. Not every ER process involves all five activities, and different ER tools and systems are designed to handle different activities in the overall ER process.

Entity Reference Extraction: ERA1

Entity reference extraction (ERA1) is only necessary when an entity reference source is presented as unstructured information. Most IT processes are designed with the assumption that information sources are in a structured format. Information is structured when it organized in such a way that all the attribute values describing a particular entity are presented in a consistent and predictable pattern, such as in the row-and-column format of a relational database management system (RDBMS). Typical record formats reflect the RDBMS model in that all the attribute values that refer to the same entity are organized into a single record and appear in the same order from record to record. Two common patterns for placing an attribute value in a record are *fixed-position field format* and *character-delimited format*. In a fixed-position field format, each attribute value is in a field of the record that always has the same starting and ending position in the record. In character-delimited formats, the attribute values are in an ordered list separated by a special character called a *field delimiter*. Commas and tab characters are commonly used for this purpose, and for this reason files in the character-delimited format are sometimes called *comma-separated value* (CSV) files.

In cases where the delimiter might occur as part of an attribute value, a *text qualifier character* is used. Usually a quotation mark or an apostrophe, the text qualifier encloses attribute values to prevent a delimiter character that is part of the field value from being erroneously interpreted as a field delimiter. Table 1.1 shows an example of this idea in the row labeled "Delimited," where the quotation character is used as a text qualifier. In this row, the first comma is the field delimiter and the second comma is part of the last-name value.

Table 1.1: JOHN SMITH, JR, in Three Structured Formats

Char position	1	2	3	4	5	6	7	8	9	10	11	12	13	14	15	16	17	18	19
Fixed position	J	O	H	N						S	M	I	T	H	,		J	R	
Delimited	"	J	O	H	N	"	,	"	S	M	I	T	H	,	J	R	"		
XML	<	D	O	C	>	<	L	>	S	M	I	T	H	,	J	R	<	/	L
(XML cont.)	>	<	F	>	J	O	H	N	<	/	L	>	<	/	D	O	C	>	

Extensible Mark-up Language (XML) also represents a structured format in which attribute values are explicitly labeled with embedded tags. XML is a very flexible and expressive format that has gained wide adoption since being introduced as a standard by the World Wide Web Consortium (W3C) (XML, 2010).

Table 1.1 shows the representation of the name JOHN SMITH in each of these three formats. Note that in the fixed-position field format, the first-name attribute value always occupies character positions 1 through 9 and the last-name characters 10 through 19. Since attribute values in the XML representation are explicitly labeled <F> for first name and <L> for last name, the values do not have to be in the same order from XML document to XML document.

In unstructured information, entity attributes are not uniformly or explicitly designated. For example, if a reference source is a photograph of a person's face, the entity attributes are the facial characteristics. Before facial characteristics can be analyzed and compared, the portion of the video image that represents the face must first be located and the identifying facial characteristics must be extracted. In image processing this process is called *feature extraction* and is the genesis of the term *entity reference extraction* to describe ERA1.

Interestingly, humans have little trouble handling unstructured information such as narrative text, sounds, and images. Reading a wedding announcement in a newspaper and recognizing the name of the bride and groom, the location and date of the wedding, and other event attributes is called *named entity recognition* (NER) and is an easy task for anyone literate in the language of such an article. However, the location of these items in the text varies from announcement to announcement and can only be found by applying a complex set of grammatical rules related to

To: Bill Jones

From: Mary Clark

Date: 11/3/2009

Subject: Sales Contact

Bill,

Possible sales lead for you to follow up. On plane from ORD yesterday I met **John Smith, Jr**, CFO for Widget Stream, Inc. I think we might have lower cost solution for their office supplies. Look up his info and see what you can do.

-mc-

Figure 1.4: Unstructured Reference to JOHN SMITH, JR

the language of the text. Computer algorithms are currently not very effective in accomplishing the same task that is done so easily by people (Chiang, Talburt, Wu, et al., 2008; Wu, Talburt, Pippenger, et al., 2007). Chapter 7 discusses the trend toward data-intensive computing and data-driven models as a way to reduce this complexity.

Figure 1.4 shows a reference to a particular JOHN SMITH in an unstructured text in the body of an email message. Web pages written in HTML are semistructured documents that can be more easily parsed than free-format text documents (Hashemi, Ford, Vanprooyan, Talburt, 2002; Bahrami, 2010). Interest in ERA1 has grown along with the realization that a great deal of an organization's useful information often resides in unstructured formats. Inmon and Nesavich (2008) suggest that more often than not, the majority of an organization's information exists in unstructured formats, most of which are documents referred to as *unstructured textual information* (UTI).

Entity Reference Preparation

Even when entity references are in a structured format, extensive preprocessing of entity reference sources is necessary before effective resolution process can take place. Collectively, these preprocess activities are called *ETL processes,* where ETL is an acronym for *extract, transform, and load.* Sometimes called *data hygiene,* the following operations are commonly used to prepare references for ER processing (Talley, Talburt, Chan, 2010):

- *Encoding.* Translating incoming data from one encoding to another, e.g., ASCII to EBCDIC character encoding.
- *Conversion.* Transforming one data representation format to another, e.g., binary integer into a numeric character string, e.g., 010111 to "23"
- *Standardization.* Transforming data representations into a common user-defined scheme, e.g., changing gender values "1" and "male" to "M" or changing "Avenue" and "Av" to "AVE."
- *Correction.* Changing values based on certified reference data, e.g., correcting a ZIP code value by looking up street, city, and state address values in postal tables.
- *Bucketing.* Grouping numeric values into ranges with an assigned code, e.g., income of $45,000 into bucket "B" for $30,000 to $50,000.

- *Bursting.* Breaking a single record into multiple records, e.g., "John and Mary Doe, Oak Street" into "John Doe, Oak Street" and "Mary Doe, Oak Street."
- *Validation.* Enforcing rules on the rationality of data values and between data items, e.g., sale transaction date for an account cannot be earlier than date account created.
- *Enhancement.* Adding information not in the original reference based on information in the reference, e.g., adding longitude and latitude coordinates based on street address.

It is during the ETL phase that the principles and practices of information quality (IQ) are applied to their greatest extent. ER and IQ are closely related because improving the quality of reference sources can dramatically improve ER process results, and conversely, integrating the references through ER improves the overall quality of the information in the system. The next chapter will explore this relationship in more depth, but it suffices to say here that many of the concepts and current practices for both ER and IQ emerged from the data warehousing movement that gained popularity in the early 1990s (Inmon, 1992; Kimball, Ross, Thornthwaite, et al., 1998; English, 1999). Most organizations at that time had no idea of the poor condition of their operational data stores and the inconsistencies among them until they attempted to integrate them into a single database.

Entity Reference Resolution: ERA3

In ERA3, decisions are made as to whether two reference instances are equivalent or not equivalent—that is, refer to the same or different entities. Often, but not always, the equivalence decision is based on the degree of similarity between the values of the identity attributes in the two references, a process called *matching.* Perhaps the greatest confusion in ER literature revolves around the use of the terms *matching* and *linking.* *Linking* two references is assigned a common identifier called a *link value* to indicate that the references are equivalent. Linking represents the outcome of an ER decision. On the other hand, *matching* two references means applying an algorithm that measures the degree of similarity between some set of attribute values. If the degree of similarity reaches a predefined threshold, the two references are said to *match* or to be *matching references.*

In almost every ER scenario there will be equivalent references that should be linked but do not match, and conversely, references that match but are not equivalent and should not be linked. For example, if a customer Mary Jones living on Oak Street marries John Smith, becoming Mary Smith, and moves to her husband's home on Elm Street, the references to Mary Jones on Oak Street and to Mary Smith on Elm Street should be linked despite the fact that they do not match on either last name or street address.

Another confusion of terminology surrounds the term *duplicate*, as in *duplicate records* or *record deduplication*. In one sense duplication implies the ultimate level of matching, namely that one reference is an exact copy of the other. However, in other contexts it may be used to mean that the references are different but similar (approximate match), and in yet other contexts it has the same meaning defined here as equivalent references (Naumann, Herschel, 2010).

ER Principle #2: ER is fundamentally about linking equivalent references, not record matching.

To avoid confusion, going forward we'll use the phrase *equivalent entity references* to mean that the references are to the same entity, and *matching entity references* will mean only that the references have a defined level of similarity for certain attribute values. The terms *duplicate* and *deduplicate* will be avoided.

The fact that linking creates an equivalence relation on a set of entity references is the underpinning of the Algebraic Model for ER (Talburt, Wang, Hess, Kuo, 2007), discussed in Chapter 3. ER is about making decisions, and linking is a way to instantiate the decision that two references are, or are not, equivalent. Although it is true that matching is one of the most important tools in the ER armamentarium, it is not the only one. Knowing that two entity references match on certain attributes can be an important factor in the decision to link the references, but it is not always the determining factor. That ER is fundamentally about linking is embodied the following statement.

Fundamental Law of ER: Two entity references should be linked if and only if they are equivalent (reference the same entity).

Many authors, even those who describe ER in terms of record matching or record deduplication, often use these terms to mean both matching in the sense of attribute similarity and in the sense defined here as equivalent references. The difficulty is that it is not always clear when there has been a shift between these two meanings from one context to another. Even in the very rigorous and pioneering ER work of Fellegi and Sunter (1969), there is a discussion about the problem of "records that should be matched that don't match." These so called *true matches* between two lists, A and B, are even designated as the subset M of the Cartesian product of A and B, where M stands for matching. Yet clearly the implication is that M comprises the record pairs of AxB that are equivalent references, not necessarily matching references.

Matching References versus Equivalent References

Given that S represents a set of entity references, the notation SxS represents the *Cartesian product* of S with itself, i.e. the set of all ordered pairs of references in S. For a given matching algorithm and defined level of similarity, a decision can be made for each pair of references that they match or they don't match according to the predefined criteria. Let M denote the subset of SxS containing all matching pairs. Further suppose that for each pair of references, there is a way to know whether the two references are equivalent or not. Let E denote the subset of SxS containing all equivalent pairs. In most large-scale ER applications, the subsets E and M will be different. Figure 1.5 shows the general case where M and E are overlapping but unequal subsets of SxS.

E represents the true entity resolution result, whereas M represents the matching results. The degree of overlap indicates the degree to which the matching process is effective in arriving at the correct ER result. Depending on the specific circumstances, matching can be a very effective process for determining equivalent records. More precisely, the smaller the sets E-M and M-E, the more effective matching is in determining equivalence.

In ER the term *resolution* speaks to making a decision (resolving) as to whether two entity references are equivalent or not. Figure 1.5 can also be interpreted in a more general sense as representing the relationship between a decision process and the correct decision outcome. Suppose that M is regarded as a decision process that says yes, two records are equivalent, or no, they are not equivalent, regardless of whether the decision is based on matching or some other methodology. Further, if the decision of the process is yes, the decision is considered a positive result. Based on this, the sets illustrated in Figure 1.5 can be named as follows:

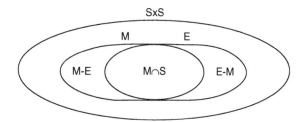

Figure 1.5: Matching References versus Equivalent References

- M-E is the set of *false positive* results. Positive indicates that the process decision was yes because the pair of records is in the set M, but a false decision because that pair is not in the set E, meaning that they are not equivalent and should not be linked.
- E-M is the set of *false negative* results—negative because the decision was no, but a false decision because the pair is in the set E, meaning they should be linked.

Following the same pattern,

- M∩E is the set of *true positive* results.
- SxS-(M∪E) is the set of *true negative* results.

Both true positive and true negative are correct decisions, whereas the false positive and false negatives are the incorrect decisions. These terms are summarized in Table 1.2.

The same terms are used in many contexts other than ER, such as in data mining and information retrieval. However, in inferential statistics, a false positive is called a *Type I decision error* and a False Negative is called a *Type II decision error* (Fisher, et al., 2006).

The False Negative Problem

In most ER contexts, false negatives are a bigger problem than false positives. The obvious reason is that E is generally not known. If all the equivalent references were known, there would be no need for an ER process in the first place. As a practical matter, E can only be determined for some sample of the entity references pairs under consideration. Furthermore, most of the attention for evaluating the ER process is focused on positive decisions. Given that an ER process brought two references together by some method, matching or otherwise, is it true that the references are equivalent? Answering this question only addresses false positive decisions and does nothing to address the issue of false negative decisions.

Table 1.2: Classification of Process Decision Outcomes

	Decision Should Be Yes	Decision Should Be No
Decision is yes	True positive	False positive
Decision is no	False negative	True negative

Evaluating false negatives requires starting with negative decisions, pairs of references that were not brought together by the ER process. In general this involves a much larger set. In particular, Figure 1.5 is not drawn to scale because for most applications the set (SxS)-M tends to be much larger than M. For example, if S has 10,000 references, SxS will have 100 million pairs. If the process only makes positive decisions for 1% of these pairs, that leaves 99 million pairs that have negative decisions. In other words, the set E-M can be a very small raft afloat in a vast sea of (SxS)-M.

Following this same example, if the ER process is primarily based on agreement between attribute values, then by definition the 99 million pairs in (SxS)-M don't exhibit these agreements, making an automated search impractical. For this reason, the best strategy for finding and evaluation false negatives is to take totally random samples of the negative decision pairs (Maydanchik, 2007).

ER Principle #3: ER false negatives are generally a more difficult problem to detect and solve than are false positives.

Another reason that false negatives tend to be a larger problem in ER is an IT legacy issue. Historically, ER has not always been very effective. Consequently, there is a certain level of expectation, or at least acceptance, that for some equivalent references the system will remain unresolved. Also, for many ER applications such as CDI, the impact of a false positive decision is considered worse than that of a false negative decision. For example, having two separate accounts for the same customer in a marketing system is generally considered to have less business impact than having one account that combines the transactions of two different customers. Making the decision that two references are equivalent may result in consolidating accounts or other information associated with those references. This leads to yet another ER principle.

ER Principle #4: ER processes are generally designed to avoid false positives at the expense of creating false negatives.

ER systems generally use four basic techniques for determining that references are equivalent and should be linked. These are:
- Direct matching
- Transitive equivalence

- Association analysis
- Asserted equivalence

Direct Matching

Direct matching is the determination of equivalence between two references based on the degree of similarity between the values of corresponding identity attributes. There are five basic methods for determining the similarity of attribute values:

1. Exact match
2. Numerical difference
3. Approximate syntactic match
4. Approximate semantic match
5. Derived match codes

Exact match simply means that the attributes' values must be identical. The requirement that all identity attributes must be an exact match is called *deterministic matching*. When attribute values are represented as character strings, exact matching is problematic because even the slightest variance prevents the values from matching. For example, the name "John Doe" is not an exact match for "JOHN DOE" or even "John Doe" if there are two spaces between the names instead of one space. The success of deterministic matching schemes relies on extensive ERA2 preparation activities, particularly standardization and cleaning.

Most large-scale ER applications employ some level of approximate match between attributes. Matching that allows for some attributes to only be similar rather than exact is called *probabilistic matching*. In the case of numeric attributes such as age, approximate matching is a matter of establishing the total amount of allowable difference between the two values. Approximate matching between numeric values is not always simple subtraction. For example, with date and time values, the difference requires more elaborate calculations that compute the difference as the number days, hours, or minutes between the values. This feature is built into many tools, such as automated spreadsheets and databases, so that subtracting the YYYYMMDD-format date 20091231 from 20100101 yields the value 1 (day) rather than the mathematic difference of 8,870.

In the case where the attribute values are represented as a string of characters, measuring the degree of similarity is not as obvious. Character strings can be considered as similar in format (syntactically similar) or similar in meaning (semantically similar). *Syntactic similarity* is measured by an *approximate string matching* (ASM) *algorithm,* also called a *string comparator metric* (Herzog, Scheuren, Winkler, 2007). What constitutes syntactic similarity is open to interpretation. As a result there are a myriad of ASM algorithms, each reflecting the designers' view of what comprises syntactic similarity. In a general sense they all consider the number of characters the two strings have in common and the order in which they occur, but they vary considerably in detail.

One of the most basic algorithms is the Levenshtein Edit Distance ASM (Levenshtein, 1966). It measures similarity as the minimum number of basic character operations required to transform one string into the other. Typically the allowable operations are inserting one character, deleting one character, and replacing (substituting) one character, although some versions also allow transposing two adjacent characters. For example, the string "ALISA" and "ALYSSA" are separated by an edit distance of two transformations; one is replacing "I" with "Y" in the first string and another inserting "S" between the "S" and "A" of the first string.

Another family of ASM algorithms focuses on the ordering of the characters. These are called *q-gram* or *n-gram* algorithms. A q-gram is a fixed sequence of characters of length q. For example, "ARM" is a 3-gram. The principle of q-gram similarity between two strings is that the more times that q-grams derived from the first string are found in the second string, the more similar is the string. Consider the two strings "JULIE" and "JULES." Here the two strings share four 1-Grams, the single letters "J," "U," "L," and "E." They also share two 2-Grams of "JU" and "UL" and one 3-Gram of "JUL." In this case the maximum value for q is 3 and, when divided by the string length of 5, gives a similarity of measure of 60%.

The q-Gram Tetrahedral Ratio (qTR) algorithm (Holland, Talburt, 2010) scores the number of shared q-grams against the total possible q-grams. The total number of q-grams (substrings) in a string of length N is the tetrahedral number of N given by

$$T_N = \frac{N \cdot (N+1) \cdot (N+2)}{6}$$

In this example, the string "JULIE" of length 5 has 35 possible substrings—that is, $T_N = 35$. Given that "JULIE" shares 7 of these with the string "JULES," the q-Gram Tetrahedral ratio of "JULIE" with respect to "JULES" gives

$$qTR = \frac{7}{35} = 0.20$$

In the case where the strings being compared are of different lengths, the calculation of qTR will depend on which string is selected to determine the tetrahedral number in the denominator of the ratio. To address these cases and make the qTR measure symmetric, an adjusted qTR measure is defined as the weighted average of the two directional measures (Holland, Talburt, 2010). If N represents the length of the first string, M the length of the second, and Q the number q-grams shared by the two strings, the adjusted qTR is given by

$$qTR_{adj} = Q \cdot \left(\frac{M \cdot T_N + N \cdot T_M}{T_N \cdot T_M \cdot (M + N)} \right)$$

Another q-gram variant is the Jaro String Comparator (Jaro, 1989). It considers the number of characters in common between two strings and the number of character transpositions. If A and B represent two strings with at least one character in common, the Jaro similarity is given by

$$J(A, B) = W_1 \cdot \frac{C}{L_A} + W_2 \cdot \frac{C}{L_B} + W_3 \cdot \frac{(C - T)}{C}$$

where W_1, W_2, W_3 are the weights assigned to the first string, second string, and transpositions, respectively, and where $W_1 + W_2 + W_3 = 1$, where C is the common character count, T is the number of transpositions, and L_A and L_B are the lengths of the two strings. For example, the strings "SHAKLER" and "SHAKEL" have 6 characters in common and one transposition of "LE" to "EL." Assuming three equal weights of 1/3 each, the Jaro similarity between these strings would be

$$J(SHAKLER, SHAKEL) = \frac{1}{3} \cdot \frac{6}{7} + \frac{1}{3} \cdot \frac{6}{6} + \frac{1}{3} \cdot \frac{(6 - 1)}{6} = 0.897$$

Some implementations of the algorithm not only require sharing the same sequence of q characters but also require that the shared sequences both start at the same or almost the same position in the strings. These types of q-grams are called *positional q-grams*. The Jaro-Winkler Comparator (Winkler, 1999) is an example of a positional q-gram algorithm. The Jaro-Winkler comparator is a modification of the Jaro Comparator that gives additional weight to the agreements on the first four characters of the two strings. If N represents the number of the first four characters that agree position-by-position, the Jaro-Winker similarity is calculated as

$$W(A, B) = J(A, B) + 0.1 \cdot N \cdot \left(1 - J(A, B) \right)$$

In the example of "SHAKLER" and "SHAKEL" the value N is 4. The Jaro-Winkler similarity of these two strings is calculated by

$$W(SHAKLER, SHAKEL) = 0.897 + 0.1 \cdot 4 \cdot (1 - 0.897) = 0.938$$

The Jaro and Jaro-Winkler algorithms are both designed so that the values they return are always between 0 and 1, and the value is 1 only when the strings are identical. This a common practice for ASM algorithms. Even the Levenshtein algorithm can be normalized to have these same properties. By its definition the edit distance between two strings cannot exceed the length of the longest string. If L represents the Levenshtein edit distance between two strings A and B, the normalized edit distance NL can be calculated as (Christen, 2006)

$$NL(A, B) = 1 - \left(\frac{L(A, B)}{\max\{L_A, L_B\}} \right)$$

The Levenshtein, Maximum Length q-Gram, Tetrahedral Ratio, Jaro, and Jaro-Winkler are only a few examples of the many ASM algorithms that are used in ER direct matching processes. A quick search of the Internet using the keywords *approximate string matching* will reveal many others along with details of their implementation.

Approximate semantic matching is when the similarity between strings is based on their linguistic meaning rather than their character structure. For example, in the English language the name "JIM" is well known and well understood as an alternate name (nickname) for the name "JAMES." Most probabilistic matching schemes for names incorporate some type of nickname or alias table to handle these situations. The problem is that the mapping of names to nicknames is not one to one. For example, the name "HARRY" could be a nickname for "HENRY," "HAROLD," or perhaps not a nickname at all—that is, the birth name was given as "HARRY."

Semantic similarity is even more problematic when dealing with business names. For example, the determination that "TOWING AND RECOVERY" represents the same business activity as "WRECKER SERVICE" is difficult to automate. The methods and techniques for making these discoveries fall into the area of research called *latent semantic analysis* (Landauer, 1998; Deaton, Doan, Schweiger, 2010).

The fifth type of approximate matching technique is the use of *derived match codes*, sometimes called *hash codes* or *hash tokens*. In a match code scheme, an algorithm is applied to the attribute value to generate a new value. These algorithms generally perform calculations on the underlying binary coding of the characters, a process called *hashing*. The hashing algorithm is designed so that similar strings (either syntactically or semantically) will produce exactly the same match code. The result is that approximate matching is converted into deterministic matching—that is, it allows the ER process to perform an exact match between the match codes of two attribute values rather than performing an approximate match between the two attribute values themselves. In addition to simplifying the match process, it is also more efficient, generating the match code only once rather than executing an ASM algorithm each time two attributes are compared.

One of the first derived match codes schemes is called the Soundex algorithm. It was first patented in 1918 (Odell, Russell, 1918) and was used in the 1930s as a manual process to match records in the Social Security Administration (Herzog, et al., 2007). The name Soundex comes from the combination of the words *sound* and *indexing* because it attempts to recognize both the syntactic and phonetic similarity between two names. As with most approximate matching, there are many variations resulting from the adaptation of the algorithm to different applications. The algorithm presented here is from Herzog, et al. (2007) using the name "Checker":

1. Capitalize all letters and drop punctuation -> CHECKER.
2. Remove the letters A, E, I, O, U, H, W, and Y after the first letter → CCKR.
3. Keep first letter but replace the other letters by digits according to the coding {B, F, P, V} replace with 1, {C, G, J, K, Q, S, X, Z} replace with 2, {D, T} replace with 3, {L} replace with 4, {M, N} replace with 5, and {R} replace with 6 → C226.
4. Replace consecutive sequences of the same digit with a single digit if the letters they represent were originally next together in the name or separated by H or W → C26 (because the 22 comes from letters CK that were next together).
5. If the result is longer than 4 characters total, drop digits at the end to make it 4 characters long. If the result is fewer than 4 characters, add zeros at the end to make it 4 characters long → C260.

Using this same algorithm, the name "John" produces the Soundex match code value J500. By using these match codes as proxies for the attribute values, the name "John Checker" would be matched to any other names that produce the same match codes, such as "Jon Cecker." Chapter 5 gives an example of an ER process using match codes generated by a proprietary algorithm in the DataFlux® dfPowerStudio® application.

ER processes often use a combination of matching schemes as a way to be more effective as well as more efficient. For example, many systems utilize partial match codes as a way to do *match prospecting*, also called *blocking* (Baxter, Christen, Churches, 2003). Prospecting is a way to narrow the search for references that are more likely to be a direct match to a given reference. For example, suppose that a target reference has a name value of "John Doe" and an address value of "123 Oak St, Anyville, AR, 72211," and the linking criteria require agreement on name and address. In this case a prospecting scheme might be to recall only those references where the last name starts with the same letter as the last name of the target reference ("D"), and the ZIP code is the same ("72211"). In a file with a large number of references, this method could significantly reduce the number of candidate references to compare against the target reference. However, it will not guarantee that every equivalent reference, or even every matching reference, in the file will be in the list of candidates. If the ZIP codes have not been standardized, matching references with missing, incorrect, or out-of-date ZIP codes would be omitted from the list of match candidates. Similarly, references where the first letter of the last name has been corrupted or where the first and last names are reversed would not appear in the candidate list.

There are many trade-offs to be considered in creating a blocking scheme. The first is striking a balance between the level match and number of candidates returned. In the previous example, requiring that the candidate ZIP codes only match the first three digits of the target zip code (722**) would potentially include equivalent records missed by an exact match, but it would also increase the overall number of candidates that must be compared to the target reference.

Another strategy is to use multiple prospecting schemes. Following the previous example, there could be two prospecting schemes. One scheme could return references in which the first letter of the last name and the full ZIP code agree with the target reference, but another could return those in which the first letter of the first name and street number agree with the target. The hope is that any equivalent references not in the candidate list of one scheme will appear in the candidate list of the other. A discussion of several blocking techniques, including *sorted neighborhood*, *Q-gram based*, *canopy clustering*, *string-map based*, and *suffix array based blocking*, can be found in Christen (2007), along with a discussion of quality and complexity measures for evaluating these techniques.

The advantage of direct matching is that it only requires the information at hand in the references being compared. Although some external information such as tables of common nicknames or abbreviations may be used, ASM is primarily an algorithmic process operating on the values of the identity attributes. The Fellegi-Sunter Model discussed in Chapter 3 is based entirely on probabilistic direct matching and provides a systematic way to structure the matching process so that the number of false positives and false negatives created are within preset limits.

ER managers like direct matching because it is easy to explain. Users of ER system results tend to focus on the records that were linked. Some of these may be wrong, but intuitively everyone agrees that the more similar the attributes, the more likely that the references are equivalent. At the same time, linking Mary Smith with Mary Jones at different addresses may be correct, but a user might want some explanation as to why it was done. Even though ER systems, especially those that perform identity management, are a class of expert systems, they rarely provide an explanation facility. An *explanation facility* is a system function that when enabled will create a log that traces all the steps and reasoning behind a decision (Hashemi, Talburt, 2000; Hashemi, Talburt, Kooshesh, 2000). Without such a facility, when Mary Smith and Mary Jones are linked incorrectly, the results can seem irrational.

In contrast to direct matching, *discovered equivalences* are created when two references do not directly match but can be determined as equivalent through other evidence. These *equivalences* can be discovered through the normal ER processing of references or by a separate data-mining process, sometimes called *entity analytics*. IBM® has an entire group of employees devoted to developing entity analytics techniques that discover nonobvious relationships (Jonas, 2005).

Transitive Equivalence

Even when two references A and B do not directly match, it may be possible to find a series of intermediate references C_1 through C_N starting at A and ending in B where consecutive pairs of references are equivalent. In other words:

A equivalent to C_1 equivalent to C_2 equivalent to... C_N equivalent to B

Determining equivalence by this process is called *transitive equivalence* or *transitive linking*. If A is a reference in a larger set of references, the set of all references that can be determined equivalent to A through transitive linking is called the *transitive closure* of A (Li, Bheemavaram, and Zhang, 2010; Zhang, Bheemvaram, Li, 2006).

Here is an example of how transitive linking might work in an *identity capture* ER system—that is, a system that collects and stores the attribute values of the references it processes. Assume that the name and at least one other attribute must agree to establish equivalence by direct matching. Consider the following references in the order shown:

```
Ref#1 name=Mary Smith, street=123 Oak, phone=555-1234
Ref#2 name=Mary Smith, street=456 Elm, phone=555-1234
Ref#3 name=Mary Smith, street=456 Elm, phone = null
```

In this example, Ref#1 does not directly match Ref#3, but an ER system that supports transitive equivalence will link them. Suppose that Ref#1 was determined to be a new identity because it is not equivalent to any of the identities already maintained by the system. The system would then use Ref#1 to seed the creation of a new identity and assign it a unique identifier, say "33." The same value of "33" would also be used as the link value appended to Ref#1. The new identity would look something like

```
ID=33, name=Mary Smith, street=123 Oak, phone=555-1234
```

Ref#2 is equivalent to Identity 33 because they agree on full name and phone number. Since Ref#2 is equivalent to Identity 33, the system would enhance Identity 33 by including the new information discovered from Ref#2 and appending the link value of "33" to Ref#2. Now Identity 33 might look something like

```
ID=33, name=Mary Smith, street={123 Oak; 456 Elm}, phone=555-1234
```

Finally, in processing Ref#3 it is found to be equivalent to Identity 33 as well because they also agree on name and address. The system would assign Ref#3 the link value 33. In this example, all the intermediate equivalences were established by direct matching, to the captured identity that merges the collective attributes of the references equivalent found equivalent to it. Transitive equivalence is essential for an ER process to produce a unique result. In the example shown, transitive equivalence was effected by creating an identity that merges the attribute values of the equivalent references. The concepts of match and merge functions form the fundamental concepts of the Stanford Entity Resolution Framework (SERF) discussed in Chapter 3. The SERF model is important in that it frames the necessary and sufficient conditions for an ER to produce a consistent, unique result. One of these conditions is transitive equivalence accomplished by way of the merge function.

Identity capture works in theory, but there are practical problems in implementing and maintaining them, namely the problems of identity *splits and consolidations*. These problems occur because the acquisition of identity knowledge is imperfect and occurs over a period of time. Suppose that the same references are processed in the order Ref#1, Ref#3, and Ref#2. Processing in this order will yield a different result. Suppose again that Ref#1 creates a new Identity 33. But now Ref#3 will not be found equivalent to Identity 33, so the system will create a new identity—say, Identity 56, based on Ref#3. Now when Ref#2 is processed last, it will be found equivalent to both Identity 33 and Identity 56. The system's response to this dilemma will depend on the design of the system and the timing of the discovery. If the three references are processed in the same run at the same time, the problem can be corrected in memory before any links are actually appended or published. In other words, it is a memory management problem. The two distinct identities 33 and 56 exist separately only within the system memory. As soon as Ref#2 triggers their consolidation, the adjustments are made in memory and at the end of the run there is only one identity linked to all three references.

A bigger problem occurs when Ref#1 and Ref#3 are processed in one run and Ref#2 is processed at a later time. In this case, the system will have given out two different link identifier values ("33" and "56") to references for the same entity (Mary Smith), thus failing to follow the Fundamental Law of ER. The correction of the problem is to consolidate Identity 33 and Identity 56. But consolidation creates problems of its own, deciding which identity identifier to keep and which to retire and how to correct the link identifiers that were given out to users of the system before the identities were consolidated.

The identity split problem is the reverse of a consolidation. It occurs when what was considered to be a single identity turns out to be an amalgam of two or more distinct identities. For example, discovering that the accumulated identity attribute values for an identity John Smith are really a mixture of attribute values from references to John Smith, Jr., and John Smith, Sr., two individuals who shared the same address and phone number for a period of time. The split of an overconsolidated identity like this can be a much harder problem to repair than the consolidation problem. For consolidations it is possible to create a consolidation list directing that references previously given link value X should be changed to link value Y. In the case of splits, previously assigned links cannot be sorted out unless the system has kept an accurate log of which previously processed references were given which links.

The use of transitive linking with ASM algorithms carries a certain amount of risk. If attribute values that are similar but not equal contribute to a match, then over a long chain of intermediate matches it is possible that the value of the attribute in the reference at the beginning of the chain can be very different from its value in the reference at the end of the chain. Like the whispering game or a word transformation puzzle, small variances at each step can lead to large change overall. This is generally not a problem with equivalence decisions that take into account negative information as well as positive information. Negative rules will not allow two references to be linked regardless of their similarity if there is disagreement on certain key attributes such as different dates of birth or gender (Whang, Benjelloun, Garcia-Molina, 2009).

Association Analysis

Transitive equivalence requires consecutive references in the chain to be equivalent. However, it is possible to discover equivalent references by exploring associations among references that don't rise to the level of equivalence. These explorations are often done using techniques borrowed from graph theory and network analysis (Bhattacharya, Getoor, 2005; Schweiger, 2009).

A simple example shows how association analysis works. Consider the following four references:

```
Ref#1, Mary Smith 123 Oak St
Ref#2, Mary Smith 456 Elm St
Ref#3, John Smith 123 Oak St
Ref#4, John Smith 456 Elm St
```

Note that none of the six possible pairings of these four references agree on both name and address. Therefore, under typical matching rules, none of six pairs would be considered equivalent. Figure 1.6 shows a graphical representation of these four references and their name and address connections.

However, given that this association is unlikely to occur by chance, it is reasonable to infer that these are the same John Smith and Mary Smith at both addresses and that their references should be linked. The decision to link would be even stronger if supported by other evidence, such as uncommon names, and if there was no conflicting evidence, such as different dates of birth.

Unlike direct matching and transitive equivalence, where decisions are made pair by pair, association analysis allows multiple relationships to be considered at the same time and multiple equivalence decisions to be made at the same time. As in this example, the equivalence decisions for both the pairs (Ref#1, Ref#2) and (Ref#3, Ref#4) are justified only when the entire configuration of relationships is considered as a whole, not by making separate decisions for each

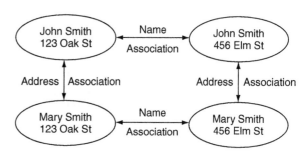

Figure 1.6: Graph of Reference Associations

pair independently. The application of graph theory and network analysis of entity relationships is a rapidly growing area of ER research, and a more detailed discussion is given in Chapter 7.

This example also shows that there is not a sharp delineation between ERA3 and ERA5. Many of the same association analysis techniques used for discovering equivalent references can also be used to explore associations between nonequivalent entities or even other entity types. Resolution through association analysis is sometimes called context-based ER in contrast to attribute-based ER using direct matching (Yongxin, Qingzhong, Ji, 2009).

Asserted Equivalence

In direct matching, transitive equivalence, and association analysis, the evidence for equivalence comes from the references themselves, either as attribute values or relationships with other references. Links created in this way are also called *inferred links* (Talburt, Zhou, Shivaiah, 2009). An *asserted equivalence* is the instantiation of a link between two references based on *a priori* knowledge that they are equivalent. For this reason, creating links in this way is also called *knowledge-based linking,* and ER systems that use this method of resolution are called *knowledge-based ER systems*. Knowledge-based ER systems and identity capture ER systems represent top-down and bottom-up approaches to identity management, respectively.

An asserted equivalence often takes the form of one record carrying the attribute values of two nonmatching references. It represents the assertion that the two references are equivalent independent of similarity or dissimilarity between their attribute values. The previous example explains how it could be possible to discover that the references to Mary Smith on Oak St. and the Mary Smith on Elm St. are equivalent through association analysis. An alternative to this scenario would simply be the assertion

Mary Smith previously residing at 123 Oak is now residing at 456 Elm

This assertion may have been self-reported, acquired from public records, or acquired from a commercial data provider, such as a magazine subscription service. If this knowledge was acquired and provisioned in the ER identity management system prior to processing reference to either Mary Smith on Oak St. or Mary Smith on Elm St., then both references would be recognized as equivalent at the time they were processed, regardless of the order in which they were received. Jonas (2005) calls ER systems that have this property *sequence neutral.*

In the case of CDI, asserted information is readily available from a number of reliable public and private sources. Acxiom®

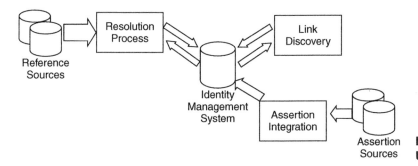

Figure 1.7: An ER System Using Asserted Links

Corporation has made asserted linking the backbone of its AbiliTec® CDI technology, managing billions of assertions for U.S. customers alone. Chapter 5 has a more complete discussion of this ER system.

The disadvantage of asserted linking is the increased storage and processing it requires to be used effectively. Asserted linking divides the overall ER process into a foreground process for resolving equivalence and a background process of integrating assertions into the identity management system. Figure 1.7 shows the principal components of an ER system that includes identity management, link discovery processes, and asserted linking.

ER Principle #5: ER systems link references through inferred and asserted equivalence. Inferred equivalence can be established through direct matching, transitive equivalence, or association analysis.

Entity Identity Management: ERA4

Another important term related to ER is *entity identity.* According to Lim, Srivastava, Probhakar, and Richardson (1993), the identity of an entity is a set of attribute values for that entity along with a set of distinctness rules that allow that entity to be distinguished from all other entities of the same class in a given context. From this definition, it should follow that ER can always be accomplished through the matching of these identity attributes. There are several reasons that direct matching fails to be a perfect ER solution:

- *An increase in the number of entities beyond the original context.* Attribute values and rules that are created to discern identity among 100 distinct entities may no longer be sufficient if 200 more are added.
- *Error or variation in the representation of the attribute values.* Spelling errors, missing values, default values, and aliases all present a challenge in the application of matching logic.

- *Not all the attributes are represented in every reference.* References typically represent only a projection of the total set of identity attributes. In the example discussed previously, even though Mary Jones on Oak St. cannot be resolved as equivalent to Mary Smith on Elm St. by matching on the name and street attributes, matching would potential work if there was another attribute present, such as a Social Security number, that would link them together.

In a small context such as a single company, a simple scheme such as combining a person's first-name initial and the first six characters of the person's last name (e.g., jsmith@abc.com) may be sufficient to identify John Smith from all other employees. However, in a larger population, more attributes are usually required to construct a distinct identity. For example, in the U.S. population, the first, middle, and last name is not sufficient. For almost every combination of values for these names there is likely to be more than one person who share that same name. Even adding date of birth is not sufficient. For common names such as John Robert Smith, there are likely to be two different people who share that same name and same date of birth.

Identity Resolution

Identity resolution is an ER process in which references are resolved against a set of previously established identities. In the general ER scenario, resolution takes place between two references from an input source. However, in the identity resolution scenario, one reference of the pair is always one of the predefined identities— that is, an input reference is compared against the set of identities maintained by the system.

If the set of identities are customers, the process is called *customer recognition*. Customer recognition systems are ER systems that resolve an entity reference against a set of customer records to determine whether the reference is for an existing customer or represents a new customer. Systems that are able to perform customer recognition in real time provide companies with a powerful CRM tool. For example, the ability of a call center to automatically identify a customer by capturing the incoming telephone number and to then have that customer's information on screen as soon as the call is answered presents the company with many opportunities to improve the customer's experience.

In the case where at least one of the entity references is to an entity in the set of known entities, entity identification can be used as a technique to accomplish entity resolution. If both references are to entities known by the system, clearly those references are either to the same or to different entities and the references are resolved. If only one is a known entity and the other is not, it is clear that the references are to different identities. Entity resolution by entity identification only fails in the case that both references are to entities outside the set of known entities. For some applications this may not be a problem. For example, resolving records of standard examination scores to student enrollment records is often guided by the assumption that a reference to a student in an examination record must also be a reference to one of the students enrolled in the school. The system only has to decide which one it is. As long as identity resolution takes place in this kind of closed context, it will be true that entity identification results in entity resolution.

However, the converse is not true. It is possible to determine whether two entity references are equivalent or not without knowing the identity of either entity. Take as an example two references to a person named John Smith. If one John Smith is 30 years old and the other is 60 years old, it is clear that that these references are not equivalent and should not be linked. Resolving that entity references are not equivalent is called *disambiguation*. However, in this example, neither reference has been identified, since there are many persons of age 30 named John Smith, just as there are many persons of age 60 named John Smith. The situation is similar to the use of fingerprints in criminal investigation. Attributes such as human fingerprints and DNA that are intrinsic to a living entity are called *biometric attributes*, as opposed to *biographical attributes* such as name and location, which are situational.

If two sets of fingerprints are found at a crime scene, an examination of the prints will show whether they belong to the same suspect or not—entity resolution. However, the identification of a suspect depends on whether his or her fingerprints are in some database that associates fingerprints with known persons—identity resolution. When identity resolution is defined to be the process of resolving an entity reference with a known entity, then it is clear that identity resolution and entity resolution are not the same.

ER Principle #6: Entity resolution is not the same as identity resolution. Identity resolution is only one form of ER.

Identity plays an important role in ER systems, regardless of whether it is an identity resolution-based system or not. Understanding the role of identity in ER goes back to the definition of entity identity as being a set of rules and attributes that distinguish among entities in a given context, and ER Principle #1, which states that ER systems work with references to entities, not real entities.

Any real entity has an uncountable number of attributes. Just take a simple product such as a plastic water bottle. There are infinitely many physical measurements that could be taken and recorded as attributes, not to mention other descriptive attributes such as style, manufacturer, UPC, stock number, and so on. However, for any given application, the data modeler or information architect for an information system will choose some finite number of attributes to represent the identity of that entity in the system. Designers of other information systems will make different choices. The constellation of attributes that comprise the identity of the bottle in the manufacturer's system will likely be different than those chosen by any of the wholesale vendors who buy that same bottle, and it will also be different than in the systems of the customers who buy from the wholesalers.

Each system strives to create a unique identity for each item in its product inventory relative to other items in its inventory. As the universe of inventory items changes, the identity requirements will change. The problem from an ER perspective occurs when different systems generate references to the same entity using different identity attributes. This is especially true for CDI, where customer identity is typically cast in terms of contact information.

The advent of social networking and Internet marketing is both an opportunity and a challenge for companies using CDI systems designed around traditional contact information such as name, address, phone, and fax numbers. Many customers now have several online identities, but gathering and linking this information is proving to be more difficult than traditional contact information. ER in social networks is an emerging area of research (Bilgic, Licamele, Getoor, Shneiderman, 2006) and is discussed in more detail in Chapter 7.

Internal versus External View of Identity

One way to describe this situation is in terms of an *internal view* versus an *external view* of identity (Talburt, Zhou, Shivaiah, 2009). Figure 1.6 illustrates the basic elements of name and address contact history for a woman born Mary Smith. Because these are records of where this woman was living, it is also called an *occupancy history*. Figure 1.8 shows three occupancy records, each with a name, an address, and a period of time that the occupancy was valid. Also note that there was a change in name between Occupancy 1 and Occupancy 2.

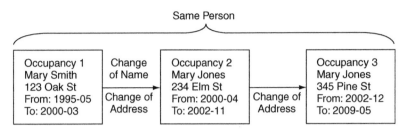

Figure 1.8: An Occupancy History

There are two ways to view the issue of identity shown in Figure 1.8. One is to start with the identity based on biographical information—e.g., Mary Smith, a female born on December 3, 1980, in Anytown, NY, to parents Robert and Susan Smith—and to follow that identity through its various representations of name and address. This internal view of identity as shown in Figure 1.8 is the view of Mary Smith herself and might well be the view of a sibling or other close relative, someone with complete knowledge about her occupancy history. The internal view of identity represents a closed universe model in which for a given set of identity attributes, all the attribute values are known to the internal viewer, and any value for one of these attributes that is not one of the known values must belong to a different identity. An ER system that possessed this information could always correctly resolve whether any given name and address reference was for this identity or not.

On the other hand, an external view of identity is one in which some number of attribute values for an identity have been collected, but it is not certain if it is a complete collection of values or even if all the values are correct. When a system based on an external view is presented with a reference, the system must always decide whether the reference should be linked to an existing identity or if it represents a new identity in the system. Therefore, an external view of identity represents an open universe model because unlike the internal view, the system cannot assume that it has complete knowledge of all identity values.

As an example, suppose that a system has only Occupancy Records 1 and 2 of the identity in Figure 1.8. In that case the system's knowledge of this identity is incomplete. It may be incomplete because Occupancy Record 3 has not been acquired or because it is in the system but has not been linked to Records 1 and 2. In the latter case, the system would treat Record 3 as part of a different identity. Even though an internal viewer would know that Occupancy Record 3 should also be part of the identity in Figure 1.8, the system has not made that decision.

In addition to the problem of incompleteness, the system may assemble an inaccurate view of an identity. When presented with a new occupancy record, the system may erroneous link it with an existing identity to which it does not belong. Accuracy and completeness are only two of the 16 dimensions of information quality described in the Wang-Strong Framework (Wang, Strong, 1996) and are another example of the close ties between ER and IQ.

In an external view, the collection of attribute values that have been linked together by the system comprises its view of the identity of the entity. In other words, an ER system based on an external view builds its knowledge about entity identities piece by piece. The external view of identity more closely resembles the experience of a business or government agency using ER tools in an effort to link their records into a single view of a customer or agency client.

All ER systems use identity at some level to resolve references, but not all ER systems have identity management functions. For example, the simplest form of ER is the merge-purge process. It uses identity by assuming that references with certain closely matching attribute values are equivalent and assigns these matching references the same link identifier. By the end of the merge-purge process, the system has an external view of the identity of each entity represented in the file based on the collective attributes of the equivalent references (match groups). However, after the merge-purge process has ended, that identity information is typically discarded. Merge-purge systems do not keep and manage entity identities for future processing. Each merge-purge process starts from scratch in assembling its identity knowledge. That knowledge is transient, existing only during the processing of a set of references.

Identity Management

Identity management in an ER system occurs when the system is preloaded with identity information, as in the case of identity resolution systems, or when it retains all or part of the entity identity information from the references it resolves in the case of identity capture systems. ER systems that support identity management have a significant advantage because they have the potential to

- Maintain persistent link values
- Allow transactional processing
- Go beyond direct matching and link records by association and assertion

Just as a merge-purge process does not retain identity information, the link identifiers it assigns to the set of references it processes are transient. Two references for the same entity may be correct resolved and assigned the same identifier in each of two different runs of the merge-purge process, but it would only be by chance that the link identifier assigned in both runs is the same. By definition, ER systems are only required to assign two entity references the same link value if, and only if, they are equivalent. Although the definition does not require an ER system to always assign the same reference the same link value, systems that do this are said to provide *persistent link values.* If an ER system supports persistent links, it means that each time it is presented with an entity reference it will assign it the same link value.

The key to assigning persistent link values is identity management. For example, identity resolution systems can assign persistent link values because they work with a set of known entities, each of which has a unique identifier. When an entity reference is recognized as referencing one of these identities, the identity identifier can be used as the link value for the reference. As long as the identity identifier does not change, the same link value will be assigned each time a reference to that entity is presented to the system.

ER Principle #7: ER systems that provide persistent link values must also implement some form of identity management.

Even ER systems that are not identity resolution systems can still support persistent links. An ER system can do this by storing the identity information it accumulates during processing, a sort of "smart" merge-purge. ER systems that build entity identities as they process references are called *identity capture systems.* In many respects an identity resolution system implements an internal view of identity in the sense that the entities and their attributes are known in advance. Other ER systems are designed to capture and save identity information as they go implementing an external view of identity. Identity capture systems start with a clean slate; when they process their first entity reference, the identity information from that reference is saved as the system's first identity and given an identity identifier. If that same reference is presented to the system again at a later time, the system will recognize it as belonging to the same identity that was created for it initially and will give it the same link value, namely the identity identifier.

Although from a conceptual viewpoint it is convenient to define ER in terms of linking two entity references, these simple examples illustrate that most ER systems don't take pairs of references as input. Except for merge-purge, which by definition must operate in a batch mode, most ER systems work on a transactional basis where the input is a single entity reference. For systems that support identity management, the input reference is compared to the identities held by the system to determine to which identity, if any, it is equivalent. For systems managing a large number of identities, it is impractical and unnecessary to compare the input reference to every identity. These systems have a scheme for narrowing, producing a smaller list of "candidate" identities that are most likely to be equivalent to the input reference. The heterogeneous join or hub systems work in a similar way. The candidate identities are filtered by the query that is posed against each of the databases by the system.

On the other hand, most ER systems really do append a link to the input reference. Even in the case of merge-purge, the final result is that a link identifier is appended to each record in the input file. Here the exception is that some ER systems, especially in law enforcement, have a graphical user interface (GUI) and do not provide a link append service. Instead they provide the user with the identities most likely to be equivalent to the input reference and leave it to the user to make the final choice.

Entity Relationship Analysis: ERA5

After equivalent references have been resolved and possibly identified, many applications ask another question: What are the various relationships among these entities? One of the first of these to be explored for customer entities was the *household relationship*. Marketing companies see value in understanding who is living with whom at the same address. Interestingly, households are still one of the hardest relationships to define and manage. The simplest definition is "all the people at the same address with the same last name." Though it is simple to apply, this definition doesn't capture the nuances of our changing culture and demographics, such as wives who keep their family names, unmarried couples, stepchildren, and extended families.

The concept of a household can also be applied to business entities in the sense of understanding whether a business entity is owned by or owns another business entity or is a local branch of a larger entity. The company Dunn & Bradstreet® is well known for its D-U-N-S® Number that encodes corporate household information. *Corporate householding* is also an area of active research (Madnick, Wang, Xian, 2004).

Exploring entity relationships is at the intersection of entity resolution and data mining. Data mining is all about discovering nonexplicit (nonobvious) relationships. A record or database instance by definition is an explicit relationship among the attribute values, namely that they are for the same entity. ER can be thought about as data mining in the sense that its goal is to make explicit which entity references are equivalent.

Like the small-world hypothesis (Watts, Stogatz, 1998), entity relationships can be categorized into levels of separation. ERA3 can be thought of as determining when two references have zero degrees separation—that is, are equivalent. One degree of separation would be when two entities have a direct association, such as the household relationship. Using the traditional definition, all household members share a matching surname and residential address. A second-degree relationship requires an intermediate association. For example, suppose that John Doe and Bill Smith share an apartment and Bill Smith and Tom Jones are members of ABC Club. Even though John Doe and Tom Jones might never have met, they share the relationship of both knowing Bill Smith. Two degrees of separation would require two intermediate associations, and so on.

Entity connections can be established through many combinations of discovered associations such as shared telephone or P.O. box address as well as asserted associations such as call records between telephone numbers or post office change-of-address records. Just as with entity extraction, the analysis of association networks has its own extensive body of research that practitioners can draw on.

Summary

Entity resolution is about determining when references to real-world entities are equivalent (refer to the same entity) or not equivalent (refer to different entities). Linking is appending a common identifier to reference instances to denote the decision that they are equivalent. Identity resolution, record linking, record matching, record deduplication, merge-purge, and entity analytics all represent particular forms or aspects of ER. In its broadest sense, ER encompasses five major activities: entity reference extraction, entity reference preparation, entity reference resolution, entity identity management, and entity relationship analysis.

Exact and approximate matching are important tools used in all five ER activities, but direct matching of references is not the only method for determining reference equivalence. Other methods include transitive linking, associative linking, and asserted linking.

There are four principal architectures for ER systems: merge-purge/record linking, heterogeneous database join, identity resolution, and identity capture. Merge-purge represents the most basic and common form of ER, where entity references are systematically compared to each other and separated into clusters (subsets) of equivalent records. Heterogeneous database join systems are a form of transactional ER system where attribute values from an input reference are translated into queries to different databases and database tables. The query results are analyzed to determine if there are references in databases that are equivalent to the input reference. In identity resolution architectures, incoming references are resolved against a set of managed identities. Each identity in an identity resolution system has a persistent identifier that can be used to link references that are equivalent to the identity, thus creating a persistent link. The identity capture architecture is a form of identity resolution in which the system builds (learns) a set of identities from the references it processes rather than starting with a known set of identities.

Review Questions

1. The definition of ER makes specific reference to "real-world" entities. Explain why you think this is important. Give some examples of entities that are not real-world entities.
2. In some database systems, the primary key for an entity can be a compound key made by combining more several attributes. Explain the circumstances in which this would be practical. Discuss the advantages and disadvantages of a compound primary key made up of identity attributes versus one that is a single-valued, assigned identifier.
3. Investigate and explain how the Entity-Relation Model compares to newer object modeling techniques such as Unified Modeling Language (UML).
4. Explain what you think Maydanchik meant by data decay as a source of data quality problems and how it is different from the other sources of data quality problems.
5. In the case of product identity, a master product table usually identifies a particular type of product, such as a model. On the other hand, an inventory system would keep track of each individual product, even those of the same model. Discuss some of the considerations in designing an ER system for each of these situations. What would be the entities in each case? What would entity references look like? In what situations would it be better to have one rather than the other?

6. ER is important in maintaining patient medical records. Suppose an ER system at a hospital made some false-negative and some false-positive linking decisions. Give examples of these kinds of decisions and possible adverse patient care outcomes that could result from them.

7. Calculate the normalized Levenshtein Edit Distance, Maximum q-Gram, Adjusted q-Gram Tetrahedral ratio, Jaro Comparator, Jaro-Winkler Comparator, and Soundex for each of the following string pairs: ("NICK", "NICHOLAS"), ("MICHELLE", "MITCHELL"), ("MUHAMMAD", MOHAMMAD"), ("CHARLES", "CHARLISE"), and ("JOHNSON", "JOHNSTON").

8. Explain the difference between reference linking and reference equivalence.

9. Design an association configuration among customer entities (different from the household example) where the associations are not equivalences but where the configuration of associations could lead to a equivalence (linking) decision.

10. Explain the difference between a merge-purge ER system and an identity resolution ER system.

11. Explain the difference between an identity resolution ER system and an identity capture ER system.

12. Discuss some of the differences and similarities between linking references by transitive equivalence and association analysis.

13. Identify at least five public sources and five commercial sources of asserted equivalence information for customer entities.

14. Give a real or fictional scenario of how ER has played or could play an important role in a criminal investigation.

2

PRINCIPLES OF INFORMATION QUALITY

Information Quality

Information is now increasingly viewed as an organizational asset (Redman, 2008) that not only drives operational processes but can be mined for intelligence (Chan, Talburt, Talley, 2010), which can be used to improve organizational performance and help an organization gain a competitive advantage in the marketplace. *Information quality* (IQ) is an emerging discipline concerned with maximizing the value of an organization's information assets and assuring that the information products it produces meet the expectations of the customers who use them (Talburt, 2009).

IQ versus DQ

The term *data quality* (DQ) is often used interchangeably with IQ. Most researchers agree that there is a difference between data and information, although they don't always agree on where one ends and the other begins in a given situation. On the other hand, there is considerable disagreement as to whether there is a material difference between DQ and IQ. Fisher, Luaria, Chengalur-Smith, Wang (2006) and others have argued that trying to make this distinction detracts from the more important IQ issues, while others such as Eppler (2006) make a clear distinction. As with most terminology, these differences are not a real issue as long as the writer's stance is made clear.

The view taken in this text is that IQ is a discipline, a body of knowledge and practice that includes DQ along with many other topics such as master data management (MDM) and data governance (DG). After an extensive survey and analysis of IQ practice and literature, the International Association for Information and Data Quality (IAIDQ) has defined IQ as addressing six domains of knowledge and skills (IAIDQ, 2010). These domains are:

1. *Information quality strategy and governance.* "... includes efforts to provide the structures and processes for making decisions about an organization's data as well as ensuring the appropriate people are engaged to manage information throughout its life cycle."

2. *Information quality environment and culture.* "... provide the background that enables an organization's employees to continuously identify, design, develop, produce, deliver, and support information quality to meet customer needs."

3. *Information quality value and business impact.* "... techniques used to determine the effects of data quality on the business as well as the methods for prioritizing information quality projects."

4. *Information architecture quality.* "... includes the tasks that assure the quality of the data blueprint for an organization."

5. *Information quality measurement and improvement.* "... covers the steps involved in conducting data quality improvement projects."

6. *Sustaining information quality.* "... focuses on implementing processes and management systems that ensure ongoing information quality."

In the IAIDQ IQ framework, the DQ tasks fall mainly in the last three domains. DQ focuses on the condition of data as measured against a set of specifications or requirements. IQ encompasses all six domains, including the external views of the information product user, organizational management, and information suppliers. To lay the foundation for a more in-depth understanding of IQ, it will be helpful to first discuss the concepts of data and information as described in two approaches to *information theory.*

Shannon Information Theory

The first is a theory developed by Claude Shannon (Shannon, 1948) while working at Bell Labs in the 1940s, and not surprisingly, it defines information from the perspective of communication. The underlying model developed by Shannon characterizes information as a message transmitted from a sender to a receiver in way that such that the message is understood by the receiver. In the Shannon Model, the actual content of the message is not important, nor is it concerned with whether the message is true or false. The only point of importance is the integrity of the transmission. Because all electronic transmission systems add some level of noise to the signal representing the message, Shannon's theory is primarily focused on developing efficient methods for encoding and decoding messages so that they are more resilient to transmission noise.

An important concept in the Shannon model is that it differentiates between data and information. Data are assertions about the state of a system that become information when they are placed into relationship to each other and interpreted by the receiver. Another is the formulation of the entropy of a discrete random variable X. In the case that X takes on the values {x_1, ..., x_n}, and p_j represent the probability that X will have the value x_j, then the *Shannon entropy* of X, represented by H(X), is given by

$$H(X) = -\sum_{j=1}^{n} p_j \log_2\left(p_j\right)$$

Shannon entropy can be used to estimate the number of binary digits (bits) necessary to encode messages based on the symbols that comprise the messages and their relative frequency of occurrence.

Fisher Information

A different view of information is based on a statistical model developed by R. A. Fisher (Fisher, 1925). In contrast to Shannon, *Fisher information* focuses on determining whether the value of an unknown parameter can be estimated based on a sequence of observations. When described in the message framework of the Shannon model, the observed values of Fisher information can be thought of as a series of messages trying to convey a particular value to the receiver. Fisher information focuses on the amount of information in the messages—that is, given a random variable X that depends on a parameter θ, it provides a measure of how much information the probability density function P(X|θ) carries about θ. Fisher information is the variance of the score. Because the expectation of the score is zero, this can be expressed as

$$I(\theta) = E\left[\left(\frac{\partial}{\partial x}\ln f(x|\theta)\right)^2\right]$$

Value of Information

Because of its focus on message content, one might expect that Fisher information is a better starting point for defining IQ, but this is not entirely the case. Both Shannon and Fisher contribute key concepts to the understanding of IQ. Shannon's introduction of the role of the receiver as an evaluator of the information is one of the most important aspects of IQ. However, there is yet another concept essential to the understanding of IQ that is missing from both of the Shannon and Fisher models. That concept is the intent of the message—that is, to what use will the receiver put the information, and more important, will the information have value (utility) for the receiver in the context of its intended use? These three concepts of information format, meaning, and purpose form the foundation of IQ and allow it to be anchored in measurable terms. The same three concepts also underpin the study of signs and symbols known as *semiotics,* where they are called *syntactics, semantics,* and *pragmatics,* respectively (Eco, 1976).

IQ and the Quality of Information

IQ as a discipline covers a wide range of topics and concerns. Kumar (2005) would categorize IQ as a concept rather than a variable that can be measured. To contrast IQ as a concept or discipline with the measurable aspects of IQ, it is useful to introduce the term *quality of information* (QoI) used by Gackowski (2009) and others. In this text, the quality of information is defined as the degree to which the information creates value for a user in a particular application. This definition relates IQ to a measurable variable (value) and embodies several important principles derived from the previous discussions of information theory and semiotics.

IQ Principle #1: Information only produces value when it is used in an application.

Information is dynamic, not static, and has a life cycle. For example, McGilvray (2008) describes a six-part information life cycle called POSMAD, short for *planning, obtaining, storing, maintaining, applying, and disposing,* of which only one, its application, produces value, the rest are overhead. Information stored in a database or a filing cabinet has potential value, but that value is not realized until it is made accessible, organized into a usable form, and used to drive meaningful activity. When data is processed and organized into a form needed for its application, it is called an *information product* (IP) (Wang, Lee, Pipino, Strong, 1998).

IQ Principle #2: The quality of an IP (QoI) is proportional to the value of the application it supports.

The quality of information is assessed in relation to the value it produces through its use as an IP. According to this principle, changes to an IP that increase its value in an application give the information higher quality. Conversely, changes that decrease its value in an application lower the quality of the information. The evaluation of IP quality must always take place in the context of a particular application of the information.

IQ Principle #3: The quality of an IP depends on its application. The same information can have different quality when used for different purposes.

DQ Dimensions and Measurements

Relating the quality of information to the value of its application is one of the most important and often misunderstood principles of IQ. The most common misunderstanding is that the quality of information is defined in terms of certain characteristics of the data itself. These characteristics are called *data quality dimensions*. There are a number of different frameworks for describing DQ dimensions. One of the most cited is the Wang-Strong Framework (Wang, Strong, 1996) of 16 DQ dimensions in four different categories, as shown in Table 2.1.

DQ dimensions represent measurable aspects of data, and there are many formulations or approaches to quantifying them. A particular formulation for the measurement of a DQ dimension is called a *DQ rating* or sometimes a *DQ metric*. The term *DQ rating* is preferred over *DQ metric* because metric has a mathematical definition that does not always carry over into

Table 2.1: Wang-Strong DQ Dimensional Framework

Intrinsic	Contextual	Representational	Accessibility
- Accuracy	- Value-added	- Interpretability	- Access
- Believability	- Relevancy	- Ease of Understanding	- Security
- Objectivity	- Timeliness	- Representational consistency	
- Reputation	- Completeness	- Conciseness of representation	
	- Amount of data	- Manipulability	

the DQ domain. A simple example of a DQ rating (Lee, Pipino, Funk, Wang, 2006) for the dimension of completeness would be

$$C = 1 - \frac{n}{T}$$

where "T" represents the total number of rows in a database table and "n" represents the number of rows that have a null or missing value in a particular column of the table. The value of "C" will range from 0 in the case that all rows have null value, to a value of 1 in the case that none of the rows has a null value.

Other DQ ratings can have a more complex representation. For example, Lee, et al. (2006) also give a DQ rating for timeliness as

$$T = (\max\{(1 - C/V), 0\})^S$$

where

$$C : \text{currency} = (\text{deliverytime}) - (\text{input time}) + (\text{age at input})$$

$$V : \text{volatility} = \text{length of time data is valid}$$

$$S : \text{sensitivity factor} > 0$$

In this formulation, currency is the total age of the data from its creation until the point of measurement, whereas volatility is the total amount of time for which the data is useful. The basic measurement is the ratio of currency to volatility, which is subtracted from one to reverse the scaling direction from zero to one. Also, due to the fact that its age may be longer than its useful life, the ratio of C to V may be larger than one, leading to a negative value when subtracted from one. Taking the maximum value of this expression with zero constrains the final value to always be in the interval zero to one.

A final step in the calculation is to raise the ratio to the power of S, the sensitivity factor. When S has the value of one, the ratio will be linear—that is, as the data gets 10% older, the timeliness rating will drop by 10% for a fixed volatility.

Figure 2.1 shows that when the sensitivity is S is one, the values of T are linear with respect to value of C for a fixed value V. For example, when C is one-half the value of V (50% of V), the rating T will be at 0.5; if C were at 90% of the value V, T would be 0.9, etc. Selecting a value of S different from one will tend to amplify or dampen the effects of changes in currency with respect to a fixed volatility.

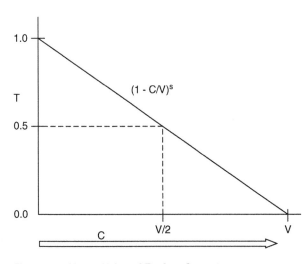

Figure 2.1: Linear Value of T when S = 1

Figure 2.2 shows the amplified values of T when the value of S is less than one. In this case, when C reaches 50% of the value of V, the value of T will still be larger than 0.5. The value of T will not drop to 0.5 until C is a much larger fraction of V. For example, if C is 3 days, V is 4 days, and S is 0.5, then

$$T = (\max\{(1 - 3/4), 0\})^{0.5} = (0.25)^{0.5} = 0.50$$

In this case, even though C has reached 75% of the value of V, the rating has only fallen to 50% of its value.

Figure 2.3 shows the dampened values of T when S is greater than one. In this case, when C ages to 50% of the value of V, the value of T will be less than 0.5. The value of T will reach 0.5 when C is a much smaller fraction of V. For example, if C is 3 days, V is 4 days, and S is 2, then

$$T = (\max\{(1 - 3/4), 0\})^2 = (0.25)^2$$
$$= 0.0625$$

In this case, when C ages to 75% of the value of V, the rating value T falls to just over 6% of its value.

In some situations it may be useful to combine multiple ratings for different dimensions or different items into a single rating—for example, to create an indicator on a DQ scorecard (Talburt, Campbell, 2006). In combining ratings, some ratings may be given more weight than others. One way to accomplish this is to use a simple weighted average (Lee, et al, 2006) given by

$$\text{Combined Rating} = \sum_{j=1}^{n} (w_j \cdot R_j)$$

where R_j, $j = 1,...,n$ are the individual ratings and w_j, $j = 1,...,n$ are a corresponding set of weights such that

$$w_j > 0, j = 1, ..., n \text{ and } \sum_{j=1}^{n} w_j = 1$$

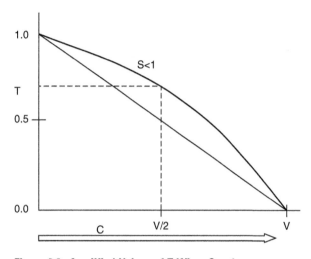

Figure 2.2: Amplified Values of T When S < 1

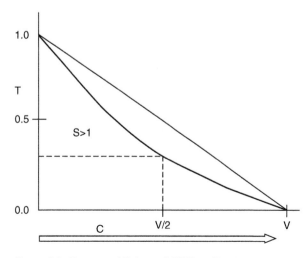

Figure 2.3: Dampened Values of T When S > 1

In addition to DQ ratings, standard techniques in descriptive and inferential statistics can also be used for DQ measurement. For large datasets it may not be practical to assess every item or record but only on samples of the data. Fisher, et al. (2006) include an excellent discussion and examples of the application of statistics in the context of DQ measurement and assessment.

DQ ratings and statistical methods both provide objective DQ quality measures, but there is also value in subjective measurements. The information quality assessment (IQA) survey developed by the Cambridge Research Group (Huang, Lee, Wang, 1999) asked system stakeholders to rate their perception of quality in each of the 16 dimensions of DQ in the Wang-Strong framework. Respondents rate the quality of each dimension using a 1-to-10 Likert scale.

Subjective measures such as the IQA survey provide insight into IQ issues in several ways. One is the comparison of average survey responses among stakeholder groups called a *role gap analysis* (Fisher, et al., 2006). For example, it can show differences in the perception of data quality between managers and database administrators or between providers and consumers. The value of the comparison is not so much in the absolute value of the average scores of these groups as it is in the differences. These gaps in perception are often related to organizational IQ issues. They also can help direct the next steps in an analysis by focusing attention on those dimensions where there is agreement that quality is low. At a minimum, data quality surveys engage stakeholders in thinking about IQ and discussing it with others, an important first step for any organization beginning to grapple with this important issue.

Another approach similar to role gap analysis is to use subjective measures in combination with objective measures. Called the *diagnostic approach* (Pipino, Lee, Wang, 2002), it results in the categorization of measurements into four groups. These groups are illustrated as the four quadrants of the graph in Figure 2.4.

The dimensions or items that have low quality by both objective and subjective measures fall in the lower-left quadrant, Q3. These are potentially the highest-priority issues to address because the low

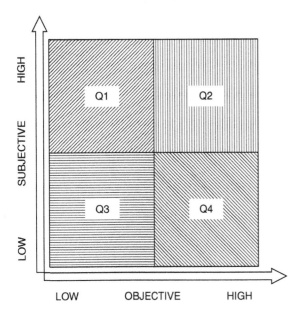

Figure 2.4: Objective vs. Subjective Assessments

objective measures confirm the stakeholders' perceptions of low quality. Conversely, those that fall into Q2 would have a lower priority. The issues that fall into the off-diagonal quadrants Q1 and Q4 require further investigation as to why there is a discrepancy between the objective and the subjective measures.

Tools and techniques such as these are important for identifying DQ issues and establishing priorities for improvement initiatives. Others include the benefit vs. cost matrix, ranking and prioritization, process impact, cost of low-quality data, and cost/benefit analysis (McGilvray, 2008).

DQ ratings are very useful tools for describing the condition of data and are an indicator of its quality, but they do not in of themselves define quality of information (QoI). The following example illustrates this point. A company periodically tries to stimulate sales by mailing its customers coupons that provide a discount for purchasing certain products. The company also measures the effectiveness of the sales campaign in terms of the total amount of sales from the products purchased with coupons. Suppose that after one of the campaigns, a great effort is made to improve the condition of the customer information because it was noted that some of the information was missing or inaccurate. A DQ assessment showed that the customer first-name field was only 80% complete and that 30% of the customer telephone numbers were incorrect. Based on this finding, an effort was made to address these problems. As a result, the completeness of the first-name field was increased from 80% to 90%, and the accuracy of customer phone numbers was increased from 70% to 85%. After the improvements were made, another coupon sales campaign was launched. Unfortunately for the company, the total sales from the new campaign turned out to be essentially the same as before the improvements were made. The conclusion is that even though the DQ was improved, the QoI was not improved for application of this IP because it did not result in any additional value.

The IQ Gap

What is missing in our sales campaign example is that the DQ assessment did not first explore which data items and which dimensions of those items were having the most impact on the value of the application in which the information was used. Establishing and improving DQ metrics is only effective in improving IQ when they are focused on the elements and dimensions that have an impact on the application. In the example, it may be the case that customers are receiving the coupons

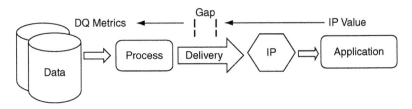

Figure 2.5: The IQ Gap

by mail even when the first name is missing. Similarly, having a correct phone number may not be relevant to the mailing campaign. It is more likely that improving the completeness and accuracy of mailing addresses to improve the deliverability of the offers would have produced more value for this application.

Figure 2.5 is meant to illustrate this problem called the *IQ gap*. In this scenario, data in an information system is organized into an information product that is delivered and used in an application. The gap is the failure to properly understand which characteristics of the data that was used to build the IP have the most impact on the QoI—that is, the value produced by the application of the IP.

Unfortunately, organizations often implement DQ metrics based on what they can conveniently measure, not necessarily what they should measure. Even in modest-sized information systems there can be thousands of combinations of elements, dimensions, and formulations to define DQ metrics around the data. The key to successful IQ is in determining which DQ metrics are most important to each IP and application. Just as a statistician often undertakes factor analysis to determine which independent variables have the greatest effect on the value of the dependent variable, the IQ analyst must work backward from the application to determine which elements and dimensions of the data are having the most impact on the value of the IP.

It is precisely for this reason that Domain 3 of the IAIDQ IQ framework addresses the knowledge and skills related to IQ value and business impact. The ability to understand and quantify the effects of data quality on an organization is as important as being able to design good DQ ratings and finding root causes of DQ problems.

IP Mapping

A valuable tool for helping to close the IQ gap is the *Information Product Map* (IP-Map). The IP-Map is a systematic way to represent the details associated with creating an IP by tracing the flow of individual data elements from their sources to the final product (Lee, et al., 2006; Shankaranarayanan, Zaid, Wang,

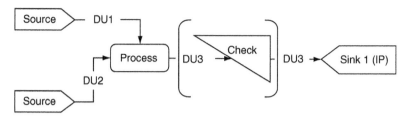

Figure 2.6: A Simple IP-Map

Figure 2.6: A Simple IP-Map

2003; Ballou, Wang, Pazer, Tayi, 1998; Pierce, 2005). Figure 2.6 illustrates some of the features of an IP-Map.

The diagram starts with the flow of data units (DU) from the two sources into Process 1. A new data unit (DU3) flows from Process 1 through a quality check. The parentheses represent a business boundary indicating that the check is performed in another business unit. Finally, DU3 flows into Data Sink 1, which represents the information product. IP-Maps are similar to traditional data flow diagrams except that the IP-Map focuses on the data requirements rather than the process requirements and specifications. IP-Maps can also span multiple systems and business units and indicate where specific data units cross their boundaries. Data flow diagrams typically document the process specifications for a single system.

Two IP Examples

Consider two information products produced by a company that manufactures and sells a product. The first is a direct pay deposit for its employees, and the second is a report on prior year sales. The direct deposit transaction represents a type of IP that is well understood in terms of the information that goes into it, the process that creates it, and the expected result of its application. For example, if it is a deposit transaction for a salaried employee, the calculation of the gross pay as a fraction of annual pay, the calculation of the net pay based on a fixed set of deductions, the schedule to generate the transaction, and the bank to which it is to be sent are easily defined and documented. From the standpoint of the employee receiving the deposit, the IP customer, the value is a binary measure rather than a continuous measure of value. The deposit amount is either correct or incorrect, and it was either deposited on the designated day or it was late.

Unlike the employee pay transaction where the salary is a well-established number, the prior year sales figures are not as clearly defined. The purpose of the prior year sales report is to inform the management (the IP customer) of past sales of their products. It also provides other insights such as which product lines, or departments, or locations, or buyers accounted for a proportional share of the sales. The value of this IP is directly related to the effectiveness of the management decisions that are based on its content. Unlike the electronic deposit IP, which either meets or does not meet user expectations, the effectiveness of the sales report IP can take on a wide range of ratings, from entirely useless to highly effective. This is further complicated by the fact that the effectiveness of the decisions made from the report are not immediately known. It may take months or years to fully evaluate their effects.

IQ Management

The examples of employee pay transactions and prior year sales reports also illustrate two broad classes of IPs that are dealt with in IQ. The pay transaction IP is this kind of information product that has inspired the analogy between information systems and the manufacturing process and has motivated the "fitness for use" view of DQ. In this analogy, data coming into the system corresponds to the raw materials, and the IT process corresponds to the machining and molding that produce a final product that conforms to a well-understood set of requirements. The analogy has been very useful in many of the principles of *total quality management* (TQM) that have been successful in improving the quality of manufactured products and have been translated into the production of IPs by information systems. One of the most useful concepts from TQM adapted to IQ is the discipline of product management (Wang, Lee, Pipino, Strong, 1998; Wang, 1998).

IQ Principle #4: Information should be managed as a product.

Lee, Pipino, Funk, and Wang (2006) set out four principles for managing information as a product. These principles are to:
1. Understand the needs of the information consumer
2. Manage information as the product of a well-defined information production process
3. Manage the information product life cycle
4. Appoint an information product manager to oversee information processes and products

One of the benefits from the adoption of the product management model for information has been to move IQM from being solely an IT function to being an enterprise endeavor. There are four principal stakeholders in the IQM process: the collectors or contributors of the data, the custodians of the data (IT personnel), the customers or consumers of the information products, and management. Playing off Einstein's famous formula,

$$E = MC^2$$

and the fact that the first three IQ management stakeholders start with the letter "C," information quality management stakeholders can be expressed as the mnemonic

$$IQM = MC^3$$

The formula indicates that successful IQM must include four primary stakeholders in an organization: "M" representing management; the first "C" represents the collectors, contributors, or compilers of the data; the second "C" represents the custodians of the information (the IT group); and the third "C" represents the customers or consumers of the information products. All too often IQM is assumed to only be the responsibility of the IT department, the information custodians. However, as organizations begin to view their information as an asset, it is seen as belonging to the entire organization as a whole, not owned and controlled by a particular group or department. This has led to the concept of *data stewardship*, the idea that certain people or groups are caretakers of information rather than its owners (Seiner, 2005).

Fitness for Use

In the context of TQM, Crosby (1979) defined the quality of a product as "conformance to requirements," and Juran (1974) defined it as "fitness for use." Because of this, "data that are fit for use" has been widely adopted as a definition for IQ (Wang, Strong, 1996; Redman, 1998). The problem with the fitness-for-use definition of IQ is that it assumes that the expectations of an IP user and the value produced by the IP in its application are both well understood. This is a fair assumption for a manufactured product and can also be true for certain types of IP that closely resemble a manufactured product. In the previous example of the electronic deposit, the IP drives an important operational process that must be completed in order to pay the company employees. The IP will meet the users' (employees') expectations when it is accurate, on time, and complete. It is not difficult for the user or the producer of the IP to evaluate its fitness for use.

However, there are many other IPs that do not fall into this category, those for which the fitness-for-use definition is much more problematic. The previous example of the prior year sales report illustrates this type of IP. In a large organization, the aggregation of prior year sales information can be a very complex issue. It may draw information from many different sources within the organization, and for each source there are questions about how the sales were calculated. Calculations may vary in terms of net versus gross sales, the handling of returns, and accrual versus received. There can also be questions about whether all the relevant sources were included, whether all the sources made their calculations in the same way, whether they all used the equivalent monetary units, and whether they all included sales for the same period of time. In addition to the questions about the sources, there are the characteristics of the IP itself, such as whether it is organized in a way that it is understandable, does the user trust it, does it have all the needed information, was it produced in the time needed? Different answers to these and many other questions could all lead to thousands of possible versions of the IP, each with a different relative value to the user. In these situations IQ is better understood in terms IP value (QoI) rather than just its fitness for use.

Casting IQ in terms value is also helpful in gaining management's endorsement of IQ projects and management practices in an organization. IQ capability and maturity vary widely across organizations, with many still operating with little or no understanding of even the most basic IQ principles. In trying to introduce IQ into an organization, there are three keys to success:

1. Always relate IQ to business value
2. Give stakeholders a way to talk about IQ—the vocabulary and concepts
3. Show them a way to get started improving IQ and a vision for sustaining it

IQ and the Organization

To this point, DQ and IQ have been discussed in relation to a specific IP and application. However most organizations produce many IPs used by both internal and external customers, and often create new or updated versions of each IP on a regular basis. Therefore another important aspect of IQ as a discipline relates to the methods and techniques needed to manage and control IP quality at the organizational level, not just for a particular project or initiative. The situation is similar to what has been learned about the software development: that long-term success depends on building an organizational capability and maturity that allow for repeatable success and continuous improvement. For example, Baskarada (2009) has developed a five-level IQM capability and maturity model in which each level is defined in terms of the maturity indicators that are satisfied.

Two domains of the IAIDQ IQ framework address IQ at the organizational level. The domain of information quality strategy and governance addresses the need to have an organizationwide understanding of how information assets will be developed and controlled. *Data governance* is defined by Thomas (2010) as "the exercise of decision-making and authority for data-related matters." One of main tenants of data governance is the concept of *data stewardship*—that data belongs to the organization, and individuals and units are accountable to management for its proper care and use. The second domain is information quality environment and culture, which addresses the basic quality principle of continuous improvement and the need for everyone in the organization, regardless of his or her role, to support information quality to meet customer needs.

IQ Principle #5: For an organization to be successful in IQM, it must be supported at the highest levels in the organization and be seen as a responsibility shared by everyone in the organization.

Information versus Process

At the most fundamental level, IQ is about information, which stands in contrast to process. Even though we are well into the so-called "information age", there has historically been a lack of parity between information (data) and process. Up to now, the information age has really been more the "technology age." Much of the disparity can be traced back to the days when computer systems had very limited memory and most problems were attacked algorithmically. The premium on internal memory also meant that information was always stored in the most concise and compact representation possible and was kept offline until it was absolutely needed.

Though software development has advanced significantly, until recently information development has not kept pace. Traditional software development projects focus almost entirely on the functionality and optimum performance of computer programs, simply assuming that any information to be processed will be available and suitable for the application at hand. Although going to great lengths to assure the quality of software through tightly controlled quality assurance and release processes, often little attention is paid to the quality of the data to be processed or the usefulness of the output. This is in spite of growing evidence that the failure of large information system projects is more often due to poor information than poorly developed software. The ascendency of Google® as a rival to the software giant Microsoft® is symbolic of the current shift in focus from process to information.

According to the Gartner research firm, inaccurate or incomplete data is a leading cause of failure in business intelligence and CRM projects (Keizer, 2004). In many ways this is just a confirmation of the long-acknowledged GIGO principle—"garbage in equals garbage out."

IQ Principle #6: Successful information systems implementation requires equal attention to both the quality of software and the quality of information.

IQ and HPC

The minimalist approach to information representation is another legacy that still haunts modern information systems despite the fact that large-scale processing and virtually unlimited memory are now relatively inexpensive. *High-performance computing* (HPC) is no longer something just for the research laboratory. The movements toward *cloud computing* and *software as a service* (SaaS) (Knorr, 2008) are putting HPC within the reach of almost every organization.

Just as the Entity-Relation Model (ERM) informs the definition of ER, the Enterprise Architecture (EA) Model provides a foundation for understanding IQ. EA has its roots in the work of John Zachman (1987) and has evolved into a widely adopted framework for designing an organization that can effectively and efficiently carry out its strategic mission. The Federal CIO Council defines EA as "a strategic information asset base, which defines the mission, the information necessary to perform the mission and the technologies necessary to perform the mission ..." (EA Guide, 2001). As this definition calls out, the EA framework is built on three basic architectural models: business architecture, information architecture, and technology architecture (sometimes divided into solution or application architecture and technology architecture).

In the EA model, the business architecture should drive the information architecture—that is, what we want to accomplish should dictate what information is needed. Decisions about mission and information needs should then drive the technology. The design of the information architecture should be the starting point for IQ in an enterprise. Historically this has not always been the case, because many organizations want to jump directly from business architecture to technology. When this happens, the technology architecture dictates the information architecture rather than the reverse.

The Evolution of Information Quality

Even though IQ has only recently emerged as a discipline, it has already gone through several phases of evolution in scope and meaning. These are the data-cleaning, prevention, product perspective, and enterprise asset phases.

Problem Recognition: The Data-Cleaning Phase

Most of the concepts and current practices that form the basis for information quality emerged from the data warehousing movement that gained popularity in the early 1990s through the work of Inmon (1992), Kimball, et al. (1998), and others. Most organizations had no idea of the poor condition of their operational data stores and the inconsistencies among them until they attempted to integrate them into a single data warehouse repository.

It was at this time that organizations recognized that much of their data was inaccurate, incomplete, inconsistently represented, and often in generally poor condition, either because it was this way from its source or because it was damaged by the processes attempting to bring the sources together. Redman (1998) provided an overview of the extent of the problem and, perhaps more important, related information quality problems to the adverse impacts they were having on the organization at both the operational and strategic levels.

The recognition that information quality problems were negatively impacting business operations spawned a new industry based on "cleaning the dirty data" in the data warehouse (English, 1999; Brackett, 1996). It was during this period that information quality focused on the immediate problem of *data cleaning*, sometimes called *data hygiene* or *data cleansing*. In the cleaning phase, most of the attention was focused on the use of ETL

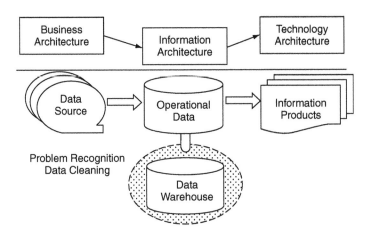

Figure 2.7: Phase 1, Data Cleaning

processes to standardize the data from different sources so that it could not only be merged into a single data warehouse but so that queries against the data would be meaningful. As Lindsey (2008) recounts an early engagement with a product manufacturer, the discovery of the many different spellings of the color beige in the product database would prevent any query where "color equals beige" from returning any meaningful results.

In Figure 2.7 the boxes above the line are meant to show the conceptual models of the enterprise, in particular the information architecture where the data models and database schemata are designed. The shapes below the line are meant to show the implementation of the models in terms of an operational information system that ingests data sources, processes them, and produces outputs, one of which is the data warehouse.

Root Cause Detection: The Prevention Phase

The next phase of IQ evolution, shown in Figure 2.8, began to draw on the principles of manufacturing quality management. In particular it focused on finding the root causes of information quality problems in an attempt to prevent them from entering the data warehouse in the first place. It is also during the prevention phase that organizations realized that simply standardizing didn't make it correct and that more attention has to be given to data accuracy (Olson, 2003).

Information as a Product Phase

One of the most important turning points in the maturity of information quality was the adoption of the perspective that information is the product of an information system, not a

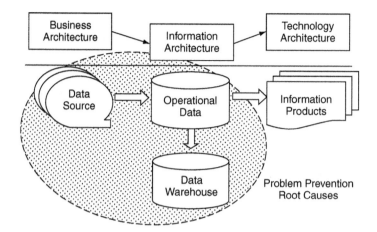

Figure 2.8: Phase 2, Root Causes

byproduct (Huang, Lee, Wang, 1999). By introducing the paradigm of "information manufacturing," whereby data sources are thought of as raw materials, the programs as the manufacturing process, and the final outputs as the products, a broad range of total quality management (TQM) principles could be applied to information systems, yielding the total data quality management (TDQM) process (Wang, Kon, 1998)

In addition to bringing into IQ management many of the principles of TQM, such as the discipline of product management, the perspective of information as a product brought focus on the uses and users (customers) of information. In the cleaning and prevention phases of IQ, the focus was on the condition of data measured in dimensions, such as accuracy, completeness, and consistency. In the product phase, it became important to understand the user's perspective and to make the connection between objective measures of the data and the user's assessment of the product's value. For example, striving to increase the completeness of a certain table column from 80% to 90% may be an improvement goal for an internal DQ measurement. However, if the data from the column goes into a report, and the user of that report does not judge that the report has any additional value as a result of meeting that goal, then information quality from a product perspective (QoI) has not been increased.

Figure 2.9 illustrates the information product view of information quality that embraces the entire production process, including all the MC[3] stakeholders: management, collectors, custodians, and consumers. It is during this phase that the concept and practice of data governance (DG) emerged.

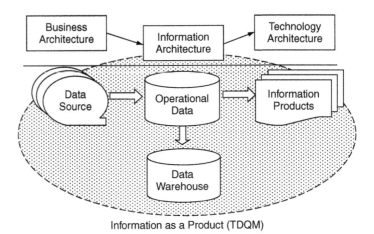

Figure 2.9: Phase 3,
Information as a Product

Information as a Product (TDQM)

Information as an Asset

IQ is now entering a new phase as information is increasingly regarded as an enterprise asset. In this new phase, information quality is moving from a passive role to an active role in the enterprise. In the recognition, prevention, and product phases, IQ was largely relegated to a passive role in the sense that IQ methods and practice were always starting with the systems and information architectures already designed and built.

Figure 2.10 shows the scope of the enterprise asset phase reaching into the modeling layer to indicate that IQ is increasingly seen as a key component of the information architecture. A well-known principle of software development is that the earlier in the process that a problem is discovered, the less costly

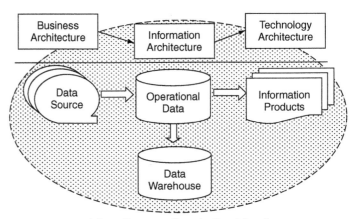

Figure 2.10: Phase 4,
Information as an Asset

Information as an Organizational Asset

it is to correct. Addressing IQ in information architecture is the application of the same principle to information, or, as Deming (1986) said, "build quality into a product throughout production." Another aspect of this phase is the focus on *master data management* (MDM), the attempt to establish *systems of record* (SOR) or *single points of truth* (SPOT) for the values of key entity attributes, such as customer name and address, product code, and so on.

IQ as an Academic Discipline

One of the reasons for the lack of attention to IQ is that until recently there has not been a widely accepted body of knowledge and vocabulary for describing and measuring DQ and the QoI. Whereas the discipline of computer science has a long history of academic research and publication in topics such as algorithm design, the theory of computation, and proof of correctness for algorithms, the same is not true for IQ. Fortunately this state of affairs is beginning to change as more conferences and journals begin to solicit and publish papers in this area. A recent paper by Ge and Helfert (2006) describes the emerging framework of IQ research.

In addition, many colleges and universities are beginning to incorporate information quality courses and seminars into their curricula. Two examples of this trend are the Massachusetts Institute of Technology (MIT) Information Quality Program and the University of Arkansas at Little Rock Information Quality Graduate Program.

TDQM and the MIT IQ Program

Responding to industry needs for high-quality data and inspired by the success of the total quality management movement in manufacturing, Dr. Stuart Madnick of the MIT Sloan School of Business led a partnership of organizations to create a research program in the early 1990s called Total Data Quality Management (TDQM). Although the short-term focus of TDQM was to create a center of excellence among practitioners of data quality techniques, perhaps its greatest impact has resulted from its long-term goal of creating a theory of data and information quality.

One of the most successful outcomes of the TDQM program is the MIT Information Quality Program (MITIQ), led by Dr. Richard Wang and based at the MIT Center for Technology, Policy, and Industrial Development (CTPID). The MITIQ program has been the leader in promoting and disseminating research in information quality through its sponsorship of the International Conference on Information Quality (ICIQ). The ICIQ has been held annually since 1996 and has created a worldwide community of academicians and practitioners who regularly present at the conference and publish their peer-reviewed papers in its proceedings. Recently, the MITIQ community worked together to organize and launch the Association for Computing Machinery (ACM) *Journal of Data and Information Quality* (JDIQ), with Dr. Madnick and Dr. Yang Lee (Northeastern University) as its editors-in-chief.

To complement the research focus of the ICIQ, the MITIQ Program began sponsoring the annual Information Quality Industry Symposium (IQIS) in July 2007. The IQIS conference promotes the sharing of best practices and technology among IQ practitioners, IQ tool vendors, and professional organizations promoting IQ.

The UALR IQ Graduate Program

Despite the rapid growth in IQ practice that arose out of data warehousing during 1990s, there was no corresponding growth in academic programs. In 2000, Craig Fisher introduced an undergraduate course titled Data Quality and Information Systems at Marist College (Fisher, et al., 2001). This course subsequently led to the publication of the first college-level textbook on IQ, *Introduction to Information Quality,* authored by Craig Fisher, Eitel Lauria, Shobha Chengalur-Smith, and Richard Wang, in 2006.

In 2005 Dr. Wang, working in collaboration with Charles Morgan, the company leader of Acxiom Corporation, headquartered in Little Rock, Arkansas, and with Dr. Mary Good, Dean of the Donaghey College of Engineering and Information Technology (EIT) at the University of Arkansas at Little Rock (UALR), conceived a plan to create the first graduate degree program in information quality. The curriculum development for the program was a joint effort among several collaborators (Lee, Pierce, Talburt, Wang, Zhu, 2007). A Master of Science in IQ was the first program developed and approved, and it enrolled its first cohort of students in the fall of 2006. The UALR IQ Graduate Program is housed in the Department of Information Science of the EIT College and now includes a graduate certificate in IQ and an IQ track in the Integrated Computing Ph.D. program.

Since 2006, several other colleges and universities have developed graduate-level programs in IQ. These include a master of science in information quality at the University of Westminster in London, U.K., and graduate studies in IQ at the University of South Australia in Adelaide.

IQ and ER

The most direct connection between IQ and ER is in the reference preparation activities (ERA2), as discussed in the Chapter 1. However, IQ and ER are connected in other ways as well. An ER process is almost always part of the creation of an IP, and the effectiveness of the ER process will have a direct bearing on the quality of the IP. In some cases, the ER process can be the IP where companies provide ER or CDI services to their clients as a product. More often, ER is an intermediate process in entity-based data integration (EBDI), a topic discussed in more detail in Chapter 4. This creates a feedback loop in which higher data quality input into an ER process produces higher-quality information products, which in turn are higher-quality inputs into successive processing, some of which may also have ER steps.

Another less obvious but equally important connection is related to growing recognition of information as an organizational asset. However, even in cases where an organization adopts this view, it is sometimes treated as a fungible asset—an asset that can be freely exchanged or replace with another of like kind. Robinson (2010) argues that when data is treated as a fungible asset, data quality suffers because data are not interchangeable. One customer or product record is not like another. A distinguishing characteristic of nonfungible assets is that they have individual identities, making entity and identity resolution key processes in IQ management.

Summary

IQ is a discipline concerned with maximizing the value of the information in an organization. The quality of information is directly related to the value it produces in its application. DQ is the practice of assessing, improving, and maintaining the condition of data with respect to established specifications or requirements and is an important component of IQ. As a discipline, IQ covers a broad array of knowledge and skills. The IAIDQ IQ framework comprises six domains that include the formulation of IQ strategy, policy, and governance; creating a culture and environment that promotes IQ; understanding, quantifying, and communicating IQ value and business impact; assuring that the organization's information architecture supports IQ; measuring and improving IQ; and sustaining IQ.

DQ dimensions define the measurable aspects of data. The measurements often take the form of DQ ratings, formulas for representing data quality on a scale from zero to one.

Review Questions

1. How is an "asset" defined from an accounting standpoint? Describe some of the ways that information fits this definition and also some of the aspects of information that don't seem to fit.
2. What is the unit of measure for the quality of information?
3. Give an example of a situation in which the same information is of high quality for one application but of much lower quality for another.
4. Find a book or article describing an IQ or DQ dimensional framework. Explain how it differs from the Wang-Strong Framework. Describe what the two frameworks have in common.
5. Explain how the definition of IP quality based on application value and the definition of IP quality as fitness for use are related to each other. Look up definitions for information utility and materiality of information, and explain how these concepts are related to IQ.
6. How can an organization know that it is experiencing the IQ gap? What are some strategies for avoiding it?
7. For an information system that is available for you to analyze, identify an IP and a single data unit of that IP. Create an IP-Map that traces the creating of the IP data unit from the source data units.
8. Describe at least two points at which you think that product manufacturing does not seem to fit as a paradigm for the production of an IP from an information system.
9. Give an example of where data could replace an algorithmic approach to the solution of an important problem.
10. Explain the difference in treating information as a fungible asset versus a nonfungible asset. Give specific examples.

3

ENTITY RESOLUTION MODELS

Overview

This chapter presents three models of ER. The models are complementary in that they address different levels and aspects of the ER process. The first and earliest model discussed is the *Fellegi-Sunter Model,* a methodology for linking equivalent references by direct matching. The Fellegi-Sunter Model provides a specific algorithm for of resolving pairs of references through probabilistic matching. The second model is the *Stanford Entity Resolution Framework* (SERF), which defines a generic model of ER in terms of matching and merging operations that act on pairs of references. Unlike Fellegi-Sunter, the SERF model does not define a specific implementation for the match (or merge) operation but instead focuses on methods for resolving a large set of references by the systematic application of the pairwise operations. The third is the *Algebraic Model,* which describes ER from an even higher level of abstraction. It focuses on the outcome of the ER process and on metrics for comparing the outcomes of different ER processes acting on the same set of references. The Algebraic Model views an ER process as defining an equivalence relation on a set of references. The Algebraic Model extends beyond the ER process to include a model for *entity-based data integration* (EBDI), discussed in more detail in Chapter 4.

The Fellegi-Sunter Model

Historically, government census, welfare, and taxation programs have been the first organizations to deal with the problem of entity resolution in attempting to tabulate and summarize information about a large population of people and businesses. To gather accurate statistics about the population, it is important to know if two records collected at different times or by different agencies and canvassers are for the same entity. In 1969, I. P. Fellegi and A. B. Sunter, statisticians working at the Dominion Bureau of Statistics in Canada, published a paper, *A Theory for Record Linkage* (Fellegi, Sunter, 1969), that described a statistical model for entity resolution. Know as the *Fellegi-Sunter Model* (FSM), it was one of the first attempts to describe ER as record linking in a rigorous way.

In addition to its historical significance, the paper still offers ER practitioners useful guidance on how to extend the linking of references from entirely deterministic matching to probabilistic matching as well as providing a methodology for creating a set of probabilistic matching rules that will not exceed given false positive and negative rates. FSM does have some limitations, however. First, it only addresses linking by direct matching of references and does not consider any of the other three linking methods discussed in Chapter 1. Another is that it is framed in the context of finding equivalent references between two lists (files) of references under the assumption that there are no equivalent references within each list—that is, all the equivalences are across lists, not within a list.

Deterministic and Probabilistic Matching

Deterministic matching is an ER method in which two references are linked if and only if all corresponding pairs of attributes have identical values (Herzog, et al., 2007). In essence, deterministic matching says that linked references are exact duplicates of each other, at least with respect to their identity attributes. This method represents the most basic form for record linkage and reflects the true meaning of the term *duplicate records*.

Fellegi and Sunter realized that deterministic matching is too restrictive and, at least in census work, leads to far too many false negatives—that is, references that should be linked but are not. Because of inconsistencies, variations, and commonly occurring data entry errors, many pairs of equivalent references will not have identical values across every one of their identity attribute pairs. The FSM extends the naïve notion of deterministic matching to the method of *probabilistic matching*. Probabilistic matching relaxes the constraint of deterministic matching by allowing some of the corresponding identity attributes to have different values. For example, if there are several identity attribute pairs and all pairs except one have the same values, that may still be deemed sufficient evidence to decide that the two references are equivalent. In cases where not all identity attribute pairs agree in value, the decision to link or not link may depend not only on how many pairs agree but also which of the pairs agree.

School Enrollment Example

The FSM can perhaps be best understood through a simple example. Suppose that at the beginning of each academic year, a public school creates one record for each student enrolled in all grades. The ER objective is to link the enrollment records for the same student across enrollment files of two consecutive grades over two consecutive years. The ER linking method is direct matching using the identity attributes of first name, last name, and date of birth. The expectation is that there will be a fairly large overlap between the files because most of the

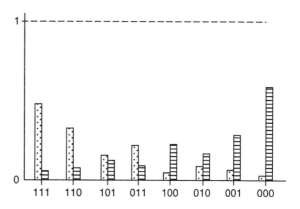

Figure 3.1: True and False Positive Probabilities for Student Records

students will be enrolled in both years, only having been promoted to a higher grade. However, there will be cases where new students enter the second year and where students enrolled in the first year leave the school before the start of the second year.

The graph in Figure 3.1 shows an evaluation of probabilistic matching patterns for the student enrollment example. On the horizontal axis the binary numbers are a coding of the possible combinations of agreement or disagreement of the identity attributes between two references. In this coding, the value 1 means that both attribute values are present (not missing) and that the two values are the same, whereas the value 0 means that either one or both values or missing or the values are present and have different values. For three attributes, there will be eight (2^3) possible patterns. When the first bit of the binary number is 1, it means that the first-name attribute values agree in both enrollment records, whereas the value 0 means that they don't agree or are missing according to the previously stated rule. Similarly, the second bit represents agreement or disagreement on the last-name attribute pair, and the third bit represents agreement or disagreement on the date of birth. For example, the coding 111 represents the case of deterministic match in which all three attributes agree.

For simplicity, the coding in Figure 3.1 has only two possible conditions (agree or disagree), but as noted in the original paper (Fellegi, Sunter, 1969), the model allows for a more complex coding—for example, a coding that separates the case of both values being different from the case where one or both values are missing. In this scenario a coding string might look like "BCA," where the "B" indicates that in the first pair of attributes one or both values are missing, the "C" that both values in the second pair of attributes are present but disagree, and the "A" that the values in the third attribute pair are present and agree. The coding could be even more complex and could take into account the nature of the values being matched, such as the first-name match is between two common first names or even to the level that the two names have a particular value such as "JOHN."

In Figure 3.1, the vertical axis measures probability on a scale from 0 to 1. On this scale, each binary coding is plotted with two vertical bars. The first bar is the probability that a pair of references for the same student (equivalent references) will satisfy this pattern. The second bar represents the probability that two references not belonging to the same student will satisfy this pattern. Taken together, these two measures indicate the effectiveness of using the pattern to make either a positive or negative a linkage decision. It is important to consider both probabilities because the Fundamental Law of ER from Chapter 1 requires that two references should be linked if, and only if, they reference the same entity. Also note that because the patterns are mutually exclusive and all patterns are included, each set of probabilities must add to 1.

The two probabilities are similar to the metrics of *precision* and *recall* (Baeza-Yates, Ribeiro-Neto, 1999) used to evaluate the effectiveness of *information retrieval* (IR) processes such as database queries. Considering the set of all possible pairings of first- and second-year enrollment records, the first probability (proportion) indicates the probability that pairs for the same student (equivalent pairs) would be found by the pattern—that is, its power to find or recall equivalent records. The second probability indicates the probability that nonequivalent pairs would also satisfy the pattern—that is, its power to discriminate or be precise in linking. In ER there is always a trade-off between these two constraints. An agreement pattern, or any other ER method, that finds many equivalent pairs is a good thing as long as it doesn't create too many false positives. On the other hand, being too conservative and using only highly precise rules may leave many equivalent pairs undiscovered and unlinked, creating a large number of false negatives. The FSM is a guide for designing a probabilistic matching scheme that does not exceed a given level (tolerance) for each of these types of errors. In the following discussion, the maximum acceptable rate for false positive linking errors is designated by μ and the maximum acceptable rate for false negative linking errors is designated by λ.

The theory behind the optimization with respect to μ and λ relies on a systematic examination of the probabilities for each pattern, as shown in Figure 3.1. For example, consider the deterministic pattern 111, where all three attributes must agree. The probability that equivalent records will satisfy this pattern is less than 50%. That means that if the decision to link were based only on this pattern, fewer than half of the equivalent records (true positives) would be linked, leaving the remaining equivalent records as false negative errors. The reason that this probability is not higher is that the example assumes that many of the values for date of birth are missing. Therefore many pairs of records for the same student will not be found by this pattern, because at least one of the records in the pair fails to have a date of birth. Even in the cases where all three attributes are recorded in two enrollment records for the same student, it is still possible that they might not agree on all three attributes. The disagreement could be caused by a number of factors, such as a data entry mistake, using a nickname one year and not the next, or possibly a legal name change. On the other hand, the probability that two enrollment records for different students will agree on all three of the attributes is relatively small, but not zero. Certainly within a large school it is possible, or even likely, that two different students could have the same date of birth and share a commonly occurring name. Therefore, in this example, the decision to link based upon the most demanding agreement pattern (111) will contribute some false positive errors.

Another example is the pattern 010, which indicates that there is agreement on the last name but not on first name or date of birth. Linking enrollment records that fit this pattern would find some equivalent pairs—for example, where one record has a complete first name and the other a nickname, and one record is missing a date-of-birth value. Even though a decision to link on the 010 pattern will find some equivalent records, it carries higher risk of creating false positives by linking nonequivalent pairs in cases where different students happen to share the same last name. Consequently this pattern is a better candidate for a not-to-link decision.

Pattern Weights and Linkage Rules

An optimal linkage rule based on probabilistic matching can be constructed if the probabilities for each pattern are known as shown in Figure 3.1. The probabilities for the patterns can be estimated by testing a sample of pairs, by using previously known characteristics about the population, or by using values established in previous work. Once the probabilities have been established, each pattern is assigned a weight based on the ratio of the first probability to the second probability. The weight ratio is a way to combine the two probabilities into a single number. The patterns with the highest weight ratios are better for decision to link because they have a high probability finding equivalent records (numerator) and a low probability of creating false positive links (denominator). Conversely, the patterns with low weight ratios are better for not-to-link decisions because they will create more true negatives and fewer false negatives. Because these ratios can take on a wide range of values from very large to very small, the weight of the pattern is expressed as the logarithm of the ratio.

$$\text{Pattern Weight} = \log_2\left(\frac{\text{Probability pattern finds equivalent pairs}}{\text{Probability pattern finds non} - \text{equivalent pairs}}\right)$$

After calculating the weight ratios for the patterns and probabilities shown in Figure 3.1, the results are arranged in descending order by value:

$$W_{111} \geq W_{110} \geq W_{011} \geq W_{101} \geq W_{010} \geq W_{001} \geq W_{100} \geq W_{000}$$

Figure 3.2 shows the same patterns and probabilities as in Figure 3.1 except that the patterns have been reordered on the graph from highest to lowest weight ratio according to the preceding sequence.

A *Fellegi-Sunter Linkage Rule* is based on choosing two values, T_μ and T_λ, where

$$W_{111} \geq T_\mu \geq T_\lambda \geq W_{000}$$

then making a linkage decision for each pair of references based on the weight of the pattern according to the following rule:

$$\text{Decision for Pattern P} = \begin{cases} W_P \geq T_\mu & \text{Positive Link} \\ W_P \leq T_\lambda & \text{Positive non Link} \\ T_\lambda > W_P > T_\lambda & \text{Possible Link} \end{cases}$$

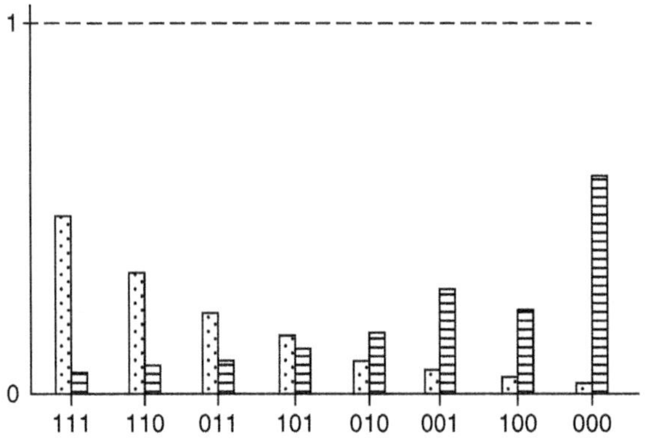

According to this rule, reference pairs that satisfy the leftmost patterns in Figure 3.2 (weights greater than T_μ) are always linked (positive link), and pairs that satisfy the rightmost patterns (weights less than T_λ) are never linked (positive nonlink). The rule also allows for patterns for which an automatic decision cannot or should not be made. Reference pairs with pattern weights that fall between T_μ and T_λ will have to be manually inspected and, presumably, correctly resolved. Figure 3.3 illustrates how T_μ and T_λ limit

Figure 3.2: Enrollment Matching Patterns Ordered by Weight

the false positive error accumulating from left to right and the false negative error accumulating from right to left.

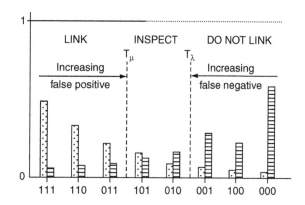

Figure 3.3: Ordered Patterns by Rule Category

The reason for the notation is that the choice of T_μ limits the false positive error rate (μ) for the positive link decisions, and the choice of T_λ limits the false negative error rate (λ) for the positive nonlink decisions. The false positive rate for this rule can be calculated by simply summing the false positive rates for the agreement patterns with weights greater than T_μ, and the false negative rate can be calculated by summing the true positive rates for the link patterns with weights less than T_λ. Therefore, if T_μ is selected so that the accumulated false positive rate is less than μ, and T_λ is selected so that the accumulated false negative rate is less than λ, then the linkage rule is optimal in that it maximizes the number of true positive and true negative links without exceeding the given error levels for each while at the same time minimizing the number of links requiring inspection. Fellegi and Sunter call this the *fundamental theorem of record linkage* (Fellegi, Sunter, 1969).

Since its original publication, a number of authors have developed and published papers describing improvements to the FSM. Most notably William Winkler at the U.S. Bureau of the Census has published on the application of expectation-maximization methods (Winkler, 1988), ways to adjust for lack of conditional independence among attributes (Winkler, 1989a), and the automation of weight calculations (Winkler, 1989b).

Calculating Weight Ratios

Herzog, Schuren, and Winkler (2007) give an excellent exposition of the FSM, including a method for calculating pattern weights from the estimated probabilities of agreement and disagreement on individual identity attributes. However, the use of this technique is based on the assumption that the attributes are conditionally independent—that is, the probability of agreement or disagreement in the value of one identity attribute does not affect the probability of agreement or disagreement in another identity attribute. Given that the attributes are conditionally independent, the pattern weight calculation is

n = number of attributes

m_i = probability that equivalent records agree on attribute i

u_i = probability that non-equivalent records agree on attribute i

$$
w_i = \begin{cases} \log_2\left(\dfrac{m_i}{u_i}\right) & \text{if agreement in attribute i} \\[2ex] \log_2\left(\dfrac{(1-m_i)}{(1-u_i)}\right) & \text{otherwise} \end{cases}
$$

$$\log_2(W_P) = \sum_{i=1}^{n} w_i$$

Using this calculation, the estimate for each pattern weight can be calculated by summing the ratios associated with individual attributes. Using the example of student enrollment records and the pattern 101, then,

$$\log_2(W_{101}) = \log_2\left(\frac{m_1}{u_1}\right) + \log_2\left(\frac{(1-m_2)}{(1-u_2)}\right) + \log_2\left(\frac{m_3}{u_3}\right)$$

Comparing Attribute Values

In the student record example shown in Figure 3.1, the pattern 011 indicates a disagreement on the value of first name but that the last name and date of birth agree. However, as noted earlier, the simple binary coding does not specify the nature of the disagreement. It could be that one or both first names are missing, but it's more likely that they are simply different values. However, when both values are present, there can be degrees of difference.

Consider the following three pairs of first-name values that might cause this disagreement: (JAMES, DALE), (JAMES, JMAES), and (JAMES, JIM). The first pair (JAMES, DALE) would appear to confirm a positive nonlink decision because the names appear to be completely unrelated. On the other hand, the pairs (JAMES, JMAES) and (JAMES, JIM) illustrate two reasons that different attribute values might be still considered similar and possibly confirm a positive link. In the case of (JAMES, JMAES) the strings are considered similar because they are made up of the same letters only slightly rearranged. The string "JMAES" doesn't appear to be valid name, but it can be transformed into the valid name "JAMES" by simply transposing the second and third letters, a common keyboard entry mistake. Algorithms that measure the difference in strings based on their character composition and order are called *approximate string matching* (ASM) algorithms. As discussed in Chapter 1, there are many different ASM algorithms, each having its own advantages and disadvantages in a given ER application (Navarro, 2001).

Both ASM and semantic matching of identity attributes can enhance the performance of probabilistic matching by allowing the simple binary agreement/disagreement patterns to be refined into a broader range of patterns. For example, an alternate coding for the agreement patterns of the school enrollment example discussed previously might use the code "E" for exact match, "A" for approximate match, "S" for semantic match, "M" if one or both of the values are missing, and "X" if none of the previous conditions are satisfied. Expressed in this coding, the false positive rate for linking references satisfying the probabilistic match pattern "SEE" is likely to be much lower than for accepting those that satisfy "XEE." The additional expressiveness of the coding allows a much sharper delineation of the cases, but at the same time it dramatically increases the number of patterns to be considered. With five possible codes for each of the three attributes, the total number of patterns increases from 8 to 125.

The term *fuzzy matching* is also used sometimes to describe probabilistic matching. However, the use of this term can be ambiguous. In some contexts, fuzzy matching refers to the use of ASM or semantic matching algorithms at the attribute level. In other contexts it is used to mean the same as probabilistic matching, in which some attributes are allowed to be approximate string or semantic matches. In any case, the term *fuzzy* is somewhat misleading in the sense that when ASM or semantic matching techniques are used, a fixed limit of variance must be established. Any implementation must still be reduced to a discrete coding with rules that explicitly define what is meant by similar—for example, the minimum allowable edit distance between two strings. There are no universal guidelines for establishing these similarity thresholds. Properly they should be established empirically by experimentation with sample pairs of references from the target population, but often they are simply based on intuition.

SERF Model

The Stanford Entity Resolution Framework (SERF) was developed by the research group at the Stanford Infolab led by Hector Garcia-Molina (Benjelloun, Garcia-Molina, Kawai, Larson, Menestrina, Su, Thavisomboon, and Widom, 2006). In the SERF Model, the pairwise resolution of two references is abstracted as a *match function M* that operates on a pair of entity references and returns a Boolean value of true or false, which indicates whether the references are equivalent or not. In addition to the match function M, the model also introduces a *merge function* μ that also operates on pairs of equivalent references to produce a third reference that is said to be *derived* from the two original references.

Given an initial set of entity references R, the objective of SERF Model is to define what is meant by the *generic entity resolution* of R, represented as ER(R), and to find a set of conditions that guarantee that ER(R) will actually exist and also be finite and unique.

Match and Merge Functions

Let D represent the domain of the match function M, where

$$R \subseteq D \text{ and}$$

$$M : D \times D \rightarrow \{True, False\}$$

Unlike FSM, the SERF model does not specify a particular matching methodology. However, to achieve a uniquely defined ER(R), M must satisfy certain constraints that are discussed later.

The merge function μ abstracts the concept of combining the attribute values from both references. It also operates on the same domain D as M, but only for matching references where

$$\text{If } r1, r2 \in D \text{ and } M(r1, r2) = \text{true, then } \mu(r1, r2) \in D$$

This means that derived references are comparable not only to the initial set of references R but also to other derived references. The functions M and μ can be thought of as comprising recursive production rules that generate D starting from R and adding derived references generated from pairs of matching references.

In the case that

$$M(r1, r2) = \text{True and } \mu(r1, r2) = r1$$

then r1 is said to *dominate* r2. In thinking of the merge function as combining attributes values, r1 dominating r2 indicates that r2 has no new attribute values to contribute beyond what r1 has already contributed to the derived (merged) reference.

Generic ER Defined

According to the SERF ER Model, Generic ER is defined as follows: Given a set of references R, a match function M with domain D, and merge function μ as previously defined, then

$$ER(R) \subseteq D$$

such that:
- Any record that can be derived from R is either in ER(R) or dominated by a record in ER(R)

- No two records in ER(R) match (are equivalent), and no record in ER(R) is dominated by any other

However, without further constraints on the match and merge functions, ER(R) may not exist for a given R, or it may not be unique. A trivial example would be where R, M, and μ are defined as

a) R={x, y}
b) M(x, x)=M(y, y)=M(x, y)=M(y, x)=True
c) μ(x, x)=μ(x, y)=x
d) μ(y, x)=μ(y, y)=y

In this case, there are two distinct solutions:

$$ER(R) = \{x\} \text{ and } ER(R) = \{y\}$$

Because x matches y, the second requirement of Generic ER prevents both x and y from being in ER(R). However, since x dominates y by (c) above, the solution ER(R) containing only x is sufficient. At the same time, (d) also says that y dominates x, allowing ER(R) containing only y to be a solution as well.

Both solutions are possible because of the lack of symmetry in the definition of the merge function. Our intuitive expectation of merge is that the order of merging should not matter. Adding this condition along with some other constraints on the behavior of the match and merge functions mitigates these problems.

Consistent ER

According to the SERF Model (Benjelloun, et al., 2006), when the match function M and the merge function μ satisfy certain conditions, then ER(R) is said to be consistent, meaning that ER(R) exists, is finite, and is unique. The additional constraints on M and μ that define *Consistent ER* are:

1. If r1, r2 ∈ D, then M(r1, r2)=M(r2, r1) and μ(r1, r2)=μ(r2, r1)
2. If r ∈ D, then M(r, r)=True and μ(r, r)=r
3. If r1, r2 ∈ D, then M(r1, μ(r1, r2))=M(r2, μ(r1, r2))=True
4. If r1, r2, r3 ∈ D, then μ(r1,μ(r2, r3))=μ(μ(r1,r2),r3)

R-Swoosh Algorithm

In addition to defining Generic ER and Consistent ER, the InfoLab research group has also developed a series of algorithms for systematically applying the match and merge functions to arrive at ER(R). The most fundamental is the R-Swoosh algorithm (Benjelloun, et al., 2006). The input to R-Swoosh is the initial set of references R and its output is ER(R). The steps of the R-Swoosh algorithm can be described as follows:

1. Set D = R and ER(R) = ∅
2. Take the first reference x in D and the first y in ER(R)

3. Evaluate M(x,y)

  a. If M(x,y) is True

  i. Generate z=μ(x,y)

  ii. Remove y from ER(R) and remove x from D

  iii. Append z to D

  iv. Restart at Step 2

  b. Else repeat Step 3 with next y in ER(R)

4. If M(x,y) is not true for any y in ER(R), then

  a. Move x from D to ER(R),

  b. If there are more references in D to process, then repeat Step 2, otherwise the algorithm is finished.

As an example of R-Swoosh, consider the set of five references R in Table 3.1 that represent student enrollment records.

If x and y represent two references, then matching function M(x, y) returns a value of True only when one or both of the following conditions hold:

1. (x.First = y.First) and (x.Last=y.Last) and (x.DOB = y.DOB)

2. (x.Last = y.Last) and (x.DOB = y.DOB) and (x.SCode = y.SCode)

Of the 10 distinct pairs of references in R, only three pairs—(r1, r3), (r3, r5), and (r2, r4) —will return True for the match function M.

The merge function is defined as creating a new reference by collecting the distinct attribute values from x and y so that

- μ(x,y).First={x.First, y.First}
- μ(x,y).Last={x.Last, y.Last}
- μ(x,y).Last={x.DOB, y.DOB}
- μ(x,y).Last={x.SCode, y.SCode}

Using R from Table 3.1 along with the definitions for M and μ above, the initial state for D and ER(R) from Step 1 of the R-Swoosh algorithm is shown in Table 3.2.

Because there are no values to select in ER(R) in Step 2, Step 3 is not satisfied for any values in ER(R); consequently, by Step 4, the first reference r1 is moved to ER(R), as is shown in Table 3.3.

Table 3.1: Starting Reference Set R

	First	Last	DOB	SCode
r1	Edgar	Jones	20001104	G34
r2	Mary	Smith	19990921	G55
r3	Eddie	Jones	20001104	G34
r4	Mary	Smith	19990921	H17
r5	Eddie	Jones	20001104	H15

Table 3.2: Initial Conditions of R-Swoosh Algorithm

	D				ER(R)			
	First	Last	DOB	SCode	First	Last	DOB	SCode
r1	Edgar	Jones	20001104	G34				
r2	Mary	Smith	19990921	G55				
r3	Eddie	Jones	20001104	G34				
r4	Mary	Smith	19990921	H17				
r5	Eddie	Jones	20001104	H15				

Table 3.3: R-Swoosh After Processing r1

	D					ER(R)			
	First	Last	DOB	SCode		First	Last	DOB	SCode
r2	Mary	Smith	19990921	G55	r1	Edgar	Jones	20001104	G34
r3	Eddie	Jones	20001104	G34					
r4	Mary	Smith	19990921	H17					
r5	Eddie	Jones	20001104	H15					

Table 3.4: R-Swoosh After Processing r2

	D					ER(R)			
	First	Last	DOB	SCode		First	Last	DOB	SCode
r3	Eddie	Jones	20001104	G34	r1	Edgar	Jones	20001104	G34
r4	Mary	Smith	19990921	H17	r2	Mary	Smith	19990921	G55
r5	Eddie	Jones	20001104	H15					

In the next iteration of Step 2, r2 is selected as the first record in D. Because it does not match r6 in ER(R), r2 is moved from D to ER(R) according to Step 4. The result is shown in Table 3.4.

In the next iteration of Step 2, r3 is selected as the first record in D. In this case, r3 matches r1. According to Step 3, r3 and r1 are removed from D and ER(R), respectively, and μ(r3, r1) is appended to D. The result is shown in Table 3.5.

In the next iteration of Step 2, r4 is selected as the first record in D. In this case, r4 matches r2. According to Step 3, r4 and r2 are removed from D and ER(R), respectively, and μ(r4, r2) is appended to D. The result is shown in Table 3.6.

In the next iteration of Step 2, r5 is selected as the first record in D. However, ER(R) is empty, so according to Step 4, r5 is moved from D to ER(R). The result is shown in Table 3.7.

Table 3.5: R-Swoosh After Processing r3

	D					ER(R)			
	First	Last	DOB	SCode		First	Last	DOB	SCode
r4	Mary	Smith	19990921	H17	r2	Mary	Smith	19990921	G55
r5	Eddie	Jones	20001104	H15					
r6	{Eddie, Edgar}	Jones	20001104	G34					

Table 3.6: R-Swoosh After Processing r4

	D				ER(R)			
	First	Last	DOB	SCode	First	Last	DOB	SCode
r5	Eddie	Jones	20001104	H15				
r6	{Eddie, Edgar}	Jones	20001104	G34				
r7	Mary	Smith	19990921	{H17,G55}				

Table 3.7: R-Swoosh After Processing r5

	D					ER(R)			
	First	Last	DOB	SCode		First	Last	DOB	SCode
r6	{Eddie, Edgar}	Jones	20001104	G34	r5	Eddie	Jones	20001104	H15
r7	Mary	Smith	19990921	{H17,G55}					

In the next iteration of Step 2, the merged record r6 is selected as the first record in D. In this case, r6 matches r5. According to Step 3, r6 and r5 are removed from D and ER(R), respectively, and μ(r6, r5) is appended to D. The result is shown in Table 3.8.

In the next iteration of Step 2, r7 is selected as the first record in D, and again because ER(R) is empty, r7 is moved from D to ER(R). The result is shown in Table 3.9.

In the last iteration of Step 2, r8 is selected as the first record in D. Because it does not match any of the records in ER(R), r8 is moved from D to ER(R). D is now empty, ending the algorithm. The final result of R-Swoosh is shown in Table 3.10.

Table 3.8: R-Swoosh After Processing r6

| | D | | | | ER(R) | | | |
	First	Last	DOB	SCode	First	Last	DOB	SCode
r7	Mary	Smith	19990921	{H17,G55}				
r8	{Eddie, Edgar}	Jones	20001104	{G34, H15}				

Table 3.9: R-Swoosh After Processing r7

| | D | | | | | ER(R) | | | |
	First	Last	DOB	SCode		First	Last	DOB	SCode
r8	{Eddie, Edgar}	Jones	20001104	{G34, H15}	r7	Mary	Smith	19990921	{H17,G55}

Table 3.10: The Final Result of R-Swoosh After Processing r8

| | D | | | | ER(R) | | | |
	First	Last	DOB	SCode	First	Last	DOB	SCode
					r7	Mary	Smith	19990921	{H17,G55}
					r8	{Eddie, Edgar}	Jones	20001104	{G34, H15}

A distinguishing feature of the SERF Model not found in the FSM is the merge function. In the FSM, equivalence is determined by a single pairwise comparison. In other words, the FSM match function result True means that the references are equivalent, and if they don't match they are not equivalent. The reason for this is the underlying FSM assumption that there are no equivalent references in either of the lists being linked—that the only equivalences are between the two lists. This eliminates the situation where two distinct references in List A match a single reference in List B, making the two references in List A equivalent and violating the assumption.

In the R-Swoosh algorithm, it is true that any two of the original references that match are deemed equivalent. However, if two references don't match, their equivalence or nonequivalence is not determined until the algorithm is complete. The net effect of R-Swoosh is that any two references that are part of (have contributed to) the same merge record in the final ER(R) set are equivalent. In this example, the original references r1, r3, and r5 have all been merged into a single record r8, despite the fact that M(r1, r5) is false—that is, r1 does not match r5. By keeping the merged records, the R-Swoosh algorithm is able to perform transitive linking and create the transitive closure of r1, r3, and r5, as described in Chapter 1. This is also the foundation for the Identity Capture ER Architecture discussed in Chapter 1 and the internal logic of the OYSTER open-source entity resolution system described in Chapter 6.

Other Swoosh Algorithms

In addition to the basic R-Swoosh algorithm, the research group at InfoLab has also developed other algorithms intended to optimize ER performance in parallel and distributed system architectures. The D-Swoosh algorithm (Benjelloun, Garcia-Molina, Kawai, Larson, Menestrina, Thavisomboon, 2006) is for distributed processor architectures, and the P-Swoosh algorithm (Kawai, Garcia-Molina, Benjelloun, Menestrina, Whang, Gong, 2006) is for parallel architectures. The Bufoosh algorithm addresses issues related to buffering algorithms for ER (Kawai, Garcia-Molina, Benjelloun, Larson, Menestrina, Thavisomboon, 2006).

Other ER Algorithms

In addition to the Swoosh algorithms, there are a number of other methods for systematically comparing reference pairs to determine equivalent references. Most are focused on improving the efficiency of the algorithm with minimum cost to its effectiveness. Given a set of N references, the worst case is that all possible pairs of records are compared, resulting in a total number of comparisons equal to

$$\frac{N(N-1)}{2} = \frac{(N^2 - N)}{2}$$

This means that number of comparisons increases as the square of the number of references—that is, doubling the number of references increases the comparisons by four times. Brizan and Tansel (2006) call this method "brute force" and discuss other algorithmic approaches, such as "canopy," "sliding window," "bucketing," and "hierarchical," and their relative computation efficiency. These algorithms, along with the Swoosh algorithms, fall into the category of merge-purge algorithms, though often the merge operation is virtual rather than explicit. Virtual merging takes place when the equivalent records are successively grouped by a common identifier (link) rather than actually merged into a single structure. A reference that is determined to be equivalent to any one of the references in the group (by matching or other means) is considered equivalent to all the references in the group and becomes a member of the group.

In addition to the difference in implementation between actually merging references versus virtual merging into groups or clusters, there is also a logical difference. Merging the identity attributes from difference references can create "phantom" references. For example, one reference could contribute the value x for attribute A1 and the value y for attribute A2. Similarly a second reference could contribute the values z and w for A1 and A2 respectively. This means that the merged reference would also match to the cross-combination of values for A1 and A2, namely the pairs (x, w) and (z, y). These value combinations may not be present in a virtual merge where combinations of value are tied directly to actual input references. For this reason there may circumstances where ER processes creating merged references will produce a different ER result than processes that rely upon clustering actual references.

Algebraic Model

Despite the complexity involved in the implementation of an ER process such as those described in the Fellegi-Sunter Model and Swoosh algorithms, its outcome can be described relatively simply in terms of an *equivalence relation*, a basic concept from abstract algebra (Rotman, 2005). First proposed as a way to approach the development of information quality metrics for entity resolution (Talburt, Wang, Hess, Kuo, 2007), the *Algebraic Model* has been extended to include a description of ER and entity-based data integration (EBDI) that is presented in Chapter 4.

Equivalence Relations

An equivalence relation is a very powerful algebraic structure that generalizes the concept of equality to the broader concept of equivalence. Equality implies that two things are exactly the same, identical in all respects, whereas equivalence carries the meaning that two things are not necessarily identical, but they are essentially the same with respect to some aspect or characteristic. As a simple example from geometry, consider the case of congruent triangles—triangles that have the same angular measurements at their vertices. Congruent triangles are not identical because they can be of different sizes, but they do have the same shape. So, with respect to shape, congruent triangles are considered equivalent, even though they are not identical—that is, they are the same with respect to shape.

Definition 3.1: An *equivalence relation on a set S* is any subset $R \subseteq S \times S$ for which the following conditions hold (Rotman, 2005):

1) $a \in S \Rightarrow (a, a) \in R$ Reflexive condition
2) $(a, b) \in R \Rightarrow (b, a) \in R$ Symmetric condition
3) $(a, b) \in R$ and $(b, c) \in R \Rightarrow (a, c) \in R$ Transitive condition

These three conditions are what one intuitively expects from an equal or identical relationship. Something is identical to itself, and if two things are identical to each other, then the order of expressing identicalness doesn't matter. To say that the first thing is identical to the second thing is the same as saying that the second is identical to the first. Finally, one also expects that if the first thing is identical to the second thing, and the second is identical to a third thing, then it would follow that the first and the third things are identical as well.

As another example of an equivalence relation, consider the set $S = \{a, b, c\}$, where

$$S \times S = \{(a, a), (a, b), (a, c), (b, a), (b, b), (b, c), (c, a), (c, b), (c, c)\}$$

Now consider the subset R of SxS, comprising the following five pairs:

$$R = \{(a, a), (a, c), (b, b), (c, a), (c, c)\}$$

Any subset of SxS is a relation on S, but only those relations that satisfy the reflexive, symmetric, and transitive conditions of

Definition 3.1 are equivalence relations on S. Each one of the three conditions must be tested to determine if R is actually an equivalence relation on S. For the reflexive condition, the test is whether each element x in S can be found as an ordered pair (x, x) in R. The answer for this example is yes because for the three elements a, b, and c in S, it is true that (a, a), (b, b), and (c, c) are also in R.

For the symmetric condition is only necessary to look at all pairs (x, y) in R, where x and y are different. In this case there are only two, (a, c) and (c, a), and it is obvious that the condition is met because for each pair (x, y) in R, the reverse pair (y, x) is also in R.

The transitive condition is somewhat harder to check. It requires looking for pairs (x, y) and (y, z) in R where the second element of the first pair is the same as the first element of the second pair. Whenever this configuration is found, it must also follow that the pair made up of the first element of the first pair and the second element of the second pair (x, z) is also in R. When either x=y or y=z, this condition is always met. The only pairs of real interest are when x≠y and y≠z. In this example, there are only two cases where this happens. One is for the case (a, c) and (c, a), which asks the question as to whether (a, a) is in R, and the answer is yes. The other is for the case (c, a) and (a, c), which asks the question as to whether (c, c) is in R, and again the answer is yes. Therefore R is an equivalence relation on S because all three conditions of Definition 3.1 have been met.

Note that only the reflexive condition requires that R must contain any pairs at all. If the set S has N elements, then R must also have at least N elements, since (a, a), (b, b), etc., must all be in R to satisfy the reflexive condition of Definition 3.1. As well as being a necessary condition, containing only the pairs of the form (x, x) is a sufficient condition to be an equivalence relation, since the symmetric and transitive conditions are trivially satisfied for such a relation. Consequently, for any set S of N elements, the simplest equivalence relation on S is the set comprising only the N ordered pairs of the form (x, x).

Equivalence Classes and Partitions

Definition 3.2: Given that R is an equivalence relation on the set S, then

$$\text{for each } a \in S, \text{ the set } \bar{a} = \{b \in S | (b, a) \in R\}$$

is called the equivalence class of a, and

$$\bar{R} = \{\bar{a} | a \in S\}$$

represents the set of all equivalence classes of R.

The equivalence class of an element is simply all the other elements of S that are related to it through the equivalence relation. Using the previous example, where

$$S = \{a.b, c\} \text{ and } R = \{(a, a), (a, c), (b, b), (c, a), (c, c)\}$$

then

$$\bar{a} = \{a, c\}, \bar{b} = \{b\}, \text{and } \bar{c} = \{a, c\}$$

Note that not every element of S generates a different equivalence class. In this example, elements a and c both generate the same equivalence class. In fact, it is easy to show that the following must hold.

Theorem 3.1: Given that R is an equivalence relation on the set S, then

$$(a, b) \in R \Leftrightarrow \bar{a} = \bar{b}$$

In other words, if two elements of S are equivalent, they will generate exactly the same equivalence class, and conversely, two elements of S that generate the same equivalence class must be related. Both arguments are straightforward applications of Definitions 3.1 and 3.2. Another property of equivalence classes is that they are either identical or disjoint.

Theorem 3.2: Given an equivalence relation R on a set S, then

$$a \in S \text{ and } b \in S \Rightarrow \text{ either } \bar{a} = \bar{b} \text{ or } \bar{a} \cap \bar{b} = \emptyset$$

This theorem simply states that two elements of S either generate the same equivalence class or their equivalence classes do not overlap (disjoint). The proof is very simple. Suppose that the equivalence classes generated by a and b are not disjoint. Then they must have an element in common—say, element c. It would then follow that both a and b would have to be related to c. By transitivity it follows that a must be related to b, and by Theorem 3.1, it follows that the two equivalence classes must be the same. When a collection of subsets of a set S has these properties, it is called a *partition of S*. Definition 3.3 gives a more formal statement of these properties.

Definition 3.3: A *partition of a set S* is any set P such that:

1. $P_i \in P \Rightarrow P_i \subseteq S$ and $P_i \neq \emptyset$
2. $P_i \in P$ and $P_j \in P$, and $i \neq j \Rightarrow P_i \cap P_j = \emptyset$
3. $\cup_{i=1}^{n} P_i = S$

A partition of a set S is simply a collection of nonempty subsets of S (Condition 1) that do not overlap (Condition 2) yet is large enough to cover all of S (Condition 3). The set of all equivalence classes of an equivalence relation R on a set S will always comprise a partition of S.

Theorem 3.3: Given that R is an equivalence relation on the set S, then a set of all equivalence classes of R over S is a partition of S—that is,

$$\bar{R} = \{\bar{a} | a \in S\} \text{ is a partition of } S$$

By definition, each equivalence class is a subset of S. Also, an equivalence class can't be empty. The reflexive property of an equivalence relation requires that every element is related to itself, therefore every equivalence class must at least contain the element that generates the class. For the same reason, the union of all equivalence classes must be the entire set S since every element of S will be in the equivalence class that it generates. By Theorem 3.2, different equivalence classes do not overlap; consequently, the set of all equivalence classes of an equivalence relation over a set form a partition of that set.

Interestingly, the process can be reversed. The following theorem shows how a partition of a set can be used to define an equivalence relation.

Theorem 3.4: Given a partition P of a set S, then the set

$$R = \{(a, b) \in S \times S | \exists P_i \in P \text{ where } a \in P_i \text{ and } b \in P_i\}$$

is an equivalence relation on S, and furthermore

$$\bar{R} = P$$

The proof of this theorem easily follows from definitions of partition and equivalence relation. The importance of this theorem is that equivalence relations and the partitions that they produce are interchangeable. In other words, there is a one-to-one relationship between equivalence classes on S and partitions of S, every equivalence class on S defines one and only one partition of S, and every partition of S defines one and only one equivalence relation on S.

ER as an Equivalence Relation

Chapter 1 introduced the terminology of equivalent entity references—that is, two entity references are equivalent if they refer to the same entity. Equivalent references do not have to be identical, but they are considered to be the same from an ER perspective.

Theorem 3.5: If E is an ER process that acts on a set of entity references S, then the relation

$$R = \{(a, b) \in S \times S | E \text{ links reference } a \text{ to reference } b\}$$

defines an equivalence relation on S.

This theorem simply states ER equivalence between entity references defines a relation on the set of references that turns out to be an equivalence relation, i.e. ER equivalence is also algebraic equivalence. It is not too difficult to show that this is true. Suppose that A, B, and C are references in S. By the unique reference assumption of the Chapter 1, A refers to one and only one entity X. Then it follows that (A, A) ∈ R because both refer to the same entity X. Hence, ER equivalence is reflexive. If (A, B) ∈ R, then both A and B refer to the same entity X. Clearly then, B and A also refer to X, since the order of reference is not important. Hence (B, A) ∈ R. Therefore ER equivalence is symmetric. Finally, suppose that (A, B) ∈ R, where both refer to entity X. Further suppose that (B, C) ∈ R, where both refer to entity Y. Again, appealing to the unique reference assumption in Chapter 1, it must follow that if B refers to both entity X and to entity Y, then X and Y must be the same entity. Consequently (A, C) ∈ R because both refer to the same entity X. Hence ER equivalence is transitive. From this it follows that ER equivalence E defines an algebraic equivalence relation according to Definition 3.1.

Again, it is important make the distinction between the ER as linking equivalent references and the actual mechanism for making pairwise linkage. As was pointed out in the R-Swoosh example from the previous section, the matching function M matches r1 to r3 and matches r3 to r5, but it does not match r1 to r5. This means that the matching function M is not transitive and by itself does not define an equivalence relation on R. However, M together with the merge function μ and the application of the R-Swoosh algorithm resolves R into two distinct merged records or identities. The final record for Mary Jones was formed by merging the references r2 and r4, and the final record for Edgar/Eddie Jones was formed by merging the references r1, r3, and r5. Even though M itself does not define an equivalence relations on R, the end result of applying R and μ to R according to the R-Swoosh algorithm does produce an equivalence relation on R with two equivalence classes {r1, r3, r5} and {r2, r4} that correspond to the final outputs of the algorithm.

It is also important not confuse the outcome of an ER process with the truth. The fact that an ER process defines an equivalence relation is just an artifact of the way in which ER processes operate. By definition, an ER process partitions a set of references into disjoint subsets (sometimes called *clusters*), where all the records in that subset are judged by the process to refer to the same entity. The partitioning mechanism is to assign each reference a single link identifier. The partition subsets are those references that share the same identifier. The link identifier can be thought of as a proxy for an entity referenced by the subset. The fact of the matter is that the ER process may be (and often is) wrong about its partitioning of the references. An outside observer may determine that two of the references with the same link identifier actually refer to different entities (false positive) or that two of the references with different link identifiers actually refer to the same entity (false negative). However, this does change the fact that the ER process has created an equivalence relation on the set of references by partitioning it into nonempty disjoint subsets of references with the same identifier.

Although there is elegance in viewing an ER process as defining an equivalence relation on a set of entity references, there are some practical issues that must also be considered. First and foremost is that in reality, some entity references may be ambiguous. Such ambiguity is often created by an incomplete set of identity attributes or by incomplete attribute values. For example, in a large school, the first- and last-name attributes may not be sufficient to uniquely identify each student, thus dictating the inclusion of additional attributes. Even if there are sufficient attributes, ambiguity can be created when the values of the attributes are missing or incomplete—for example, references where initials are used for first-name values instead of the complete first name. However, by the unique reference assumption stated in Chapter 1, it is assumed that it was originally created to refer to a unique entity—that is, entity references are not intentionally ambiguous.

ER Scenarios

Another practicality is that an ER process must act on the references is some temporal order or sequence. Not all references can be resolved simultaneously, and if the process has resolution dependencies, processing the same set of references in a different sequence may produce different resolution results—that is, it may result in a different equivalence relation and partition of the references. The following definition of an ER scenario takes this into consideration.

Definition 3.4: An *ER scenario* is a triple (E, S, ω), where E is an entity resolution process, S is a set of entity references acted on by E, and ω represents the sequence in which the references are processed.

Definition 3.5: Two ER scenarios (E1, S, ω1) and (E2, S, ω2) over the same set of references S are *equivalent* if and only if they produce the same partition of S.

By Theorem 3.5, partitions and equivalence relations on S are interchangeable; therefore Definition 3.5 also says that ER scenarios are equivalent if and only if they produce the same equivalence relation on S. Definition 3.5 requires that the scenarios be defined over the same set of references. However, different ER processes and different sequences of processing of the transactions comprise different scenarios, which may or may not be equivalent.

As a simple example, consider S as comprising the same five student enrollment records used to illustrate the R-Swoosh algorithm in the previous section. Table 3.11 shows the references and also defines the sequence of processing (ω1) by the order of the references by rows in the table (row order).

In this example, suppose that the match function M is the same as before—that is, if x and y represent two references, then the matching function M(x, y) returns a value of True only when one or both of the following conditions hold:

1. (x.First = y.First) and (x.Last=y.Last) and (x.DOB = y.DOB)
2. (x.Last = y.Last) and (x.DOB = y.DOB) and (x.SCode = y.SCode)

However, instead of the R-Swoosh algorithm, the ER process E for resolving S is defined as follows:

1. Take the first reference x from the S, assign it identifier value 1, and append x to the Output
2. Take the next reference from the S and the first reference from the Output
3. Evaluate M(x, y)
   a. If M(x,y) is True
      i. Assign x the same identifier that y has
      ii. Append x to the Output
      iii. Restart at Step 2
   b. Else continue with next y in the Output

Table 3.11: Student Enrollment Records in Row-Order Sequence ω1

	First	Last	DOB	SCode
			S, ω1	
r1	Edgar	Jones	20001104	G34
r2	Mary	Smith	19990921	G55
r3	Eddie	Jones	20001104	G34
r4	Mary	Smith	19990921	H17
r5	Eddie	Jones	20001104	H15

4. If M(x,y) is not true for any y in the Output, then

    a. Increment by one the highest value identifier already assigned

    b. Assign x the new incremented identifier value

    c. Append x to the Output

    d. If there are more references in the Input to process, repeat from Step 2, otherwise the process is finished.

Let $\omega 1$ represent the sequence of processing define by the row-ordering of S as shown in Table 3.10. Together the set references S, the row-ordering $\omega 1$ of S from Table 3.10, and the ER process E as defined previously create the ER scenario $(E, S, \omega 1)$.

In the execution of $(E, S, \omega 1)$, the first reference r1 is moved to the Output and assigned identifier value 1. The next reference r2 is compared to r1 in the Output but does not match, so the identifier value is incremented to 2, assigned to r2, and r2 is appended to the Output. When r3 is processed, it is found to match the first record of the Output according to the match function M. Therefore r3 is assigned its identifier value of 1 and appended to the Output. Similarly, r4 matches r2 and is assigned its identifier value of 2. The last reference of S, r5, does not match r1, but it does match r3, hence it also acquires the identifier value 1 and is appended to the Output. Table 3.12 shows the final output of executing $(E, S, \omega 1)$.

The results from Table 3.11 can also be represented as the partition of S, where the partition classes are formed by grouping all the references that share a common identifier:

$$(E, S, \omega 1) = \{\{r1, r3, r5\}, \{r2, r4\}\}$$

For this ER scenario, the result is the same as it was for the R-Swoosh algorithm except that each equivalence class of

Table 3.12: The Result from ER Scenario (E, S, ω1)

	S, ω1				Output (E, S, ω1)				
	First	Last	DOB	SCode	Ident	First	Last	DOB	SCode
r1	Edgar	Jones	20001104	G34	1	Edgar	Jones	20001104	G34
r2	Mary	Smith	19990921	G55	2	Mary	Smith	19990921	G55
r3	Eddie	Jones	20001104	G34	1	Eddie	Jones	20001104	G34
r4	Mary	Smith	19990921	H17	2	Mary	Smith	19990921	H17
r5	Eddie	Jones	20001104	H15	1	Eddie	Jones	20001104	H15

the E process corresponds to single merged record in ER(R) produced by R-Swoosh.

Now consider a new ER scenario (E, S, $\omega2$) that uses the same set of references S and the same ER process E, but where $\omega2$ represents a different sequence of processing S as defined by the row-ordering shown in Table 3.13.

In the execution of (E, S, $\omega2$), the first reference r1 is moved to the Output and assigned identifier value 1. The next reference r2 is compared to r1 in the Output but does not match, so the identifier value is incremented to 2, assigned to r2, and r2 is appended to the Output. When the next reference r5 is processed (according to order $\omega2$), the situation is different than before because r5 does not match either of the references r1 or r2 already in the Output. Therefore r5 is assigned an incremented identifier value 3 before being appended to the Output. As before, r4 matches r2 and is assigned identifier value 2. The last reference in $\omega2$ ordering of Table 3.12 is r3. Because r3 matches r1, the algorithm assigns r3 the identifier value of 1. Table 3.14 shows the final output of executing (E, S, $\omega2$).

The result shown in Table 3.14 represented as a partition of S yields

$$(E, S, \omega2) = \{\{r1, r3\}, \{r2, r4\}, \{r5\}\}$$

In this example, the ER scenarios (E, S, $\omega1$) and (E, S, $\omega2$) are not equivalent because they do not produce the same partitions. The reason for the difference is that the ER process E is sensitive to the order in which the references are processed.

Definition 3.5: An ER process is said to be *sequence-neutral* if and only if its partitioning of a set of references is the same regardless of the sequence in which the references are processed.

Table 3.13: Student Enrollment Records in Order ω1

	S, $\omega2$			
	First	**Last**	**DOB**	**SCode**
r1	Edgar	Jones	20001104	G34
r2	Mary	Smith	19990921	G55
r5	Eddie	Jones	20001104	H15
r4	Mary	Smith	19990921	H17
r3	Eddie	Jones	20001104	G34

Table 3.14: The Result from ER Scenario (E, S, ω2)

	S, ω1				Output (E, S, ω1)				
	First	**Last**	**DOB**	**SCode**	**Ident**	**First**	**Last**	**DOB**	**SCode**
r1	Edgar	Jones	20001104	G34	1	Edgar	Jones	20001104	G34
r2	Mary	Smith	19990921	G55	2	Mary	Smith	19990921	G55
r5	Eddie	Jones	20001104	H15	3	Eddie	Jones	20001104	H15
r4	Mary	Smith	19990921	H17	2	Mary	Smith	19990921	H17
r3	Eddie	Jones	20001104	G34	1	Eddie	Jones	20001104	G34

The R-Swoosh algorithm is an example of a sequence-neutral ER process. If W represents the R-Swoosh ER process, then, based on the examples just given,

$$(W, S, \omega1) = (W, S, \omega1) = (E, S, \omega1) \neq (E, S, \omega2)$$

Partition Similarity

Just as ASM provides a way to quantify the degree of similarity between two strings of characters, expressing ER scenarios in terms of the partitions they produce provides a way to measure their similarity—that is, two ER scenarios are similar if their partitions are similar. Several algorithms that measure the similarity between two partitions have been developed in statistics in connection with cluster analysis. Typically the similarity measure is expressed as an *index* that takes on values from 0 to 1. The primary consideration in selecting an index is the extent to which it provides adequate discrimination (sensitivity) in a particular application. Two commonly used indices for statistical cluster analysis are the Rand Index and the Adjusted Rand Index. However, in cluster analysis, the samples sizes are usually relatively small compared to ER processes, which often process millions of references. Unfortunately, the Rand, Adjusted Rand, and other statistical index calculations do not scale well. For this reason, less computationally intensive but still useful similarity algorithms, including the Talburt-Wang Index (Talburt, Wang, Hess, Kuo, 2007), have been developed.

Definition 3.6: If A and B are two partitions of a set S, the *partition overlap* of A and B is the set V of all nonempty intersections between partition classes of A and partition classes of B—that is,

Table 3.15: Intersection Matrix of (E, S, ω1) and (E, S, ω2)

A\B	{r1, r3}	{r2, r4}	{r5}	
{r1, r3, r5}	2	0	1	3
{r2, r4}	0	2	0	2
	2	2	1	5

$$V = \{A_i \cap B_j | A_i \in A, B_j \in B, \text{and } A_i \cap B_j \neq \emptyset\}$$

The overlap between partitions can best be visualized in tabular form as an intersection matrix where the each row of the matrix represents a single partition class of the first partition, each column represents a single partition class of the second partition, and the value at the intersection of a row and column is the count elements in the intersection of the two classes. For example, Table 3.15 is the intersection matrix for the two partitions generated by the ER scenarios (E, S, ω1) and (E, S, ω2) discussed previously.

In Table 3.15 there are only three cells with nonzero intersection counts, meaning that there are three overlaps between these two partitions. The information from the intersection matrix is useful for calculating the three partition similarity measures: the Talburt-Wang Index, the Rand Index, and the Adjusted Rand Index.

Talburt-Wang Index

The Talburt-Wang Index (TWI) is the simplest of the three to calculate. It does not use the size of the overlaps, only the number of overlaps. If S represents a set, then the notation S represents the size of S—that is, the number of elements in S.

Definition 3.7: If A and B are two partitions of a set S, the TWI of similarity between A and B is defined as

$$\text{TWI} = \frac{\sqrt{|A| \cdot |B|}}{|V|}$$

where V is the set of overlaps between A and B from Definition 3.6. For the example in Table 3.14,

$$\text{TWI} = \frac{\sqrt{|A| \cdot |B|}}{|V|} = \frac{\sqrt{2 \cdot 3}}{3} = \frac{2.4494}{3} = 0.816$$

Theorem 3.5: If A and B are both partition of a set S, and V is the set of overlaps between A and B, then

$$|V| \geq |A| \text{ and } |V| \geq |B|$$

Proof: Since partition classes are not empty, any given partition class X from A must contain at least one element of S. Since the partition B must cover all of S, X must overlap with at least one partition class of B. Therefore there is at least one overlap for each partition class of A, yielding the first inequality of Theorem 3.5. A similar argument holds for B demonstrating the second inequality.

Theorem 3.6: If A and B are both partitions of a set S, then

$$0 < \text{TWI} \leq 1$$

Proof: As long as S is not empty, then neither A or B can be empty. Therefore

$$|A| \geq 1 \text{ and } |B| \geq 1 \Rightarrow |A| \cdot |B| \geq 1 > 0$$

From Theorem 3.5,

$$|V| \geq |A| \geq 1 > 0$$

Therefore

$$\frac{|A| \cdot |B|}{|V|} > 0 \Rightarrow \text{TWI} > 0$$

Also using Theorem 3.5,

$$|V| \geq |A| \Rightarrow 1 \geq \frac{|A|}{|V|} \text{ and } |V| \geq |B| \Rightarrow 1 \geq \frac{|B|}{|V|}$$

$$\Rightarrow 1.1 \geq \frac{|A| \cdot |B|}{|V| \cdot |V|} \Rightarrow \frac{|A| \cdot |B|}{|V| \cdot |V|} \leq 1$$

$$\Rightarrow \sqrt{\frac{|A| \cdot |B|}{|V| \cdot |V|}} \leq \sqrt{1} \Rightarrow \sqrt{\frac{|A| \cdot |B|}{|V|}} \leq 1 \Rightarrow \text{TWI} \leq 1$$

Theorem 3.7: If A and B are both partitions of S, then TWI = 1 if and only if A = B.
Proof: If A = B, then

$$|A| = |B| = |V| \Rightarrow \text{TWI} = 1$$

Now suppose that A ≠ B. Then there must exist a partition class X of A and a partition class Y of B where X ≠ Y. This means that either X must have an element that is not in Y or Y must have an element that is not in X. Suppose the former—that is, there is an element in X that is not in Y. That means that X must overlap with at least one other partition class of B—that is, X overlaps with at least two partition classes of B. Thus,

$$|V| > |A| \Rightarrow \frac{|A|}{|V|} < 1$$

By Theorem 3.5

$$|V| \geq |B| \Rightarrow \frac{|B|}{|V|} \leq 1$$

Together these mean that

$$\frac{|A| \cdot |B|}{|V| \cdot |V|} < 1 \Rightarrow \sqrt{\frac{|A| \cdot |B|}{|V| \cdot |V|}} < \sqrt{1} \Rightarrow \text{TWI} < 1$$

Theorems 3.6 and 3.7 show that the TWI has the characteristics of a good similarity index in that it takes on values between 0 and 1 and only takes the value 1 when the two partitions are the same.

Rand Index and Adjust Rand Index

The Rand Index (Rand, 1971) and the Adjusted Rand Index (Yeung, Ruzzo, 2001) are both commonly used indices to compare clustering results against external criteria (Hubert, 1985). The computation of these indices is more complex than the TWI and involves the formula for counting the pairwise combinations—that is, given N things, the total number of pairs (ignoring order) that can be made from these N things is denoted by C(N, 2) and calculated as

$$C(N, 2) = \frac{N \cdot (N - 1)}{2}$$

Note that both C(1, 2) = 0 and C(0, 2) = 0.

In the intersection matrix, V_{ij} represents the count of elements in the intersection between partition class A_i of partition A and the partition class B_j of partition B. When $V_{ij} > 0$, it represents an overlap between the partitions. Each row sum S_{i*} is equal to the number of elements in the partition class A_i, and the column sum S_{*j} is equal to the number of elements in the partition class Bj. The sum S_{mn} is equal to the number of elements in the underlying set S.

The calculation of both the Rand Index and Adjusted Rand Index can be expressed in terms of four values, x, y, z, and w, defined as follows:

$$x = \sum_{i, j} C(V_{ij}, 2)$$

$$y = \sum_i C(S_{i^*}, 2) - x$$

$$z = \sum_j C(S_{*j}, 2) - x$$

$$w = C(S_{mn}, 2) - x - y - z$$

$$\text{Rand Index} = \frac{x + w}{x + y + z + w}$$

$$\text{Adjusted Rand Index} = \frac{x - \left(\dfrac{(y + x) \cdot (z + x)}{x + y + z + w}\right)}{\dfrac{(y + z + 2x)}{2} - \left(\dfrac{(y + x) \cdot (z + x)}{x + y + z + w}\right)}$$

Applying these formulas to the numbers in the intersection matrix of Table 3.14 yields the following:

$$x + C(2, 2) + C(0, 2) + C(1, 2) + C(0, 2) + C(2, 2) + C(0, 2)$$
$$= 1 + 0 + 0 + 0 + 1 + 0 = 2$$
$$y = C(3, 2) + C(2, 2) - 2 = 3 + 1 - 2 = 2$$
$$z = C(2, 2) + C(2, 2) + C(1, 2) - 2 = 1 + 1 + 0 - 2 = 0$$
$$w = C(5, 2) - 2 - 2 - 0 = 10 - 2 - 2 - 0 = 6$$
$$\text{Rand Index} = (2 + 6)/(2 + 2 + 0 + 6) = 8/10 = 0.80$$
$$\text{Adjusted Rand} = 0.545$$

Note that Talburt-Wang Index gives a very similar result to Rand in this case but with much less computation.

Other Measures of ER Outcomes

Menestrina, Whang, and Garcia-Molina (2010) discuss the "pairwise" comparison and "cluster-level" comparison measures and propose a new measure called *merge distance*. The pairwise measure is similar to the Rand Index measure in that it counts pairs within partition classes (clusters). However, in the case of the pairwise measure, only distinct pairs are counted. Using the partitions

$$A = \{\{r1, r3, r5\}, \{r2, r4\}\} \text{ and}$$
$$B = \{\{r1, r3\}, \{r2, r4\}, \{r5\}\}$$

as shown in Figure 3.14, partition A generates a set of four distinct pairs:

$$\text{Pair}(A) = \{(r1, r3), (r1, r5), (r3, r5), (r2, r4)\}$$

and B generates a set of two distinct pairs:

$$\text{Pair}(B) = \{(r1, r3), (r2, r4)\}$$

Pair Precision is defined by

$$\text{PairPrecision}(A, B) = \frac{|\text{Paris}(A) \cap \text{Pairs}(B)|}{|\text{Pairs}(A)|} = \frac{2}{4} = 0.5$$

and Pair Recall is defined by

$$\text{PairRecall}(A, B) = \frac{|\text{Paris}(A) \cap \text{Pairs}(B)|}{|\text{Pairs}(B)|} = \frac{2}{2} = 1.0$$

The pairwise comparison measure (pF) is defined as the harmonic mean of the Pair Precision and Pair Recall measures:

$$\text{pF}(A, B) = \frac{2 \cdot \text{PairPrecion}(A, B) \cdot \text{PairRecall}(A, B)}{\text{PairPrecion}(A, B) + \text{PairRecall}(A, B)} = \frac{2 \cdot 0.5 \cdot 1.0}{0.5 + 1.0}$$
$$= 0.667$$

The cluster-level comparison (cF) has a similar calculation except that the precision and recall count the partition classes in the intersection of the actual partitions—that is,

$$\text{ClusterPrecision}(A, B) = \frac{|A \cap B|}{|A|} = \frac{2}{2} = 1.0$$

$$\text{ClusterRecall}(A, B) = \frac{|A \cap B|}{|B|} = \frac{2}{3} = 0.67$$

$$\text{cF}(A, B) = \frac{2 \cdot 1.0 \cdot 0.67}{1.0 + 0.67} = 0.802$$

The cluster-level comparison is very close the TWI and Rand Index values of 0.816 and 0.800, respectively.

Brizan and Tanzel (2006) define a measure called the *efficacy* of an ER process. The efficacy measure presumes that for a collection of M references, the true number of entities to which they refer is known—say, N. For each entity, the precision and recall of the ER process P with respect to that entity can be calculated. For a given entity E, the precision of P w.r.t. E is the number of references assigned to E by P that are correct, divided by the total number of references assigned to E by P. Similarly, the recall of P w.r.t. E is the number of references assigned to E by P that are correct, divided by the total number of correct references for E in the reference set. The efficacy of the ER process P is the average harmonic mean of the precision and recall for each entity.

$$\text{Efficacy}(P) = \frac{1}{N} \left(\sum_{i=1}^{N} \frac{2 \cdot \text{precision}_i \cdot \text{recall}_i}{\text{precision}_i + \text{recall}_i} \right)$$

The efficacy measure works well in the case of identity resolution, where there is a fixed set of identities to which references can be associated. The problem is that in most cases the true set of identities is not known; hence the value of N is not known. Take as an example the two partitions A and B shown in Table 3.14. Each partition represents the outcome of an ER process where one claims that there are two entities while the other claims that there are three entities.

ER Metrics

In addition to the partition similarity indices, there are also a number of other useful metrics for comparing to ER scenarios, such as:

- Number of references
- Number of partition classes
- Average class size
- Number of single element classes
- Maximum class size

Again, using the two ER scenarios,

$$(E, S, \omega1) = \{\{(r1, r3, r5\}, \{r2, r4\}\}, \text{and}$$

$$(E, S, \omega2) = \{\{(r1, r3\}, \{r2, r4\}, \{r5\}\}$$

Table 3.16 shows a comparison of these two scenarios using these measures.

ER Consistency

Although the metrics in Table 3.16 do not give any indication as to which scenario is more accurate, they do provide a measure of consistency between the scenarios. This could be useful in a number of situations. One situation would be to compare the

Table 3.16: Metrics Comparing Two ER Outcomes

Metric	(E, S, ω1)		(E, S, ω2)
References	5		5
Nbr. of classes	2		3
Avg. class size	2.50		1.67
Single element	0		0
Max. class	3		2
Talburt-Wang		0.81	
Rand Index		0.80	
Adj. Rand		0.545	

relative performance of two different ER systems acting on the same set of references, perhaps as part of a purchase decision. In cases where references are grouped differently by the two systems, there will be pairs of reference for which the two systems have made different linking decisions. If for some of these pairs it is possible to determine which linking decision is correct, some general assessment can be made as to which system is providing better linking.

Another situation where a relative comparison is helpful is for system modifications. Again, by comparing the premodification and post-modification results, an analysis of differences can suggest whether the changes are producing more or less accurate results. It is also a good safety check to be sure that the programming changes do not produce undesirable side effects or runaway errors.

A third situation is where the reference set is changed while the ER process remains fixed. Of particular interest is the effectiveness of the data-cleaning processes that applied to the references. For example, what is the effect of address standardization? Is it bringing together more references (increased average class size)? Are the new links true positives or false positives? The same questions can be posed for other ETL operations performed prior to the ER process. This would also include sorting the reference set into different sequences in the case where the ER process is not sequence-neutral.

ER Accuracy

In the case where the correct partition is known, the similarity between the ER scenario and the correct partition provides a metric for accuracy. Of course, just as with data quality accuracy, if the true facts were known in all cases, data cleansing and the ER process would not be necessary. In most practical situations the true links are only known for some subset of the reference set. In this case the similarity index of the true partition compared to the partition produced by the ER process represents an estimate of the accuracy of the process.

Synthetic Data Experiment

As discussed in Chapter 1, most ER processes only have access to external views of the entities. As they try to assemble a correct internal view from these references, it is difficult to assess the correctness of the results because the internal view is not known. However, in an academic environment, it is possible to know the complete internal view by creating it. This allows the process to be reversed, starting with a synthetically generated internal view of a set of entities, then creating various external views of these entities. When an ER process is used to reassemble the external views, it is then possible to compare the ER results with the true internal view to judge its effectiveness.

As part of an instructional project in 2009, a system called SOG (Talburt, Zhou, Shivaiah, 2009) was designed to create a set of synthetic occupancy histories for 20,067 individuals. Each individual was created with a name, date of birth, gender, and Social Security number. Using real addresses from publicly available data, the synthetic identities were randomly assigned to a series of 1 to 9 addresses, creating the address (occupancy) history for each individual. In some cases a male and a female identity shared the same sequence of addresses. During the sequence of shared addresses, the last name of the female identity was changed to the last name of the male identity. Each occupancy record was created with a complete street address and 10-digit telephone number, with some records also having a post office box address. In all, 84,515 occupancy records were generated.

As a second step in the process, four files with different formats were created from the occupancy records. Each file retained only some aspects of the complete record. For example, the one file was created with the first and middle names together in one field, the last name in another field, one address (either the street or PO box), and telephone number. Another field contained other information such as name, date of birth, and telephone number. In this case the name and telephone were shared attributes between the two files that would allow them to be linked.

In addition to the reformatting of the information from the occupancy records, data quality problems were also injected into the files. This included such things as missing values, corrupted values, and variations of spellings and abbreviations (ST, St, Str, Street, STR, etc.). Each occupancy record was copied into at least two of the files and in some cases in three or all four of the files. In total, the four files comprising the external view of the 20,067 entities contained 271,142 records. As the records of the four files were generated, they were also given a record identifier. The record identifier was recorded along with the correct entity identifier in a fifth cross-referenced file that correctly linked each record in the four files to the entity to which it should refer.

As an exercise, the four files were given to the students who were asked to create an ER process to link equivalent references. The students returned their results as an unduplicated list of the 271,142 record identifiers along with a second entity identifier that indicated which records should be grouped together as referencing the same entity—essentially a partition class identifier. Using the cross-reference file, the correct entity identifiers could be added

Table 3.17: Metrics for Student ER Results using Synthetic Data

	TRUE	Team 6	Team 4	Team 3	Team 1	Team 2	Team 5
TWI	1.00000	0.52853	0.49305	0.41863	0.41692	0.38091	0.36875
Class cnt	20,067	54,905	78,880	114,313	111,502	138,027	147,531
Overlap cnt	20,067	62,803	80,693	114,409	113,456	138,166	147,553
Avg. class size	13.5	4.9	3.4	2.4	2.4	2.0	1.8
Class Distribution							
1	158	31,485	41,721	79,919	42,263	98,162	85,526
2	397	5,069	9,803	8,403	32,301	12,080	30,377
3	594	5,218	10,404	11,156	17,390	14,016	20,315
4	759	1,594	2,497	2,272	6,603	2,734	3,031
5	913	903	1,180	1,680	4,666	2,076	2,071
6	969	1,020	2,534	1,835	3,031	2,068	4,522
7	984	695	1,058	1,187	2,080	1,322	149
8	969	583	865	1,001	1,325	1,087	597
9	948	1,023	1,676	1,029	800	959	943
10	1,049	694	1,005	860	432	771	0
10+	12,327	6,621	6,137	4,971	611	2,752	0
Max. size	52	2,260	542	41	33	31	9
Rank		1	2	3	4	5	6

to each record, allowing the student partition to be compared to the correct partition. Table 3.17 shows the results for five teams working on this problem. The results are ranked according to the TWI, but other metrics are shown as well.

The results exhibit the typical tendency to be cautious and err on the side of false negatives (underconsolidation) rather than false positives (overconsolidation), although Team 6 did create a single class of 2,260 references to the same entity. The largest average class size for any team was only five, compared to the actual average of more than 13.

ENRES Meta-Model

Although not a model of ER per se, Malin and Sweeny (2005) have proposed a semantic framework called ENRES for specifying ER models—that is, a meta-model. The ENRES framework comprises entities, attributes, and tuples (vectors) of attribute values. The tuples correspond to entity references as defined in Chapter 1. The attributes are classified into three semantic types:

* *Personal.* The attribute refers to the entity itself.
* *Locational.* The attribute refers to where the data was collected.
* *Social.* The attributes refer to relationships between entities.

The framework allows three types of relations between framework elements:

* Entity-to-entity
* Tuple-to-entity
* Tuple-to-tuple

In addition it has a "truth resolution function" that maps each tuple to one and only one entity (corresponding to the unique reference assumption of Chapter 1).

The paper describes how three broad classes of ER models can be mapped to the ENRES framework. These model classes are:

* Record linkage and deduplication, which includes the Fellegi-Sunter and SERF Models
* Location-based linkage
* Social linkage and depulication, which are discussed further in Chapter 7

The framework is also used to derive a new ER model called *topological linkage* that can be applied to problem of identification in unlabelled (anonymous) social networks.

Summary

The Fellegi-Sunter Model represents the first attempt at defining a formal theory of entity resolution in the context of record linking. It still provides practical guidance on constructing and analyzing probabilistic match rules. The SERF Model provides a more generalized model of ER that does not prescribe the method for determining reference equivalence but focuses on the conditions that linking and merge operations must satisfy to ensure that there will be a unique ER outcome. It also introduces the notion of a merged reference that is a primary component of identity management and identity capture. The R-Swoosh algorithm describes the basic merge-purge method of ER. The Algebraic Model provides a way to describe ER processes as defining an equivalence relation on a set of references and that there is a one-to-one correspondence between partitions of the reference set and ER outcomes.

It also provides a simple way to compare ER outcomes through the computation of the T-W Index.

Review Questions

The following information will be needed for review Questions 1, 2, and 3. Visit the Downloads page of the ERIQ Laboratory website (ualr.edu/eriq/) and download the data sets ListOne.txt, ListTwo.txt, and TruthFile.txt. ListOne.txt is a list of 284 records. Each record has two fields:

- Field 1 is the record number (1 to 284).
- Field 2 represents four identity attributes of the record. Each attribute takes on single character values A through G. For example, in Record 2 of List One the attribute values are:
  - Attribute 1 = "E,"
  - Attribute 2 = "B,"
  - Attribute 3 = "C,"
  - Attribute 4 = "F"
- Note that none of the records in ListOne.txt are duplicated—that is, no two records have the same set of attribute values.
  ListTwo.txt is another unduplicated list of 272 records. The structure of List Two is the same as for List One.
  TruthFile.txt is a list of 3,104 records. It represents the true equivalent pairs between ListOne and ListTwo, i.e. the pairs of records from ListOne and ListTwo that should be linked (equivalent) independent of any agreement pattern or matching criteria. Each record in TruthFile.txt has 3 fields
- Field 1 is a record number from List One
- Field 2 is a record number from List Two
- Field 3 is the value "Y" meaning the records are equivalent. If a pair of record numbers is not in this file, assume that the two records are not equivalent. Note there are 77,248 possible pairs between ListOne and ListTwo.

1. Using the information in ListOne, ListTwo, and TruthFile as described, calculate the Pattern Weight for each of the 16 possible agreement patterns between the four identity attributes of ListOne and ListTwo, where

$$\text{Pattern Weight} = \log_2\left(\frac{\text{Probability pattern finds equivalent pairs}}{\text{Probability pattern finds non} - \text{equivalent pairs}}\right)$$

2. Following the example shown in this chapter, order the pattern weights from highest to lowest. Given that the false positive rate μ must not exceed 10% and the false negative rate λ

must not exceed 15%, establish where the cut points T_μ and T_λ will fall in the ordered sequence of weights. Which patterns fall into the middle category that requires manual inspection? Calculate how many pairs of ListOne and ListTwo records would have to be examined.

3. Using the assumption that the four attributes are conditionally independent, recalculate the 16 pattern weights by summing the individual attribute weights as discussed in the text. Compare the weights calculated in this way to the direct calculation of the weights in Question 1.

4. According to the SERF Model, given a set R, a match function M, and a merge function μ, the set ER(R) might not exist, might not be finite, or might not be unique. An example was given in this chapter that had two solutions for ER(R). Construct an example of an R, M, and μ where there is no solution—that is, ER(R) does not exist. Explain why. Construct an example where ER(R) is infinite. Explain why.

5. Let R = {1}, M(x, y) = True if x is an odd integer, and $\mu(x, y) = x + y$. According to the SERF Model, what is D? What is ER(R)?

6. Using the 284 records in ListOne.txt described above as the set of references R, perform the R-Swoosh algorithm on R where the match function M returns true if and only if all four or any three of the four attributes are the same. Let the merge function be the same as defined for the R-Swoosh example in the text, where all attribute values from a matching pair of records are retained to create the merged record. What is the size of ER(R) when the process is finished?

7. Using the set S = {a, b, c, d}, give an example of a relation on S expressed as a subset of SxS that is:
   - Not reflexive, not symmetric, not transitive
   - Reflexive, not symmetric, not transitive
   - Not reflexive, symmetric, not transitive
   - Reflexive, symmetric, not transitive
   - Not Reflexive, Not Symmetric, Transitive
   - Reflexive, not symmetric, transitive
   - Not reflexive, symmetric, transitive
   - Reflexive, symmetric, transitive

8. Let S = {a, b, c, d, e, f}, let A and B be partitions of S where A = {{a, c}, {b, d, e}, {f}}, and let B = {{a}, {b, c}, {d, e, f}}. Calculate the Talburt-Wang Index, Rand Index, Adjusted Rand Index, and Minestrina pairwise and cluster-level comparison measures between the partitions A and B.

4

ENTITY-BASED DATA INTEGRATION

Introduction

ER is often only an intermediate step in the larger process of *entity-based data integration* (EBDI). EBDI is the process of integrating and rationalizing the collective information associated with equivalent entities. Each reference may only provide a small portion of information about an entity, but combined with the information from other equivalent references a more comprehensive picture of the entity can emerge. Of course, some of the information provided by the equivalent references may be for the same attribute, a circumstance that can have both positive and negative implications. When attribute values agree, it tends to increase the level of confidence that the values are accurate. On the other hand, when there are conflicting values, it begs the question of which value, if any, is correct. Resolving these conflicts and deciding which values to keep or discard is sometimes called *knowledgebase arbitration* (Doerr, 2003; Liberatore, 1995; Revesz, 1993). The optimal selection of conflicting attribute values also has an impact on IQ. How it affects IQ is dependent on the DQ dimension under consideration and the application against which QoI will be measured. For example, if the critical dimension is accuracy, the strategy for arbitration may be different than if the critical dimension is coverage or timeliness.

In dealing with customer entities, EBDI is considered part of *customer data integration* (CDI). CDI is essential for gaining the so-called "360-degree view" of a customer's interaction with the company that forms the foundation of *customer relationship management* (CRM). In law enforcement, EBDI is an important tool for building a comprehensive investigation file.

Formal Framework for Describing EBDI

The formal description of EBDI given here extends the Algebraic Model of ER (Talburt, Wang, Hess, Kuo, 2007) from the previous chapter, in which an ER process is defined in terms of an equivalence relation on a set of entity references (Holland, Talburt, 2009; Talburt, Hashemi, 2008). The formal description of EBDI begins with the concept of an *integration context*. The integration context provides an explicit mechanism to describe both entity equivalence (the ER part) and attribute equivalence (the integration part) across a collection of information sources. Both entity and attribute equivalence must be considered in dealing with entity-based integration.

Definition 4.1: An *information source* $S = (E, Q, V, f)$ is a quadruple where
1) E is a non-empty, finite set of entity references
2) Q is a non-empty, finite set of attributes
3) V is a finite set of values that may include the null value
4) f is a function where f: $E \times Q \rightarrow V$

This definition of an information source used here is equivalent to a relation scheme (Ullman, 1989) and is a generalization of an information system (Pawlak, 1984).

Definition 4.2: An *integration context* $G = (C, X, Y)$ is a triple where
1) $C = \{S_1, S_2, \ldots, S_n\}$ is a finite collection of information sources where each
2) $S_i = (E_i, Q_i, V_i, f_i)$, for $1 \leq i \leq n$
3) X is an equivalence relation over the combined set of entities $U_{i=1}^{n} E_i$
4) Y is an equivalence relation over the combined set of attributes $U_{i=1}^{n} Q_i$

Definition 4.3: An *integration entity* of the integration context G is any member of $\overline{X}$ the set of all equivalence classes defined by the entity equivalence relation X over $U_{i=1}^{n} E_i$—that is, $\overline{X} = \{\overline{e} | e \in U_{i=1}^{n} E_i\}$, where $\overline{e}$ represents the equivalence class of the entity e

Definition 4.4: An *integration attribute* of the integration context G is any member of $\overline{Y}$, the set of all equivalence classed defined by the attribute equivalence relation Y over $U_{i=1}^{n} Q_i$—that is, $\overline{Y} = \{\overline{q} | q \in U_{i=1}^{n} Q_i\}$, where $\overline{q}$ represents the equivalence class of the attribute q.

The integration context provides the formal mechanism for expressing both entity equivalence and attribute equivalence, features that distinguishes entity-based integration from data integration in general. The model does not define or depend on the mechanisms used to implement either of the equivalence relations X or Y. X represents the outcome of some ER process applied to the totality of entities in the integration context G (Talburt, Wang, Hess, Kuo, 2007).

On the other hand, the integration attributes of $\overline{Y}$ may involve some type of data transformation to arrive at equivalence (Bilenko, 2003; Naumann, 2002)—for example, an attribute such as "Employee Age" in one information source may be mapped (transformed) to an equivalent attribute value of "Employee Date of Birth" in another source based on the date at the time of the mapping (Welty, 2001).

A useful concept that relates the entity equivalence classes and the attribute equivalence classes is the value range.

Definition 4.5: For $\bar{e} \in \bar{X}$ and $\bar{q} \in \bar{Q}$ the *value range* of $\bar{e}$ over $\bar{q}$ represented by $R(\bar{e}, \bar{q})$ is defined as

$$R(\bar{e}, \bar{q}) = \{v \in U_{i=1}^{n} V_i | \exists e_j \in \bar{e} \text{ and } q_j \in \bar{q} \text{ s.t. } f_j(e_j, q_j) = v\}$$

By this definition, $R(\bar{e}, \bar{q})$ is the set of all attribute values taken on by a set of equivalent entities over a given set of equivalent attributes—for example, if S_1 has an entity e_1 and attribute a_1 that has value v_1, and S_2 has an entity e_2 with attribute a_2 that has value v_2. If e_1 and e_2 are equivalent entities and a_1 and a_2 are equivalent attributes, then v_1 and v_2 would belong to the set $R(\bar{e}, \bar{q})$. The expectation is that v_1 and v_2 are the same value because they come from equivalent entity references for the same (equivalent) attribute—for example, age. However, this is not always the case, because equivalent references may report different values for the same or equivalent attributes. In the case of age, it may be because the references were created at different times. The age value may actually be correct for each reference in its given time context but leads to conflicting values when the two are brought together. This is why age and other time-dependent values should always be stored with point of reference. If age is given in each source with a point of reference such as date of birth or date of acquisition, the values can be rationalized. In any case, $R(\bar{e}, \bar{q})$ is the set of all these values and, consequently, the set of choices for a single value to represent the integration attribute of the integration entity.

Definition 4.6: An *integration selection operator* for an integration attribute $\bar{q}$ is any function $\sigma_{\bar{q}}$ such that

1) $\sigma_{\bar{q}} : X \rightarrow U_{i=1}^{n} V_i$ and

2) $\sigma_{\bar{q}}(\bar{e}) = v$ where $v \in R(\bar{e}, \bar{q})$

Definition 4.6 simply says that an integration selection operator must assign to an entity class a value for the attribute provided by one of the underlying entities that comprise that class. The following example will help clarify these concepts.

Example 4.1: Consider two information sources S_1 and S_2 with the following characteristics:

$S_1 = (E_1, Q_1, V_1, f_1)$ where,

$U_1 = \{e_1, e_2, e_3\}$,

$Q_1 = \{q_1, q_2, q_3\}$,

$V_1 = \{-1, 0, 1, 3, +4, \text{``AB''}, \text{``X''}\}$, and

f_1 is defined by Table 1.

$S_2 = (E_2, Q_2, V_2, f_2)$ where

$E_2 = \{e_4, e_5, e_6, e_7\}$,

$Q_2 = \{q_4, q_5, q_6\}$,

$V_2 = \{1, 2, 3, 4, 123, 643, 901, \text{"AB"}, \text{"M"}, \text{"RS"}, \text{"X"}\}$, and

f_2 is defined by Table 4.2. Note that (–) indicates a null or missing value.

Now consider the integration context $G = (C, X, Y)$, where

$C = \{S_1, S_2\}$ as above,

X defines five integration entities (entity equivalence classes) as

$\overline{X} = \{\{e_1, e_6\}, \{e_2, e_4\}, \{e_3\}, \{e_5\}, \{e_7\}\}$

Y defines four integration attributes (attribute equivalence classes) by

$\overline{Y} = \{\{q_1, q_4\}, \{q_2, q_5\}, \{q_3\}, \{q_6\}\}$

Table 4.1: Definition of f_1

E_1	q_1	q_2	q_3
e_1	3	"AB"	0
e_2	1	"X"	−1
e_3	0	"AB"	+4

Table 4.2: Definition of f_2

E_2	q_4	q_5	q_6
e_4	1	"M"	123
e_5	2	"X"	643
e_6	3	"RS"	–
e_7	4	"AB"	901

Table 4.3: Value Ranges

	$\{q_1, q_4\}$	$\{q_2, q_5\}$	$\{q_3\}$	$\{q_6\}$
$\{e_1, e_6\}$	$\{3\}$	$\{$"AB", "RS"$\}$	$\{0\}$	–
$\{e_2, e_4\}$	$\{1\}$	$\{$"X", "M"$\}$	$\{-1\}$	$\{123\}$
$\{e_3\}$	$\{0\}$	$\{$"AB"$\}$	$\{+4\}$	–
$\{e_5\}$	$\{2\}$	$\{$"X"$\}$	–	$\{643\}$
$\{e_7\}$	$\{4\}$	$\{$"AB"$\}$	–	$\{901\}$

Each cell in Table 4.3 shows the value range from Definition 4.5 for each combination of an integration entity and integration attribute in the integration context (G, X, Y), as defined in Example 4.1.

For example, $R(\bar{e}, \bar{q}) = \{$"AB", "RS"$\}$. This example also shows that $R(\bar{e}, \bar{q})$ may only contain the null value because none of the entities in the integration entity provided a value for the attribute. Using this same example, Table 4.4 defines one possible integration selection operator $\sigma_{\bar{q}_2}$ for $\bar{q}_2$.

Because a selection operator for $\bar{q}_2$ would have two choices of values for $\bar{e}_1$ and two choices for $\bar{e}_2$, Table 4.4 represents only one of the four possible selection operators for $\bar{q}_2$.

Integration selection operators are defined at the integration attribute level for two reasons. One is to simplify the description of the formalization framework; second, this is typically how integration is approached in practical applications. Knowledge base arbitration is used to describe the process in which the selection operator must choose among the sometimes conflicting values offered for a given integration entity and integration attribute.

Table 4.4: An Integration Selection Operator for $\bar{q}_2$

$\bar{e}$	$\sigma_{\bar{q}_2}(e)$
$\bar{e}_1$	"RS"
$\bar{e}_2$	"X"
$\bar{e}_3$	"AB"
$\bar{e}_5$	"X"
$\bar{e}_7$	"AB"

Optimizing Selection Operator Accuracy

A common problem in EBDI is to optimize the accuracy of an integration selection operator. The fact that records from different sources may have conflicting values for an attribute is both a problem and an opportunity. The problem is deciding which value to select, but the opportunity is to increase the overall accuracy of the integrated sources by having more choices. If at least one source provides the correct value and that value is selected, the accuracy of the combined sources can exceed the accuracy of any one source.

As a simple example, suppose that two sources both have only two entities and that the first entities and second entities in each source are equivalent, resulting in two integration entities. For an equivalent attribute shared by the sources, suppose that the first entity of the first source provides a correct value, but the second entity has an incorrect value, and that for the second source the situation is reversed: the first entity provides an incorrect value for the attribute, but the second entity is correct. In this case, each source is only 50% accurate for this attribute. However, if a selection operator were constructed that chooses the value provided by the first entity in the first source and the second entity in the second source, the attribute selection operator would be 100% accurate for this attribute.

In a real-world situation where the sources have a large number of entities, it is only practical to estimate the overall accuracy of each source. In some cases it may just be a subjective judgment of the perceived accuracy of each source, but in other cases the estimate may be more informed by verifying the correct attribute values for a sample of entities from the source. A collection of entities in which the attribute values are known or can be verified to be correct is sometimes referred to as a *truth set authoritative source,* or *benchmark* (Talburt, Holland, 2003). For each entity in a source that corresponds to an entity in the truth set, the correctness of the attribute value from the source can be determined and the overall accuracy of the attribute in the sample set can be used to estimate the overall accuracy of the attribute in the source.

Naïve Selection Operators

A simple way to construct a selection operator is to choose attribute values based on some characteristic of their contributing source. The *naïve strategy* for optimizing the accuracy of a selection operator is to make this choice based on the overall accuracy of the contributing sources. More precisely, for an integration entity $\bar{e}$ and integration attribute $\bar{q}$, the strategy is to always select the (nonnull) value v from $R(\bar{e}, \bar{q})$ that was contributed by the information source that is known or estimated to have the overall highest accuracy for attribute q.

Suppose that in Example 4.1, it was deemed that the values of attribute q_2 in S_1 are overall more accurate than the values of the equivalent attribute q_5 of S_2. Table 4.5 shows the integration selection operator $N_{\bar{q}_2}$ for the attribute $\bar{q}_2$ based on the naïve strategy.

In cases where S_1 contributes a value, that value is always chosen. If a value is not available from S_1, the value is chosen from S_2 if available. In a case where there are more than two sources and a value is not available from either S_1 or S_2, it would be chosen from S_3, and so on.

A description of the naïve approach in terms of the formal framework is as follows: For a particular $\bar{q} \in \bar{Y}$, assume that the information sources in the integration context G are placed in rank order from most to least accurate with respect to the accuracy of $\bar{q}$—that is, the sequence of information sources are ordered as $S_1, S_2, \ldots, S_n$, where $i < j$ implies that overall the attribute $\bar{q}$ is more accurately represented in S_i than in S_j. For a value $v \in R(\bar{e}, \bar{q})$, define

$$\rho(v) = \min(i | v \in S_i)$$

In this context, the naïve integration operator over $\bar{q}$ can be defined in the following way:

Definition 4.7: The *naïve integration selection operator* $N_{\bar{q}}$ for optimizing the accuracy of attribute $\bar{q}$ is defined as follows:
1) $N_{\bar{q}}(\bar{e}) = $ null when $R(\bar{e}, \bar{q})$ contains only the null value, else
2) $N_{\bar{q}}(\bar{e}) = v$, where $\rho(v) - \min\{\rho(v) | v \in R(\bar{e}, \bar{q}) \text{and v in not null}\}$

Table 4.5: Naïve Integration Operator for $\bar{q}_2$

$\bar{e}$	$N_{\bar{q}_2}(\bar{e})$	Source
$\bar{e}_1$	"AB"	S_1
$\bar{e}_2$	"X"	S_1
$\bar{e}_3$	"AB"	S_1
$\bar{e}_2$	"X"	S_2
$\bar{e}_7$	"AB"	S_2

The selection operator is called *naïve* because it is intuitive and easy to implement. However, the naïve integration selection operator will not necessarily be the integration operator that gives the highest possible accuracy for a given integration context. This is because it is possible for a source ranked lower in overall accuracy to assert a correct value of the attribute, even though all sources with a higher accuracy rank assert an incorrect value.

Selection Operator Evaluation

The evaluation of selection operators is best illustrated by example. Table 4.6 shows an integration context of three sources S1, S2, and S3 for which the entity equivalence relation X creates 10 integration entities. The columns labeled S1, S2, and S3 contain the values contributed by each of these sources for a particular integration attribute that can take on any one of five values A, B, C, D, or null. Furthermore, the column labeled True shows the correct value of this attribute for each of the 10 integration entities.

By definition, the set of true values is 100% accurate. The source S1 is correct for five values, giving it an accuracy of 50%. Source S2 has an accuracy of 40% and Source S3 only 30%. The column labeled Naïve shows the values that would be

Table 4.6: Accuracy of Sources and Selection Operators

	True	S1	S2	S3	Naïve	Best	Worst
1	B	A	–	–	A	A	A
2	C	–	C	A	C	C	A
3	A	A	A	D	A	A	D
4	B	B	B	C	B	B	C
5	D	C	D	D	C	D	C
6	C	C	B	·	C	C	B
7	D	–	–	D	D	D	D
8	B	–	D	B	D	B	D
9	A	A	–	B	A	A	B
10	B	B	A	C	B	B	A
	100%	50%	40%	30%	70%	90%	10%

chosen by the naïve selection operator. The 70% accuracy of the naïve operator in this example is higher than the accuracy of any one of the sources S1, S2, or S3.

The attraction of the naïve strategy is that it is very simple to implement, and it will perform no worse than the most accurate contributing source. In most cases there is the expectation that it will perform better than the best source (as in Table 4.6) because other less accurate sources may provide a correct choice when the most accurate source does not provide a value. For example, in Table 4.6, Source S2 provides the correct value C for the second integration entity in Row 2, and Source S3 provides the correct value D for the seventh integration entity in Row 7.

Despite its better performance than Source S1, the naïve strategy does not always result in the most accurate selection operator. The columns labeled Best and Worst show the upper and lower limits for a selection operator selecting nonnull values in this integration context. The column Best shows that for all but one integration entity, there is a correct choice available. It is only for the first integration entity (Row 1) that no source provides a correct choice. The problem is that correct choice is not always the naïve choice. An example is the integration entity shown in Row 5. Here the naïve choice is the value C from Source S1, even though the correct choice of D is provided by both S2 and S3.

The column labeled Best represents what would happen if a selection operator for this integration context could always make the correct choice whenever it is provided by one of the sources. Similarly, the column labeled Worst represents what would happened if a misguided selection operator always made the wrong choice whenever an incorrect, nonnull value was provided by one of the sources. Table 4.6 shows that worst selection operator would not have accuracy lower than 10%. The reason is that in Row 7 there is only one nonnull choice and that choice is correct. In all other cases, an incorrect, nonnull choice could be made.

The best and worst selection operators represent the performance limits for any selection operator defined for this integration context, and it also illustrates the dilemma in the design of a selection operator. On one hand, using the naïve selection strategy it is a relatively safe choice, but it may fall short compared to the best operator. On the other hand, it might be possible to design selection rules that provide higher accuracy than the naïve operator, but the risk is that the accuracy of a poorly designed rules could result in an operator with accuracy as low as the worst case.

Figure 4.1 illustrates the critical values for selection operators as a graphic. The interval between the performance of the naïve

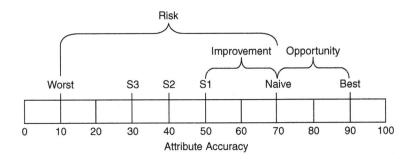

Figure 4.1: Selection Operator Evaluation Scale

operator and the best possible selection represents the opportunity for improvement. The interval between the naïve selection and the worst selection represents the risk of a poorly designed selection operator.

Strategies for Optimizing Selection

Of course, in an actual integration context, if all the true choices were known, none of this discussion would be necessary. However, the example shown in Table 4.6 and Figure 4.1 does illustrate how such an analysis could be done if the true values could be obtained or verified for a representative sample of the integration entities. It would also provide a way to build and test alternative selection models. Of course, as with any model, there is always the risk that its performance on the truth set might not extrapolate to the entire integration context.

Although the naïve selection operator is commonly used for EBDI, there are many other ways to design selection operators and strategies for optimizing their performance. Another simple strategy that can be used when there are three or more sources is the *voting strategy*. The voting strategy is based on the assumption that whenever there is a predominant value, it is more likely to be correct. In the case there is not a predominate value, the naïve rule could apply. The results of applying this combined voting/naive strategy to the example in Table 4.6 is shown in Table 4.7.

In this example, the voting rule only applies to three of integration entities in Rows 3, 4, and 5. In Rows 3 and 4, the voting agrees with the naïve selection, so the selection is not changed. However, in Row 5, the voting selection is the correct value D, which supersedes the incorrect value C selected by the naïve rule. The result is that the voting operator has 80% accuracy versus the 70% accuracy of the Naïve operator without voting.

Table 4.7: Accuracy of Sources and Selection Operators

	True	S1	S2	S3	Naïve	Voting	Best	Worst
1	B	A	–	–	A	A	A	A
2	C	–	C	A	C	C	C ˙	A
3	A	A	A	D	A	A	A	D
4	B	B	B	C	B	B	B	C
5	D	C	D	D	C	D	D	C
6	C	C	B	–	C	C	C	B
7	D	–	–	D	D	D	D	D
8	B	–	D	B	D	D	B	D
9	A	A	–	B	A	A	A	B
10	B	B	A	C	B	B	B	A
	100%	50%	40%	30%	70%	80%	90%	10%

Although it did not occur in this example, it is also possible that the voting selection could be incorrect and may override a correct naïve selection. However, the assumption of voting is that the former is more probable than the latter.

In the integration context of this example, even the voting operator fails to achieve the best possible accuracy. The value D selected by the naïve rule for the integration entity in Row 8 is incorrect and for this entity, the voting rule does not apply. To achieve the highest possible accuracy for this integration context, there would have to be an additional rule, a rule that would override the naïve selection of the incorrect value D from Source S2 in Row 8 and instead select the correct value of B from Source S3.

There are many ways to design a rule set that would solve this problem. A simple way would be to have an additional rule: If the sources only provide the two values B and D, always select the value B. A new operator that first applies the voting rule; second, the new "B over D" rule; then third, the naïve rule would be an operator that achieves the best possible accuracy for this integration context.

Although this rule would achieve the best-case accuracy for this integration context, it is clearly contrived to solve this one case. If the same situation occurred for other integration entities, there is no reason to believe that choosing B or D would give the correct result in those cases. To justify including rules like these, it is necessary have a much large truth set so that

- More examples of a given combination of values can be observed and analyzed, and
- A portion of the records matching the truth set can be set aside for testing the effectiveness of the rules

This is a common practice for data mining and machine learning, where the combination of inputs and desired outputs is called a *training set*. Some of the input/output combinations are randomly selected for the process of building the rules, a process sometimes called *supervised learning*. After the rules are built, their performance is measured against the input/output combinations that were not used for building the rules. In some cases the selection-build-testing sequence is repeated several times as a way to prevent the development of rules that only perform well for the input/output cases that were used in the creation of the rules, a situation described as *overfitting*.

There are many supervised learning strategies that have been developed that try to derive approximate solutions to complex problems by analyzing a sample of cases in which the correct or desired result is known. Collectively these are known as the area of *soft computing*, which includes techniques such as *artificial neural networks, fuzzy computing, evolutionary computing, classification algorithms,* and *support vector machines.*

More Complex Selection Rules

The EBDI discussed so far has been limited in two respects

- The context of analysis has been limited to a single integration attribute.
- Integration is limited to the selection of an attribute value provided by one of the source entities in the integration entity—that is, a value from $R(\bar{e}, \bar{q})$.

Relaxing either of the constraints leads to a more complex analysis of EBDI.

Selection Based on Multiple Attributes

One of the important aspects of IQ assessment embodied in data profiling is testing for determinant-dependency relations among the columns of a database table (Lindsey, 2008). From an IQ perspective the purpose is to detect certain types of data redundancy. It is often the case that data profiling can discover a partial, or even complete, dependency relationship between columns. This simply means that the value in one column (the determinant value) can often predict the value in another column (the dependent value). When one column can predict the values in two or more other columns with 100% accuracy, this is an indication that the table is not in third normal form and that it can be decomposed into two tables where the determinate value is a foreign key into a new table created from the dependent values.

From the standpoint of EBDI, it means that there may also be determinate-dependency relations among the integration attributes of an integration context—relationships that can be exploited to further optimize the performance of integration selection operators. In the previous examples such as Table 4.6 and 4.7, the basis for designing the selection rules was limited to the values of a single integration attribute. However, in most integration contexts, each source will have several attributes yielding many integration attributes.

Table 4.8 shows the same integration context as Table 4.6 except that the original integration attribute has been labeled Q1 and a second attribute Q2 that takes on numeric values has been added. Taking into consideration only one additional attribute can lead to an explosion in the number and complexity of selection rules. The complexity of a set of selection rules is related to possible relationships under consideration. For example, the naïve strategy only considers the relation that the value of Q1

Table 4.8: Selection Using Multiple Attributes

	True	S1		S2		S3		Naïve	Q1Q2	Best	Worst
		Q1	Q2	Q1	Q2	Q1	Q2				
1	B	A	1	–	1	–	0	A	A	A	A
2	C	–	3	C	3	A	2	C	C	C	A
3	A	A	0	A	3	D	0	A	A	A	D
4	B	B	2	B	2	C	1	B	B	B	C
5	D	C	4	D	4	D	2	C	D	D	C
6	C	C	2	B	3	–	0	C	C	C	B
7	D	–	0	–	3	D	4	D	D	D	D
8	B	–	3	D	1	B	2	D	B	B	D
9	A	A	2	–	3	B	2	A	A	A	B
10	B	B	2	A	3	C	2	B	B	B	A
	100%	50%		40%		30%		70%	90%	90%	10%

for a source is either null or not null. In the following examples of rule-based selection, the notation S1.Q1 indicates the value of attribute Q1 in source S1, S1.Q2 indicates the value of Q2 in S1, and so on.

Naïve Selection Rule:

```
If (S1.Q1 not null) Then Select S1.Q1 value
Else If (S2.Q1 not null) Then Select S2.Q1 value
Else Select S3.Q1 value
```

However, the voting integration operator considers Q1-to-Q1 relations.

Voting Selection Rule:

```
If ((S2.Q1 not null) AND (S2.Q1 = S3.Q1)) Then Select S2.Q1 value
Else If (S1.Q1 not null) Then Select S1.Q1 value
Else If (S2.Q1 not null) Then Select S2.Q1 value
Else Select S3.Q1 value
```

An example of a rule that takes advantage of the additional attribute Q2 adds Q2-to-Q2 relations. Moreover, because Q2 has numeric values, there is an increase in the types of comparisons from only equal or not equal to include less- and greater-than comparisons. Consider the following rules set:

Q1Q2 Selection Rule:

```
If ((S3.Q1 not null) AND (S2.Q2 < S3.Q2)) Then Select S3.Q1
Else If ((S2.Q1 not null) AND (S1.Q2 = S2.Q2)) Then Select S2.Q1
Else If (S1.Q1 not null) Then Select S1.Q1 value
Else If (S2.Q1 not null) Then Select S2.Q1 value
Else Select S3.Q1 value
```

The column labeled Q1Q2 of Table 4.8 shows the results of applying this rule and that it will achieve best accuracy attainable through selection. Clearly, the Q1Q2 rule is only one of an unlimited number of possible rules sets that can be designed around logical combinations of null-not-null, Q1-to-Q1, and Q2-to-Q2 relationships. The choices grow exponentially as additional attributes are included.

Statistical, data mining, or soft computing techniques can be useful aids for developing rule sets that optimize integration accuracy. Often the final choice is a compromise between accuracy and the efficiency of implementation, since these analysis techniques may lead to very complex rule sets that are difficult to implement or inefficient in operation. In some cases, complex rule sets can be replaced by much simpler sets with only a minimal loss of accuracy while realizing large gains in computing efficiency.

Nonselection Integration Operators

Although only integration selection operators were defined for the formal Integration Context Model, there can be situations in which the best value for an integration operator is not one of the attribute values contributed by one the original sources. As a simple example, consider the case where the sources are providing a numeric value. In cases where there is not a predominate value among the conflicting values, it may be that instead of trying to select one of the conflicting values, a better choice would be to use the computed average of the nonnull values. Even in cases in which the attribute value is a string value, the best choice may be a *default value* that is different from any of the source values.

Definition 4.8: An *integration operator* for an Integration Attribute $\bar{q}$ is any function $\delta_{\bar{q}}$ such that

1) $\delta_{\bar{q}} : \bar{X} \to R$, where

2) $\bar{q} \in \bar{Y}$, and

3) R is the set of admissible values for the range of operator $\delta\bar{q}$

Definition 4.8 extends the definition of an integration selection operator (Definition 4.6) to provide for a more general class of integration operators that can provide values that are not in $R(\bar{e}, \bar{q})$. The following definition shows how the example of average value as a nonselection operator could be defined using the algebraic framework.

Definition 4.9: The *average-value integration operator* for a numeric integration attribute $\bar{q}$ is the integration operator $\alpha_{\bar{q}}$ where

1) $\alpha_{\bar{q}} : \bar{X} \to \mathbb{R}$, where $\mathbb{R}$ the set of real numbers, and

2) $V = \{v \in R(\bar{e}, \bar{q}) | v$ is not null$\}$

3) $\alpha_{\bar{q}}(\bar{e}) = \begin{cases} \Sigma_{v \in V}(v)/|V| & \text{if } V \neq \emptyset \\ \text{null} & \text{Otherwise} \end{cases}$

Summary

EBDI is a two-step process in which the first step is an ER process and the second step integration of attributes. The Algebraic Model for ER, discussed in Chapter 3, can be extended to provide a formal framework for defining the integration process. In particular the concept of entity equivalence is also applied to attribute equivalence to create integration entities and integration attributes, respectively. In the extended framework, an integration operator is defined in the context of a particular integration attribute as a function that assigns a value to each integration entity. An integration operator that always assigns a value provided by one of the underlying sources is called a *selection operator.* In cases where sources provide conflicting values, there are several strategies for deciding which value to select. Guidance in the design of selection rules is best provided by observing and analyzing a sample of integration entities for which the correct choice is known.

Review Questions

1. Give an example of a commonly used data integration process that is not entity-based. Explain why it is not EBDI.
2. For an integration context $G = (C, X, Y)$ there is nothing in the definition of the entity equivalence relation X that requires equivalent entities to be in different sources. Many integration contexts start the EBDI process with sources that contain unresolved references. The same is true for the attribute equivalence relation. Using the same sources S_1 and S_2 defined in Example 4.1, create a new integration context using the following entity equivalence and attribute equivalence relations:

    $X = \{\{e_1, e_4, e_7\}, \{e_2, e_5, e_6\}, \{e_3\}\}$
    $Y = \{\{q_1, q_3, a_4\}, \{q_2, q_5\}, \{q_6\}\}$

    Rebuild Table 4.3 using the value ranges that result from these new definitions of X and Y.
3. Using the new table of value ranges created in Question 2, calculate how many distinct integration selections operators can be defined for the integration attribute $\bar{q}_2$; for the integration attribute $\bar{q}_3$.
4. Following the notational style used to define the naïve integration operator in Definition 4.7, write a formal definition of the voting/naïve integration operator.
5. Visit the Data Download page of the website (ualr.edu/eriq/) and download the dataset "Three-Sources-One-Attribute." This download file has 1,001 rows of data. The first row contains the column names T, S1, S2, and S3. The remaining 1,000 records each have four comma-separated values all representing values for the same attribute. The first value is the true value of the attribute. The second is the value provided by the first source S1, the third is the value provided by S2, and the fourth is from S3. Using this data:
    a. Determine the rank order of the sources from most to least accurate as measured against the true values.
    b. Compute the best and worst accuracy for an integration selection operator in this integration context.
    c. Build the naïve integration operator and compute its accuracy.

d. Build the voting/naïve hybrid operator as described in the chapter.

e. Plot the accuracy of the sources, the best case, worst cases, naïve operator, and the voting/naïve operator on an evaluation scale similar to Figure 4.1.

f. Using a data-mining algorithm such as J48 classification or some other analysis technique, try to design a set of selection rules with fewer than 20 comparisons that results in higher accuracy than either the naïve or voting/naïve operator.

6. Visit the Data Download page of the website (ualr.edu/eriq/) and download the dataset "Three-Sources-Two-Attributes." This download file has 1,001 rows of data. The first row contains the column names T, S1Q1, S1Q2, S2Q1, S2Q2, S3Q1, and S3Q2. The remaining 1,000 records each have seven comma-separated values representing the values of two distinct integration attributes Q1 and Q2. The first value is the true value of attribute Q1. The second is the value provided by the first source S1 for Q1, the third is the value for Q2 from S1, the fourth is the value for Q1 from S2, the fifth is Q2 for S2, the sixth is Q1 for S3, and the seventh is Q2 for S3. Using this data:

a. Plot an evaluation scale for integration selection operators defined on Q1.

b. Define a selection operator for Q1 that uses comparisons on both attributes Q1 and Q2 to achieve accuracy better than either the Naïve or Voting-Naïve operators.

7. Following the notational style used to define the average-value integration operator for a numeric integration attribute $\bar{q}$ in Definition 4.9, write a formal definition of the naïve/default operator $\omega_{\bar{q}}$ that behaves the same as the naïve operator except that when all the attributes values are null, the operator gives a default value d.

5

ENTITY RESOLUTION SYSTEMS

Introduction

This chapter discusses three commercial ER systems that demonstrate how some of the features and functions discussed in the previous chapters have been implemented in real applications. The three discussed here are only offered as examples and not a comprehensive survey, evaluation, or endorsement of any one of the many commercial systems currently available.

The first example is a basic merge-purge process of customer references performed on a single-user desktop system. The second example shows how a server-based system based on the heterogeneous database join architecture can be used to perform search and discovery processes on entity relationships. The third example discusses the architecture of a large-scale, hosted identity resolution system.

DataFlux dfPowerStudio

DataFlux® started out in 1997 as a developer of data-cleansing software (DataFlux 2010). In 2000, it was acquired by the SAS Institute® and has evolved to provide a broader range of applications, including data integration and master data management (Rasmussen, 2000). DataFlux has been consistently listed in the Magic Quadrant® for Data Quality Tools, published by the Gartner Research Group® (McBurney, 2010).

In the scenario described here, a single-user version of DataFlux dfPowerStudio® 8.2 is used to carry out a typical merge-purge operation on customer data that involves reference preparation activities (ERA2) and a resolution step (ERA3).

In this scenario, three lists of customer references of different formats are combined and resolved. The three lists were built from 20,067 synthetic occupancy histories generated by the SOG system (Talburt, Zhou, Shivaiah, 2009) using U.S. name and address formats. Each list is stored as a separate table in a Microsoft® Access database named DataChallenge.mdb. Each list has a different layout, with all columns defined as text (character strings). The layout descriptions are:

1. List_A table (94,306 rows):
   a. *RecID*. A unique record identifier formed by the character "A" followed by a six-digit sequence number.
   b. *Name*. Customer first, middle, last names in a single field.
   c. *Address*. Street address, including street number, directional, name, and secondary address if any (e.g., Apt #) in a single field.
   d. *City State Zip*. City, state, and ZIP code for the street address in a single field.
   e. *PO Box*. Post office box address (optional).
   f. *PO City State Zip*. City, state, and ZIP code for the box address.
   g. *SSN*. Nine-digit Social Security number.
   h. *DOB*. Ten-digit date of birth.
2. List_B table (100,777 rows):
   a. *RecID*. A unique record identifier formed by the character "B" followed by a six-digit sequence number.
   b. *Name*. Customer first, middle, last names in a single field.
   c. *Address*. Street address, including street number, directional, name, and secondary address if any (e.g., Apt #) in a single field.
   d. *City State Zip*. City, state, and ZIP code for the street address in a single field.
   e. *Phone*. Ten-digit telephone number.
3. List_C table (76,059 rows):
   a. *RecID*. A unique record identifier formed by the character "C" followed by a six-digit sequence number.
   b. *Contact*. Customer first, middle, last names in a single field.
   c. *SSN*. Nine-digit Social Security number.
   d. *DOB*. Ten-digit date of birth.
   e. *Phone*. Ten-digit telephone number.

In addition to extracting information from various SOG occupancy records to generate the three lists, the list generator also injected data quality problems into the references in the form of missing fields, name variations, alternate formatting, and character string corruptions. The three lists were also built to include both intra- and inter-list equivalent references. The goal of the scenario is to resolve the combined list of 271,142 references into subsets of equivalent references that represent unique customer identities.

The ER strategy for this scenario is to perform the following steps:

1. Establish an initial set of identity attributes and agreement (matching) rules.
2. Assess the quality and characteristics of each list.
3. Perform data-appropriate data cleansing and standardization operations.
4. Convert to common layout and combine lists.
5. Generate match codes (hash tokens) for the attributes used in the agreement rules and aggregate into clusters of equivalent records.
6. Evaluate the results.

As is often the case in ER processes, much of the effort is expended in the preparation and data quality (ERA2), such as Items 2, 3, and 4 above.

Establish Agreement Rules

The agreement patterns for the matching rules are based on the following seven identity attributes:

1. First Name
2. Last Name
3. Street Address
4. City
5. DOB
6. SSN
7. Phone

Using these seven attributes, an initial set of agreement patterns are selected as a starting point for the ER process. Once equivalence classes are generated based on the initial rule set, the results can be analyzed for false positive and negative results. Based on the analysis the rule set may be changed and the resolution steps repeated until satisfactory results are obtained. The initial agreement rules for the scenario are as follows:

Rule 1: SSNs agree:

- This rule has the advantage of creating true positives regardless of changes in the customer's name, address, or telephone number whenever this value is present and correct on both references.
- False positives are possible. For example, it could be that a wife is associated with her husband's SSN through joint business dealings. Although unlikely, it could also be caused by chance when a corruption of a number causes it to match the SSN for another customer.
- False negatives will occur if either value is missing or corrupted.

Rule 2: First Names, Last Names, Street Addresses, and Street Cities agree:

- This rule creates true positives for references to a customer at the same street address. The requirement for state names and ZIP codes to agree is omitted because their inclusion is unlikely to prevent a false positive and is more likely to create a false negative by their variation or absence.
- False positives could be caused by members of a household at the same street address also having the same or similar names, such as John Doe, Jr., and John Doe, Sr. They could also occur by chance when two different customers with the same first and last names occupy the same address at different times. They can also occur when secondary address information is missing. For example, different customers with a common first and last name could be present at the same apartment complex having the same street address, but disambiguating apartment numbers are not included in the address.
- False negatives will occur when the name, street address, and city name are missing or corrupted. They will also occur when the references are to different addresses for the same customer or if the customer's name has changed.

Rule 3: First Names, Last Names, and DOBs agree:

- This rule has a higher false positive risk than the others, but it is another rule that can create true positives when the customer's address or telephone number has changed or is missing or when the SSN is missing.
- False positives could be caused by chance where two customers with relatively common names share the same DOB. It could also be caused by twins with very similar first names being brought together by approximate matching.
- False negatives will occur when the first or last name or the DOB is missing or corrupted.

Rule 4: First Names, Last Names, and Phones agree:

- This rule can create true positives in cases where the customer's address has changed and the SSN or DOB values are missing.
- False positives could be caused by chance where two customers with very similar names in the same household report the same phone number.
- False negatives can occur when the first or last names or the phone is missing or corrupted.

The rules as expressed here are somewhat different than the Fellegi-Sunter agreement rules in that they are not mutually exclusive. In this expression, if an attribute is not listed, it does not matter if its values match or not. For example, a pair of references that agreed on all seven of the identity attributes would satisfy all four rules.

The dfPowerStudio® application provides for approximate matching through the generation of hash tokens called *match codes*. The match code algorithm is designed so that attribute values that are syntactically or semantically similar will generate the same match code value. The user can set parameters for the match code algorithm that tell it what type of data is being matched and what level of match sensitivity is desired. Thus by applying the agreement rules to the match codes of identity attributes rather than the attribute values themselves, the rules will actually employ approximate matching. For example, if the First Name values were "JAMES" and "JIM," they would not match as attribute values. However, the match codes generated for these two values are likely to be identical in the case where the match code algorithm is given parameters that tell it that the values are U.S. first names and that a sensitivity of less than exact match is allowed.

Another issue is that three of the identity attributes specified for the match rules are not fields in the layouts of original lists. These attributes are First Name, Last Name, and City. First Name and Last Name are components of the larger combined Name field, and City is a component of the larger combined City State Zip and PO City State Zip fields. To solve this problem, an additional step must be added to separate the larger field into its logical components through a process called *parsing*. Similar to match code generation, the parsing operation needs to know the type of values that will be in the field being parsed. The type of the value also determines what components will be available for output from the parsing process.

Assess Quality

The first step in data assessment is to look at the data. Curiously, many data owners and data custodians never examine data in detail. They often make unwarranted assumptions about its content and condition without ever attempting to verify those assumptions. Sometimes just scrolling through a few records can reveal significant issues. References in flat files can be loaded into a text editor for viewing. Most relational database systems also include a command to display table contents as well.

The dfPowerStudio® application can connect to various file and database formats and display their contents. Figure 5.1 shows a portion of the DBViewer screen where a connection has been made to List B in the database and the first few references are displayed.

From just this sample it is clear that List B has a number of data quality issues that could defeat the proposed agreement rules. For example, in the Name field there is no consistency in the use of upper- and lowercase letters. Some names are all in uppercase, some lowercase, and many in mixed case. In addition, some names are given only as initials, such as "L Brown."

The same letter casing issue is also present in the Address and City State Zip fields, but in addition these fields also show considerable variation in abbreviations—for example, there are three representations of "Avenue," "Ave," and "Av" just in the small sample shown in Figure 5.1. Similarly, there is an inconsistency in the representation of state names, such as "Texas" and "TX." Another issue is that values in the Phone field have been punctuated differently, with a mixture hyphens, periods, and parentheses.

In addition to DBViewer, the application also provides a data-profiling tool. Whereas viewing allows detailed examination of a small number of references, profiling gives a summary of statistics and exceptions over the entire list. Figure 5.2 shows a portion of the Profile Viewer Screen that displays the pattern frequency distribution for the Phone field of List B. The distribution shows that this field is well populated, with only 2,532 missing (in this case, blank) values. However, the phone numbers have been formatted in six different styles.

Figure 5.1: A Sample of References in List B

ID	NAME	ADDRESS	CITYSTATEZIP	PHONE
B898229	ALBERTO J hibler	2528 ROYAL TERNS CT	LEAGUE CITYP TX 77573	(281)682-5401
B898228	SEAN N CIENEGA	16127 FORECASTLE ST	crosby texas 77532	281-350.7367
B898227	STEVEN J Odom	2090 WELDON LN	Bay Point cali. 94565	925.814-5024
B898226	L brown	4120 Cockroach Bay Rload Lot 803	Ruskin fl 33570	813-487.6672
B898225	denins ENRIQUE Rivera	10303 HIGHWAY 63 N	Bono ar 72416	870.160-3330
B898224	armando G P	719 n eucadlyptus ave	Inglewood ca 90302	310-473.7832
B898223	r GNOZALEZ	740 W OWENFS AVENUE	TULARE CALI 93274	559.107-1208
B898222	JOSEPHINE M ADAMS	36625 SINGLETARY RD	Myakka City fl 34251	(941)310.3815

Field: Phone

Defined type: varchar
Defined length: 255 chars

Column Profiling	Frequency Distribution	Pattern Frequency Distribution	Percentiles	Outliers	Notes

Pattern	Alternate	Count	Percentage
999-999-9999	9(3)-9(3)-9(4)	16467	16.34
(999)999.9999	(9(3))9(3).9(4)	16435	16.31
999.999.9999	9(3).9(3).9(4)	16429	16.30
999-999.9999	9(3)-9(3).9(4)	16368	16.24
(999)999-9999	(9(3))9(3)-9(4)	16335	16.21
999.999-9999	9(3).9(3)-9(4)	16211	16.09
		2532	2.51

Figure 5.2: Pattern Frequency Distribution for Phone in List B

The Column Profiling tab of the Phone profile (not shown) indicates that there are no null values for Phone. This means that the 2,532 Phone values shown in Figure 5.2 that have no pattern are strings of blank characters rather than null values. The difference between missing values that are blank versus missing values that are null (an undefined database value) can be an important distinction in many computer operations and algorithms, as will be noted later in this scenario.

A similar assessment of Lists A and C show additional inconsistencies in the formatting of the SSN and the DOB fields that should be addressed as well. Based on these assessments, several data quality issues can be identified:

- Inconsistent upper/lowercase letter casing in the Name, Address, and CityStateZip fields
- Initials for first and last names in the Name field
- Lack of standard address abbreviations in the Address and CityStateZip fields
- Inconsistent formatting of Phone, DOB, and SSN values.

Data Cleansing

Most of the data representation issues can be addressed through built-in standardization functions provided with the dfPowerStudio® application. To further facilitate the processing, the application of standardization and other functions can be automated through a graphical workflow interface called Architect®. Architect allows the user to drag and drop symbols that represent these functions onto a palette and connect the symbols with arrows to indicate the order of processing. Figure 5.3 shows a portion of the Architect screen where the three lists undergo standardization.

The standardization functions were selected from the left-hand drop-down list and connected into the workflow in proper sequence. After a function has been added to the workflow, its specific action is determined by setting its properties. These settings are managed through a property dialog box. Figure 5.4 shows the settings made in the property dialog box for the Standardize C standardization function shown in Figure 5.3.

Here four of the five fields from List C are standardized using standard definitions provided with the application. Name is standardized with the built-in Name definition and the standardized output is put into a new field named "name_Stnd." Because there is not a built-in standardization definition for SSN, another definition for removing nonnumeric characters is applied. DOB is standardized using the built-in YMD Date definition and Phone using the built-in Phone definition.

An examination of the results from the Standardize A process shows the effects of these operations. For example, the name

Figure 5.3: A Segment of the ER Process Workflow

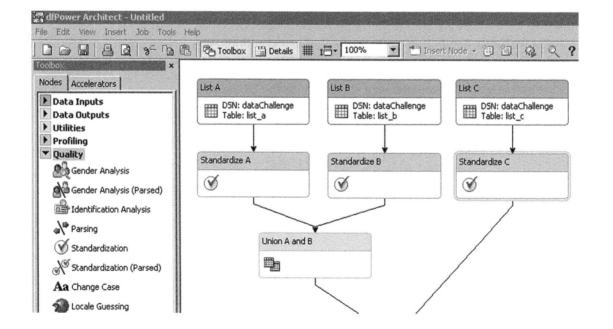

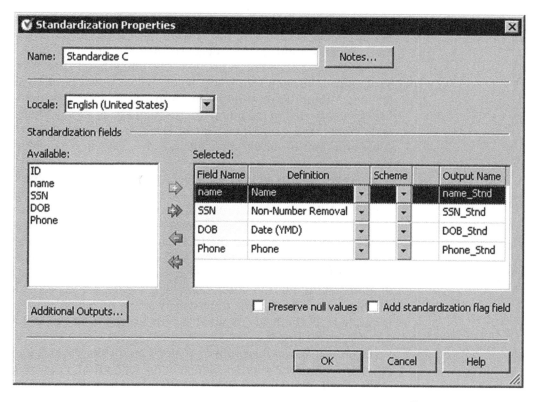

Figure 5.4: Property Dialog Box for Standardize

"christine urias" is standardized to "Christine Urias" from all lowercase to proper case. The address "alameda, california 94501" is standardized to "Alameda, CA 94501," and the SSN "176-19-2715" is standardized to "176192715" by removing the nonnumeric characters.

Convert to Common Layout

The final preparation step before starting the resolution process is to combine the three lists into a single list with a common layout. This can be done through the Union function that is provided with the application. It allows two files to be appended and their fields to be mapped into a common set of field names. The standardized values of Lists A and B share the fields Name, Name_Stnd, Address, Address_Stnd, CityStateZip, and CityStateZip_Stnd. Because these fields are used by the agreement rules, they are carried forward into the union of the two lists under their common names. The PO Box Address and PO City State Zip fields of List A were not carried forward into the standardization process because they are not used in the initial set of agreement rules. On the other hand, the SSN, SSN_Stnd, DOB, and DOB_Stnd fields of List A will be needed for matching to corresponding fields in List C. Therefore these fields are included in the union of Lists A and B, as are the Phone and Phone_Stnd fields from List B. List C has no new field to contribute and is simply mapped into the collective names of Lists A and B.

However, there is another problem. Agreement Rules 2, 3, and 4 specifically refer to First Name, Last Name, and City, none of which is defined in the layout of the combined list. As an additional step, the First and Last Names must be parsed from the combined Name field, and the City name must be parsed from the combined City State Zip field. The application provides a built-in parsing function than can be used to extract these fields in preparation for the resolution step. Figure 5.5 shows the workflow that includes the union and parsing operation needed to produce all the fields required for the execution of the initial set of agreement rules.

Figure 5.6 shows the property dialog box for the Parse Name function shown in Figure 5.5. Note that the target field for parsing is the standardized name field and that the function recognizes six logical name components for U.S. names. Only the Given Name (First Name) and Family Name (Last Name) are selected for output.

Cluster Equivalent Records

In the ER scenario presented here, some of the agreements defined in the match rules are allowed to be approximate matches. In particular, matches between first names, last names, addresses, and city names can be approximate matches. The approximate matching for these fields is accomplished by comparing the match codes for these attributes values rather than the actual attribute values. As noted earlier, the algorithm that the application uses for generating the match codes provides a level of approximate matching between fields. For example, in this scenario the Last Name values "BUSONICK" and "BSONICK" generate the same match code value of "M4B3 $$$$$$$$$$$$$$$$." The exact nature of the algorithm for generating the match codes is proprietary and the details of its operation are hidden by the application.

Although it is convenient to use the match code algorithm provided by the application, there is nothing to prevent users

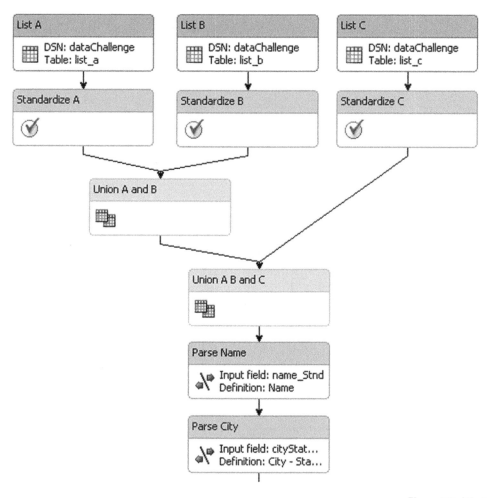

Figure 5.5: Workflow of Reference Preparation Activities

from implementing their own approximate matching algorithms, since the application allows custom functions to be inserted into the workflow. Matching for SSN, DOB, and Phone are required to be an exact match. Figure 5.7 shows the Property dialog box for generating the match codes for First Name, Last Name, Address, and City.

The sensitivity setting for each field represents the degree of approximate match on a scale from 0 to 100. The default value of 85 is selected in all cases. As in the standardization and parsing, the match code generation is guided by knowing the type of

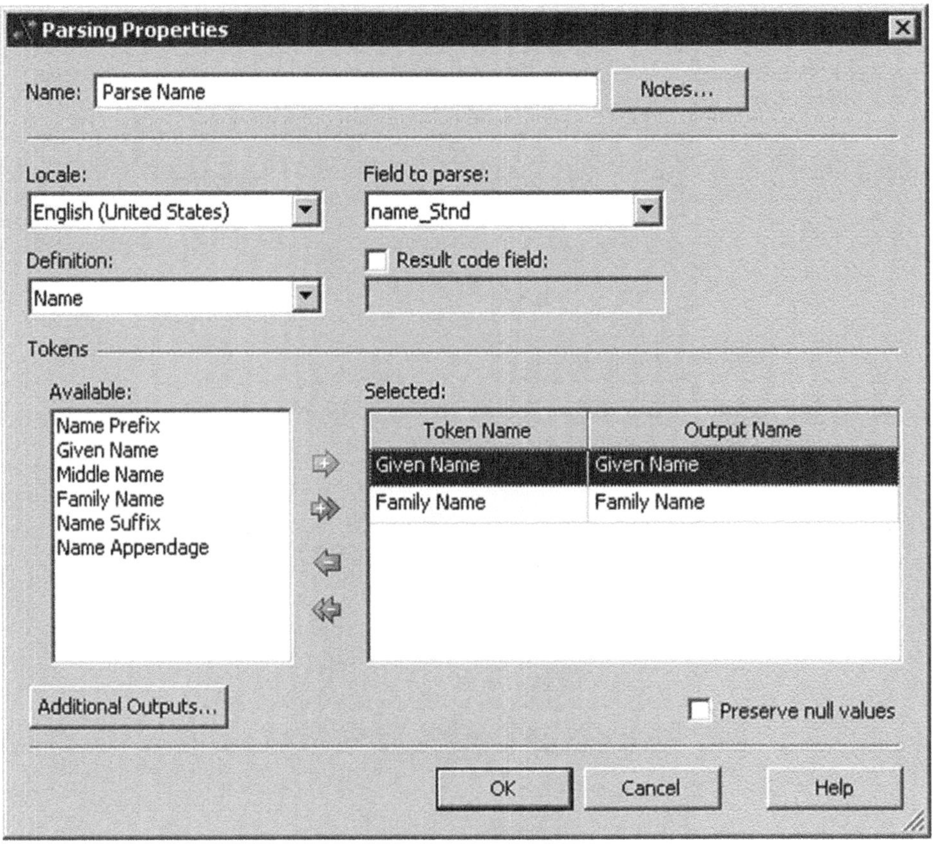

**Figure 5.6: Property Dialog
Box for Parse Name Function**

field that is specified by the predefined setting in the Definition column. Note that match codes are generated for the standardized SSN, DOB, and Phone values, even though approximate matching does not apply to these fields. As discussed earlier, some of these fields have a mixture of null and blank missing values. By generating match codes with the option to generate null match codes for blank fields (see the checked box in Figure 5.7), the two cases are handled uniformly. Figure 5.7 also shows that these three fields are designated as Exact in the Definition column.

The final step of the ER process is to identify and cluster the references that are deemed to be equivalent by satisfying one or more of the agreement rules. Figure 5.8 shows the Property dialog box used to set up the four initial agreement rules. Note

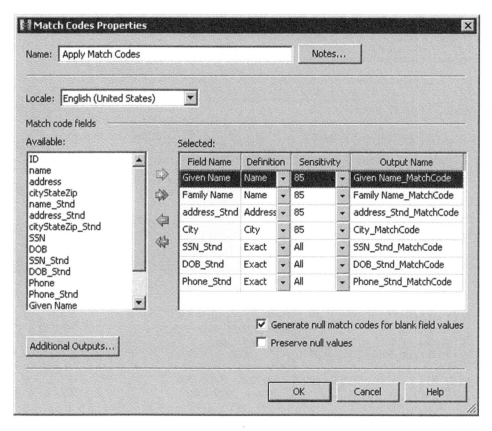

Figure 5.7: Property Dialog Box for the Apply Match Codes Step

that only Rules 1, 2, and 3 are visible in the window shown in Figure 5.8.

The application implements its own logic for resolving the pairwise comparison into clusters of equivalent references. However, instead of using a merge function to create "super" references as described in the R-Swoosh algorithm discussed in Chapter 3, equivalent references are linked together in groups or clusters by assigning equivalent references the same identifier, called the *cluster identifier*. Figure 5.8 indicates that the field defined for the cluster identifier is named "Entity_ID." By retaining access to the identity attributes of previously resolved references, either by grouping or merging, the process is able to link records by transitive matching as well as by direct matching. Figure 5.9 shows the entire workflow for the first iteration of the resolution process.

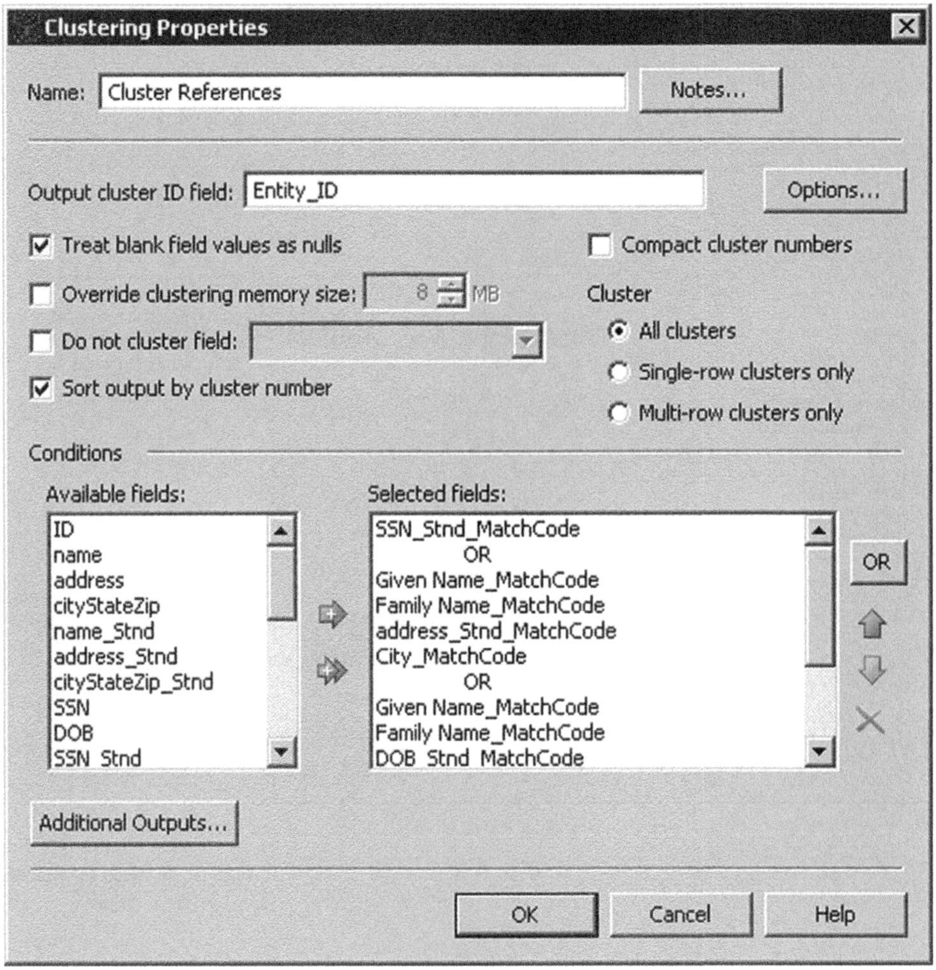

Figure 5.8: Property Dialog for Defining Resolution Rules

Evaluation of Results

The execution of the ER process shown in Figure 5.9 reduces the initial combined list of 271,142 references into 93,981 distinct customer identities. Because Lists A, B, and C were generated from an original set of 20,067 occupancy histories, the true linkages between pairs of references is known. Table 5.1 shows the results of the initial ER process compared against the true linkages based on the T-W Index described in Chapter 3.

The fact that the overlap count is very close to the class count (94,011 versus 93,981) is an indication that the links made in the

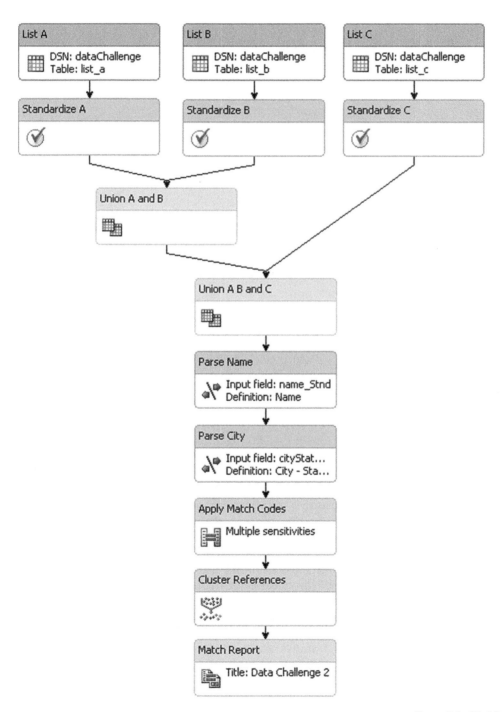

Figure 5.9: Workflow for the First Iteration of ER

Table 5.1: First-Run Results Compared to True Linkage

	TRUE	First Run
T-W Index	1.00000	0.46194
Class cnt	20,067	93,981
Overlap cnt	20,067	94,011
Avg. class size	13.5	2.88
Class Distribution		
1	158	53,248
2	397	12,109
3	594	11,843
4	759	2,342
5	913	1,641
6	969	2,480
7	984	1,314
8	969	1,056
9	948	1,464
10	1,049	1,047
10+	12,327	5,437
Max. size	52	44

initial iteration are predominately true positive links. The closeness of these two numbers means that the equivalence classes produced from the process are almost entirely subsets of the true partition classes. It means that the process is making good (true positive) links but that it is also leaving a large number of equivalent references unlinked (false negatives). In the next section, some of the reasons for the large number of false negatives are investigated using a different kind of ER tool. The lessons learned can then be used to improve the workflow and the resolution results.

Table 5.2 shows an example of three customer references from Lists A, B, and C brought together as Identity 396 by the first iteration of the ER process.

Rule 1 links the first reference from List A to the second reference from List C by agreement on SSN. Rule 4 links the second reference from List C to the third reference from List B by

Table 5.2: Customer Identity 396

List ID	Name	Address	SSN	DOB	Phone
A905091	Jaime Galhouse	1202 KENTUCKY AVE FORT PIERCE, FL 34950	189546658	08 Jan 190	
C951918	Jamie galhouse	6841 Meadowlark Lane Chino, Ca 91710	189-54-6658	2930	772.581.6316
B923695	JAMIE galhouse	12444 OFFICE BOX FORT PAIERCE, FLA. 34979			772.581-6316

agreement on First Name, Last Name, and Phone. Thus even though there is no rule that directly links the first reference from List A to the third reference from List B, they are both assigned to same identity by transitive closure.

Infoglide Identity Resolution Engine

Infoglide Software®, founded in 1996, is a privately held company headquartered in Austin, Texas. It develops and markets identity resolution software for government and commercial markets. The company's application serves as the platform for passenger screening within the Secure Flight program of the Transportation Threat Assessment and Credentialing (TTAC) department of the Transportation Security Administration (TSA) (Infoglide, 2010).

This section will describe two scenarios that use its Identity Resolution Engine® Version 2.2 (IRE). The IRE is based on the heterogeneous database join architecture, where the engine acts as a hub that connects to and queries multiple databases and database tables. The query results are then combined and presented to the user. Although the IRE can be operated either interactively or in batch mode, it is primarily positioned as an interactive tool for exploring and finding nonobvious relationships among entities, tasks that fall into ERA5. In the first scenario the IRE is connected to the same Lists A, B, and C used in the previous section to search for some of the false negatives created in the first DataFlux scenario. The IRE discovery scenario will also illustrate some of its capabilities to explore and visualize up to four degrees of separation among entities of interest.

Search Scenario

Figure 5.10 shows the home screen for the IRE Desktop, showing icons for the functions Search, Discover, Decide, Cases, and Favorites. In this scenario the Search function will be used to explore the same Lists A, B, and C that were used in the

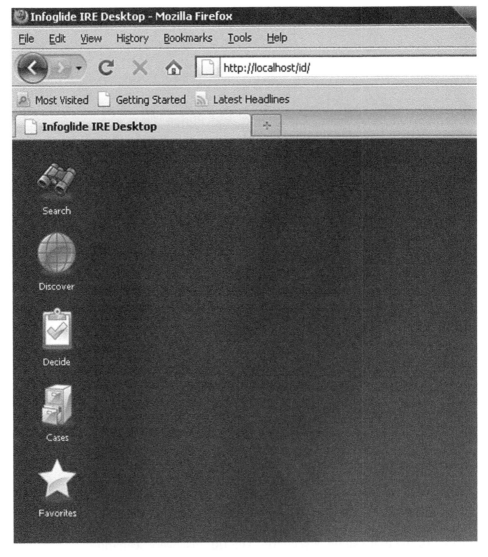

Figure 5.10: IRE Desktop Homepage

previous merge-purge process. The objective is to find examples of false negatives and try to identify their root causes.

Configuring the system to make these searches requires three steps:

1. Connecting to data sources
2. Defining the attribute structure
3. Mapping the structure to each source

IRE can be connected to several different databases, although in this scenario Lists A, B, and C are just different tables in the same database. Figure 5.11 shows the dialog box for establishing a connection to the Data Challenge database.

As was evident in the previous scenario, different reference lists will contain different identity attributes. For example, List B has Name, Address, and Phone attributes but not SSN or DOB that are in List A and List B. IRE uses the concept of a "structure" as a way to define a collection of identity attributes (similar to the Union operation of the previous scenario) that will be applied to different sources. Figure 5.12 shows the dialog box for creating a structure named Data Challenge that defines the six attribute types in the three lists.

IRE provides several predefined attributes types as shown in the column labeled Similarity Type in Figure 5.12. It also allows each attribute to be assigned a relative weight in scoring and prioritizing search results. In this example the default value of 1.0 is selected for all attributes.

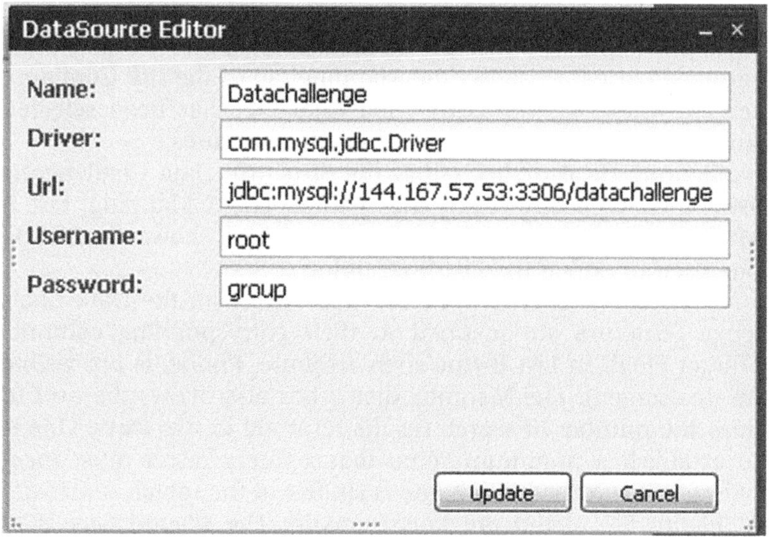

Figure 5.11: IRE Dialog Box for Connecting to a Data Source

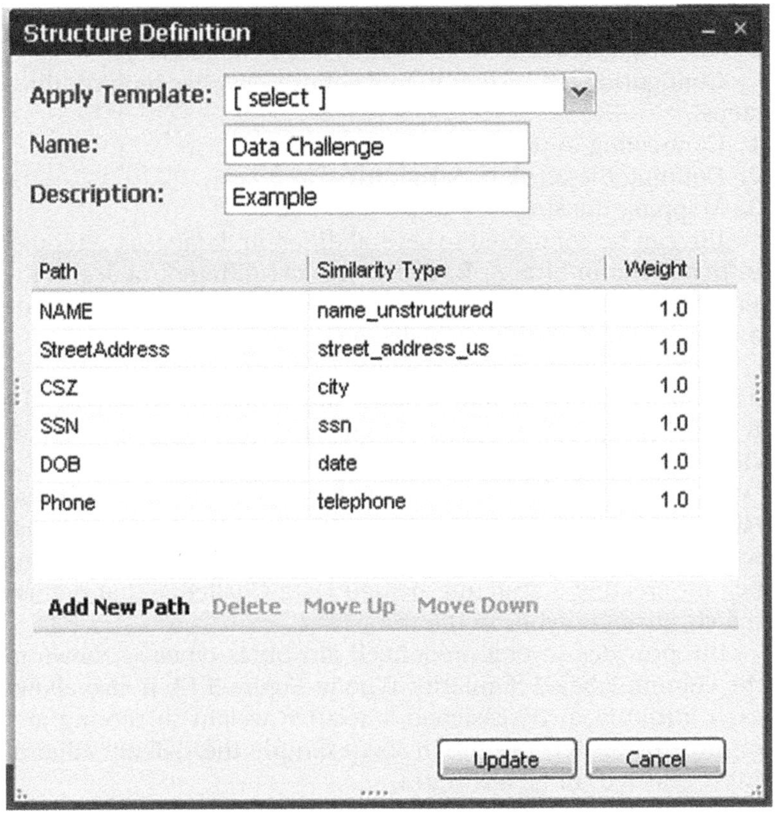

Figure 5.12: Dialog Box for Data Challenge Attribute Structure

The last configuration step is to map the attribute types defined in the structure to the actual attributes in each data source. Figure 5.13 shows the Mapping tab of the IRE Configure screen, where the Structure Data Challenge has been selected from the drop-down menu of available structures.

Figure 5.13 also shows that the Structure Data Challenge is associated with three mappings named List A Mapping, List B Mapping, and List C Mapping. Figure 5.14 shows the dialog box used to define the List B Mapping.

Here four of the six attribute types (Path) in the Data Challenge Structure are mapped to their corresponding columns (Target Field) in List B (the sixth attribute, Phone, is not visible on this screen). The Mapping dialog box also allows the user to limit the number of search results returned in two ways. One is to establish a minimum score that a query result must meet before it is returned, a scheme is similar to the match sensitivity in Figure 5.7 in the previous scenario. The second way is to

Figure 5.13: Mapping Tab of the Configure Screen

simply limit the total number of results that can be returned from the source.

Once the configuration is complete, the Data Challenge Structure can be called from the Search function to find references in Lists A, B, and C based on any combination of the six attribute types. Figure 5.15 shows the Search screen with the Data Challenge Structure selected.

Here all three lists are selected as targets for the query on the name value "Jamie Galhouse" and SSN value "189-54-6658." These values were taken from Identity 396 (Table 5.2) of the previous scenario. Figure 5.16 shows the 17 references found by the search.

The results shown in Figure 5.16 demonstrate how different ER tools can be used to analyze different aspects of data and work together and to improve ER results. The IRE also has a function to cluster matching records, but for this scenario the search function is used. In this case, the search function has located several records that were not grouped into the same identity by the initial set of matching rules of the first scenario.

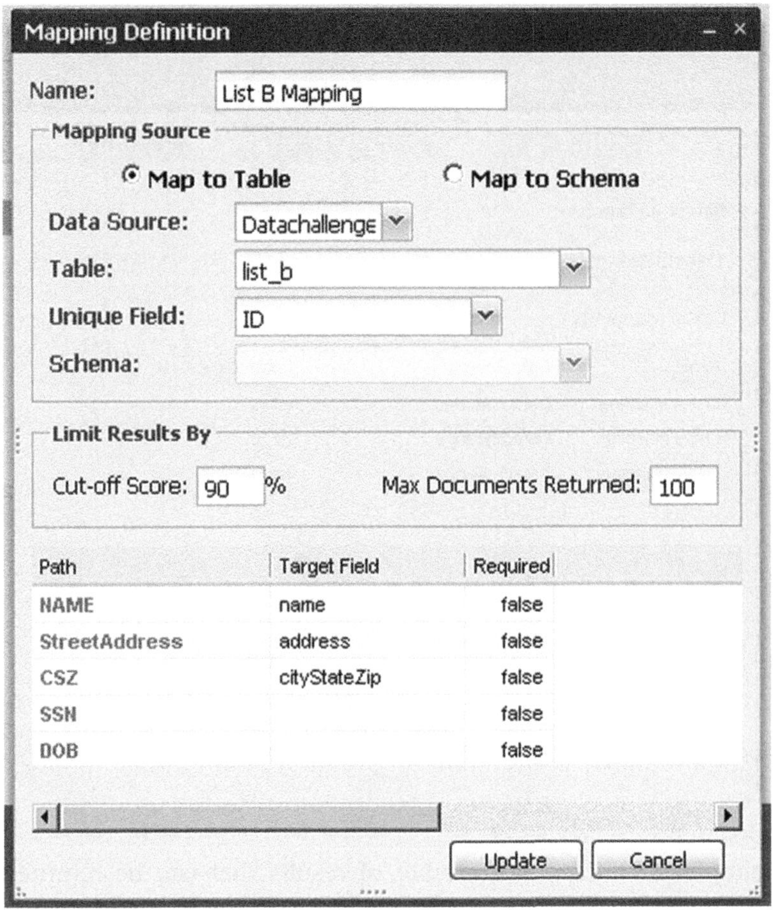

Figure 5.14: Dialog Box Defining List B Mapping

The three original references from Table 5.2 are enclosed in rectangles. It appears that the first 14 references in the list shown in Figure 5.16 are equivalent and should have been included as part of Identity 396 of Table 5.2.

One immediate observation from the results in Figure 5.16 is that seven of the references have an SSN value that is different from the value for the two records in Identity 396. The difference is due to a transposition of the fourth and fifth digits of the SSN. This suggests that one of the reasons that Identity 396 shown in Table 5.2 did not include the additional records is because Rule 1 was written to require an exact match on the SSN value. The IRE search found these references because by default it employs approximate matching in its search logic. Much of the IRE match logic is customized for particular types of attributes such as SSN,

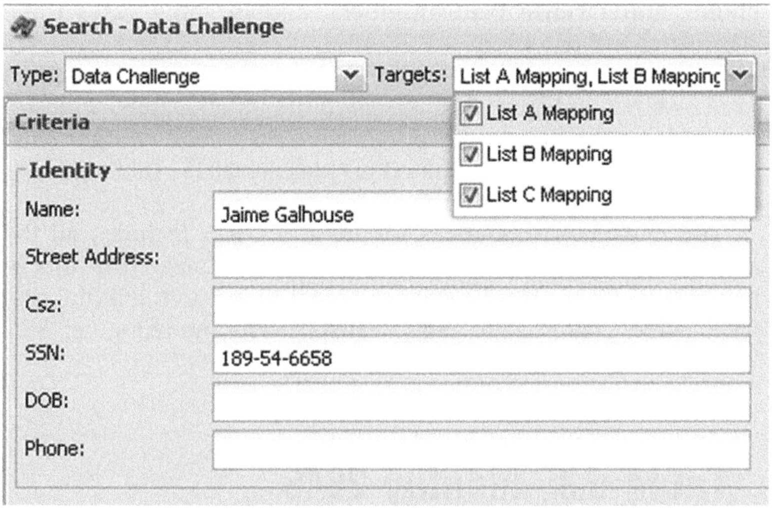

Figure 5.15: Data Challenge Search Screen

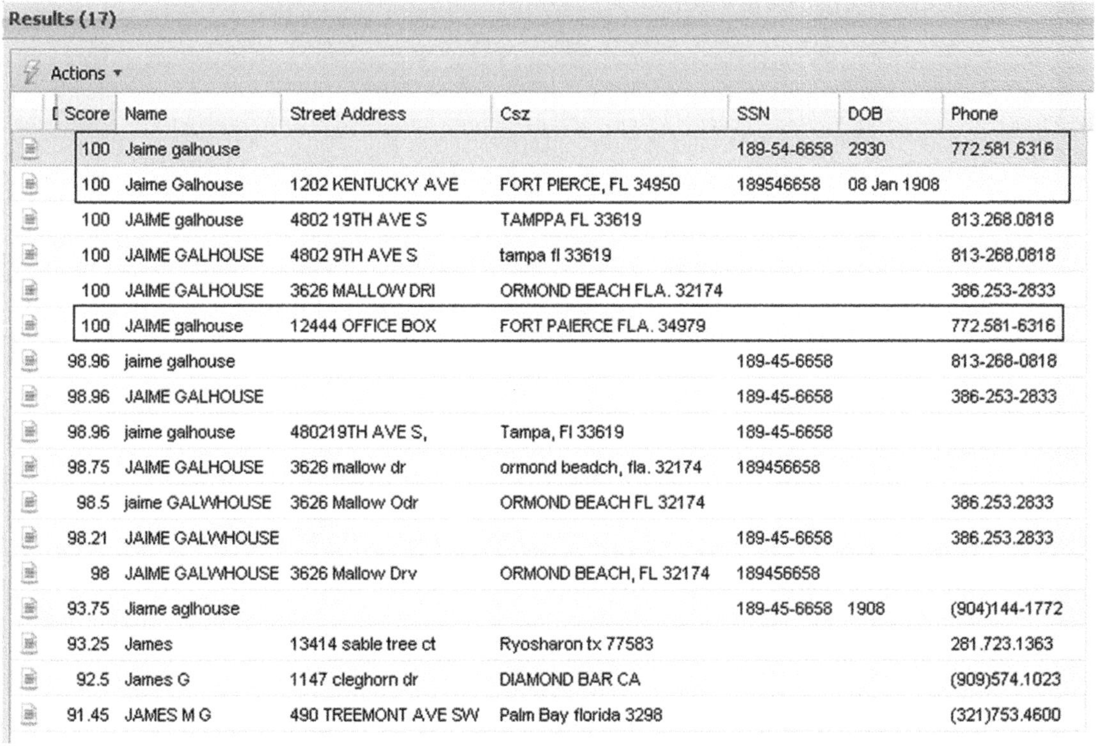

Figure 5.16: Results from Search in Figure 5.15

Phone, and License Plate numbers, and in some cases these algorithms are patented.

Using the alternate SSN value "189-45-6658" from the search results shown in Figure 5.16 to search the initial DataFlux cluster results from the first merge-purge scenario reveals another cluster of 13 references, designated as Identity 2645. Table 5.3 lists the references in this identity.

The cluster of references for Identity 2645 includes all the additional references discovered from the IRE search results in Figure 5.16. These results suggest that if Rule 1 in the initial scenario were changed to allow transposition matching on SSN

Table 5.3: Identity 2645

List ID	Name	Address	SSN	DOB	Phone
C960587	JAIME GALHOUSE		189-45-6658		386-253-2833
B956790	Jaime GALWHOUSE	3626 Mallow Odr ORMOND BEACH FL 32174			386.253.2833
B962183	JAIME galhouse	4802 19TH AVE S TAMPPA FL 33619			813.268.0818
A938319	JAIME GALHOUSE	3626 mallow dr ormond beadch, fla. 32174	189456658		
C930655	Jiame aglhouse		189-45-6658	1908	(904)144-1772
A907387	JAIME GALWHOUSE	3626 Mallow Drv ORMOND BEACH, FL 32174	189456658		
A917648	JAIME GALHOUSE	4802 19th ave s tampa, fl 33619			
C932355	JAIME GALWHOUSE		189-45-6658		386.253.2833
A992293	jaime galhouse	480219TH AVE S Tampa, Fl 33619	189-45-6658		
B917760	JAIME GALHOUSE	3626 MALLOW DRI ORMOND BEACH FLA. 32174			386.253-2833
C969456	jaime galhouse				(813) 268.0818
B942545	JAIME GALHOUSE	4802 9TH AVE S tampa fl 33619			813-268.0818
C989029	jaime galhouse		189-45-6658		813-268-0818

values, Identities 396 and 2645 would merge into a single identity. However, this change must be undertaken with care. There is always a risk that a change to correct one problem can have unintended consequences. In this case it might be wise to further modify Rule 1 to also require corroboration on other fields, such as Name or DOB. Allowing Rule 1 to link based only on approximate match of SSN values could create unwanted false positive links where SSN values for different customers are very similar.

A second iteration of the DataFlux scenario using the same four initial rules plus an additional rule that allows linking based on approximate First Name, Last Name, and SSN gives the results shown in Table 5.4.

After adding the new SSN rule, the number of identities drops from 93,981 to 38,112, a number much closer to the true number of 20,067 identities known to be in Lists A, B, and C. A check of

Table 5.4: First- and Second-Run Results Compared to True Linkage

	TRUE	Initial Run	Second Run
T-W Index	1.00000	0.462	0.644
Class cnt	20,067	93,981	38,112
Overlap cnt	20,067	94,011	42,895
Avg. class size	13.5	2.88	7.11
Class Distribution			
1	158	53,248	8,408
2	397	12,109	4,453
3	594	11,843	7,935
4	759	2,342	1,603
5	913	1,641	1,337
6	969	2,480	1,545
7	984	1,314	1,124
8	969	1,056	1,038
9	948	1,464	1,062
10	1,049	1,047	900
10+	12,327	5,437	8,707
Max. size	52	44	1,000

the actual cluster results also verified that Identity 396 in the second run comprises 16 references that included the three references originally in Identity 396 (Table 5.2) plus the 13 references that previously comprised Identity 2645 (Table 5.3). However, as suggested by the Fellegi-Sunter Model in Chapter 3, as new linking rules are added to collect additional true positives, the number of false positives also tends to increase. Table 5.4 gives two indications that the number of false positives was increased by this change.

The first is the growing difference between the number of equivalence classes and the number of overlaps produced by the process. This indicates that more of the process links are crossing over true equivalence class boundaries. Another is the maximum class size of 1,000 references. This class and other large classes need to be examined to determine what is causing such large consolidations of references. Given that the only change has been to add a new SSN rule, the likely suspect is an anomaly with matching SSN values that somehow connects several distinct identities. In the discovery example, the difference between the SSN values was the transposition between consecutive digits, but the new rule only specified that the two SSN values be similar. To get better results it may be necessary to implement a more precise similarity algorithm instead of relying on the default matching function.

By iteratively adjusting the rules and analyzing the results, the ER process can be fine-tuned to give better and better results. Unfortunately, in most real scenarios, it is not possible to instantly compare ER process results against the true results as easily as was done here using synthetic data. Instead the assessment must rely on the analysis and verification of sample links (both positive and negative) to understand whether the linking results are getting better or worse. However, even in these cases, it is still possible and useful to compare ER results between consecutive iterations to understand the overall changes in clustering.

Discovery Scenario

One of the features of the IRE is that it supports the exploration and discovery of relationships among entities (ERA5). The discovery process starts by selecting the Discover icon on the IRE Home Screen as shown in Figure 5.10, which then takes the user to the Discover Screen shown in Figure 5.17.

The discover query shown here is for a First Name value of "Michelle" and Last Name value of "Midway" using the discovery context named "People" selected from the drop-down menu. The discovery context People refers to a pre-defined XML

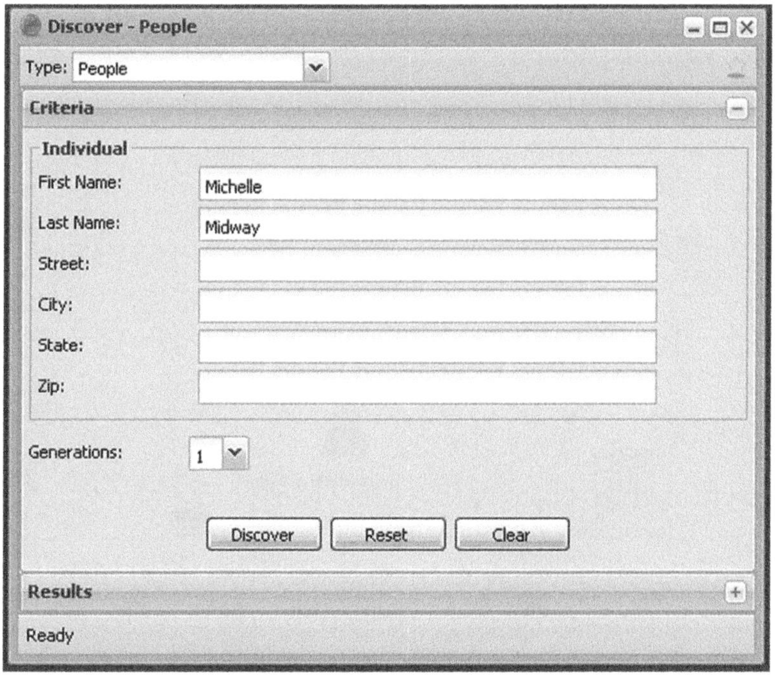

Figure 5.17: IRE Discover Screen

document called a "Linker." The Linker defines the data sources, queries, and entities that participate in the People discovery process. In this scenario they are customers, members of a watch list, product return transactions, and addresses. Figure 5.17 also shows the parameter labeled Generations. This indicates how many degrees of separation between entities are to be explored. Figure 5.18 shows the Link Chart produced using the value of 1 for the Generations parameter as shown in Figure 5.17.

The entity of interest labeled Search Criteria is shown in the center of the network, along with icons representing the first-generation connections. By approximate name matching, original search criteria "Michelle Midway" is connected to seven customer records, two watch list records, and three product returns. Using the same "Michelle Midway" search criteria for two generations yields the Link Chart shown in Figure 5.19.

At the level of two generations, connections between customer entities become clearer based on the appearance of shared residential addresses. Five of the seven customer records and both watch list records are associated with a common address, suggesting the possibility of customer fraud. The IRE provides for the exploration of up to four generations of relationships.

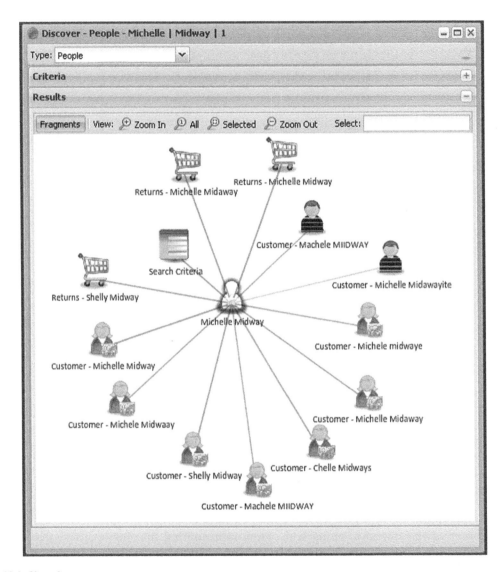

Figure 5.18: Link Chart for Michelle Midway, Generations = 1

Search and discovery results can be used to create decision rules that can be automatically applied—for example, a rule to deny a customer from making a product return if she has had five or more returns totaling $1,000 or more over the last 30 days.

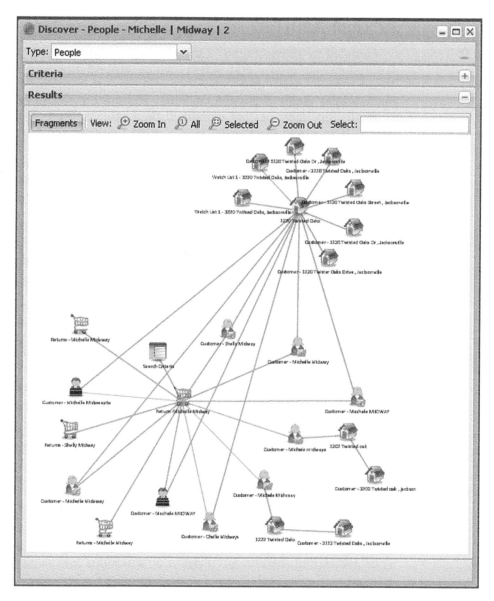

Figure 5.19: Link Chart for Michelle Midway, Generations = 2

Search and discovery results can also be saved and managed as cases. Both the Decide and Cases functions, as well as saving Favorites, can be initiated from the IRE Home Screen, as shown in Figure 5.10

Acxiom AbiliTec

Founded in 1969, Acxiom® Corporation is headquartered in Little Rock, Arkansas, and serves clients around the world, specializing in marketing technology and services that enable marketers to create profitable customer relationships (Acxiom, 2010). In the 1990s Acxiom embarked on a project to create a new CDI technology with the objective of reducing the time and effort required to execute very large merge-purge processes that in some cases could run for several days. The resulting technology, called AbiliTec® (AbiliTec, 2010), is based on the principle of reuse. Instead of repeatedly cleaning and linking the same pairs of references, linking knowledge is saved and reapplied as needed. Though sometimes called *reference-based matching* (Raab, 2010), this technique will be referred to here as *knowledge-based* or *asserted linking*, to avoid confusion between the terms entity reference and reference data.

AbiliTec is a large-scale identity resolution system. The original set of target entities consisted of all U.S. consumers (adults who purchase goods or services) and U.S. postal delivery addresses. This was later extended to include U.S. business entities. In addition, Acxiom has replicated AbiliTec services for other countries such as the United Kingdom (AbiliTec, 2008). Figure 5.20 shows the basic components of the AbiliTec linking system and their interactions.

As shown in Figure 5.20, the system has two major components that operate concurrently: the foreground process and the background identity management process (Talley, 2010; AbiliTec, 2008).

Identity Management Process

The Identity Management system stores and maintains linking knowledge in a large database. The inputs to this part of the system are two types of link assertions: existence assertions and association assertions. Existence assertions are single references from a reliable source—for example, a name, address, and phone record from a telephone directory. If the assertion represents new knowledge, it is added to the knowledge base as a new identity. If the assertion matches an existing reference, it may be able to enhance the existing reference—for example, providing an apartment number that was not in the stored reference. At a minimum it confirms the reference already in the knowledge base.

Association assertions provide an explicit link between two dissimilar references—for example, a public marriage record that

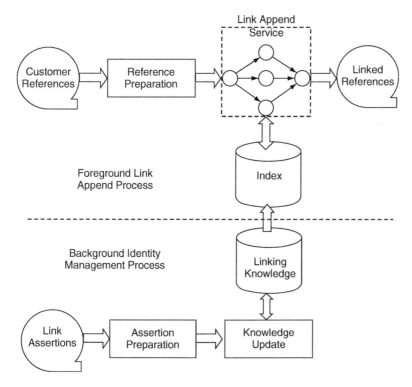

Figure 5.20: AbiliTec Component Interaction Diagram

asserts that the Mary Lee with an address on Oak Street is the same person as the Mary Doe living on Elm Street. An association assertion is essentially a combination of two single references for the same identity. Because an assertion comprises two references, there could be several outcomes to its resolution. One is that both references are new to the knowledge base and are used to produce a new identity. Another is that one reference could match an existing identity while only the other reference represents new knowledge that is added to that identity.

If both references match existing references in the knowledge base, it becomes a question as to whether the two references are already linked as part of a single identity or not. If they are already part of the same identity, the assertion confirms that association. If not, the assertion provides evidence that what was formerly believed to be two different customer identities are actually equivalent. If that evidence, perhaps along with other evidence, is considered strong enough, the conclusion is that the two identities should be consolidated into a single identity. Knowledge base consolidation is very similar to what transpired in the first scenario of this chapter where the original set of matching rules created two identities: Identity 396 (Table 5.1), a group of three references, and Identity 2645 (Table 5.2), a group of 13 references. However, after the SSN rule set was modified, it caused at least one reference in 396 to be linked to at least one reference in 2645. By transitive closure all 16 references must be consolidated into a single identity.

The reverse can sometimes also be true. It can occur that references in the knowledge base that were considered to comprise the same identity may later prove to be for different identities. When this situation is discovered, the references must be split apart into two or more identities. Again appealing to ER Principles 3 and 4 in Chapter 1, consolidations are more common than splits because the linking rules for equivalent records tend to be conservative and, when in question, err on the side of false negative. There is also a certain amount of latency in association assertions. Information about association often comes later in time than information about existence. The result is often that an existence assertion is added as new identity before an association assertion is processed that links it to an existing identity.

Of course, before any of the assertions can be processed they need to undergo standardization, cleaning, and enhancement, the normal activities of ERA2, reference preparation. Merging new assertions into the knowledge base falls under ERA3, reference resolution. Splits and consolidations and maintaining persistent identifiers fall under ERA4, identity management activities.

An important difference from the previous scenarios is that the identity identifiers in the knowledge base remain the same over time—that is, they are persistent identifiers (Raab, 2010). With the exception of identity identifier changes due to splits and consolidations, a maintained reference (that is, a reference stored in the knowledge base) will always have the same identity identifier. For this reason the identifiers in the knowledge base that link the maintained references together are called *maintained links*.

Link Append Process

The ER activities related to maintaining the knowledge base represent internal overhead. The actual delivery of ER services to clients occurs in the other part of the system called the *Link Append Service*. The basic principle of its operation is that after customer references in client files undergo standardization, enhancement, and cleaning, each reference is compared against the set of maintained references in the knowledge base. If a reference provided by the client matches a maintained reference, the link identifier from the maintained reference is appended to the reference provided by the client. Thus as an identity resolution system AbiliTec recognizes an incoming customer reference by resolving it against the set of maintained references in the knowledge base. This is different than clustering it with other references in a large customer input file, as would be done in a merge-purge process similar to that described in the first scenario. To be sure, clustering effort is expended, but only in the background maintenance process as new assertions are received, not each time a customer input file is processed. The effectiveness of this approach depends on the completeness and accuracy of the knowledge base (Raab, 2001).

An important difference between the link append and identity maintenance processes is in the handling of references that do not match the knowledge base. In the identity maintenance process, if these references meet a satisfactory level of quality, they would be used to create a new identity in the knowledge base and assigned an entity identifier. However, when the link append process fails to recognize a reference, the system does not add the reference information to the knowledge base, because it is client data. When a reference from a client file is not recognized, the link append system creates a temporary entity identifier by hashing the attribute values of the reference. Because the link identifier is derived from information in the reference and not information from the knowledge base and is not stored in the knowledge base, these link identifiers are called *derived links*. Derived links are analogous to the match codes described in the DataFlux scenario except that they are a single value that has a similar structure and format as a maintained link. Two unrecognized references that have the same or very similar attribute values would generate the same derived links.

Although U.S. consumers and businesses represent large entity identity domains, they are finite and, with the help of large-scale storage and HPC, are manageable. For example, the U.S. Census Bureau estimates that as of July 1, 2009, the adult population of the United States is approximately 232 million (U.S. Census Bureau, 2010). Even assuming that all these are consumers and that they on average have as many as 10 distinct representations, it would only mean managing around 2 billion references in the knowledge base, which is not an issue for a large-scale relational database management system.

However, the size of the knowledge base does become an issue when it comes to the transactional processing requirements of the link append process. Acxiom has solved this problem by creating an HPC grid of interconnected, off-the-shelf computers as a platform to deploy the link append service (Talley, 2010). As shown in Figure 5.20, the link append service does not directly access the knowledge base of maintained references. Instead, the maintained reference information in the knowledge base is first extracted into a large lookup table called a *link index*. The index is then partitioned into subsets of geographically related records that are small enough to fit into the RAM of the computers that function as the nodes of the grid.

In addition to AbiliTec, Acxiom uses its grid architecture to deploy other CDI services such as data cleansing, data enhancement, and workflow management. The result has been a dramatic increase in processing capacity. In 2008 the Acxiom CDI grid architecture was capable of processing more than 1.5 trillion records per month (Talley, 2010).

Summary

There are many commercial ER systems currently in use. Each has different features, architectures, and focus on different ER activities. To produce the best ER results it is often necessary to fine-tune the linking rules over several process iterations. The ER results from each iteration should be carefully analyzed to determine the best rule adjustments for the next iteration. Different ER and IQ tools can be used to assist in the analyses.

Review Questions

1. Search the Internet and other information sources to locate more information on ER systems, including those discussed in this chapter. Based on the available information, try to determine the degree to which each system addresses each of the five major ER activities. Make a table in which the rows are the systems found and with a column for each of the five ER activities. Place an indicator in each row and column to show that the system supports the activity designated by that column.
2. Using either general-purpose computer applications (spreadsheets, SQL, etc.) or an accessible ER system, try to resolve the Challenge Data discussed in this chapter. The data sets and their descriptions are available from the Downloads link on the ERIQ Research Center website (http://eriqlab.org/).
3. In the dfPowerStudio scenario, suggest ways that the second set of matching rules could be further enhanced. Explain the reasoning behind each rule.

4. In the dfPowerStudio scenario, the POBox and POCity-StateZip fields in List A were not used by any of rules. Only the Street Address field in List A was used to compare to the Street Address field in List B. What are some of the potential problems of doing this? How could you assess whether it might cause a problem? If it does, how could you fix it?

5. Compare the IRE search scenario to the DataFlux cluster scenario. Explain two ways in which their functions are similar and two ways in which they differ.

6. The IRE discovery scenarios used only one and two generations (degrees of separation). Invent a plausible fraud scenario that would only become apparent using three generations; with four generations.

7. Discuss the advantages and disadvantages of asserted (knowledge-based) linking. Is it more feasible for some types of entities than others? Explain.

8. In the AbiliTec scenario, the index of maintained references for customer entities is distributed across a grid of computers based on geography. What are some the drawbacks of using this approach? How could these drawbacks be addressed?

6

THE OYSTER PROJECT

Background

OYSTER is an open-source software development project sponsored by the ERIQ Research Center at the University of Arkansas at Little Rock (ualr.edu/eriq). OYSTER (Open sYSTem Entity Resolution) is an entity resolution system that can be configured to run in several modes of operation including merge-purge, identity capture, and identity resolution. The resolution engine supports probabilistic direct matching, transitive equivalence, and asserted equivalence. To facilitate prospecting for match candidates (blocking), the system builds and maintains an in-memory index of attribute values to identities. Because OYSTER has an identity management system, it also supports persistent identity identifiers. OYSTER is written in Java and the source code and documentation are available as a free download from the ERIQ website (ualr.edu/eriq/downloads) for use under the OYSTER open-source license.

Although the original version of OYSTER was developed to support entity resolution for student records in longitudinal studies, the system design readily accommodates a broad range of ER domains and entity types. A key feature of the system is that all entity and reference-specific information is interpreted at run-time through user-defined XML scripts.

The OYSTER Project has been guided by several design principles:
- Oyster does not use an internal database for its operation
- System inputs and outputs can either be text files or database tables
- XML scripts are used to define:
  - All entity identity attributes
  - The layout of each reference source
  - Identity rules for resolving each reference source

OYSTER Logic

The resolution engine of the OYSTER system is basically an implementation of the R-Swoosh algorithm described in Chapter 3 with the addition of an identity management system. The merged references described in the R-Swoosh algorithm correspond to the identities maintained by the OYSTER identity management system.

As shown in Figure 6.1, the OYSTER system reads two inputs and produces two outputs. The two inputs are the starting set of entity identities and one or more sources of entity references. In an ongoing operation, the entity identities input at the start of a run would be the entity identities output from a previous run. If no identities are input to the run, all the identities output at the end of the run are created from the set of references that are processed. This provides a way to bootstrap the process for the first time, producing an initial set of identities that can be updated in later processes.

In ordinary operation, information captured from the references processed during a run is used to create new identities or update existing identities. However, there is a system feature that allows this option to be turned off for a reference source. When the capture option is off for a reference source, the system will still try to resolve each reference to a particular identity. If it resolves to an identity, the identifier of that reference will be associated with the resolved identity in the link index. If not, the reference would remain unidentified, since a new identity would not be captured and created for this purpose.

There are two outputs from an OYSTER run: a set of updated entity identities (provide identity capture is turned on) and a link index file that associates each reference to an identity. At the end of the process the updated identities are written to storage as XML

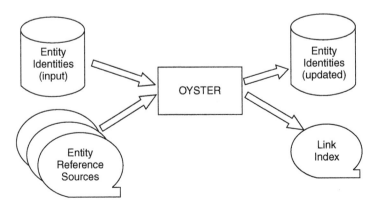

Figure 6.1: Dataflow of an OYSTER Run

documents so that they can be accessed and updated in a future run. The link index is a simple text file with one record for every reference processed in the run. Each record of the link index file contains two items. The first item is the reference identifier and the second is the entity identifier of the identity to which the reference was resolved (if any). The link index provides a way for the user of the system to append an entity identifier to the original reference to facilitate post-ER processing of the references.

An OYSTER run comprises the following steps:

1. Start Run
   a. Read Run Script
   b. Load identities into memory from stored XML documents
   c. While there are reference sources to process
      i. Read reference source
      ii. Resolve each reference to an identity
      iii. Update identities (if in capture mode)
      iv. Update link index
   d. Write updated identities to storage as XML documents
   e. Write link index file
2. End Run

All OYSTER activities are controlled by the OYSTER Run Script. The Run Script is loaded at the start of each run and provides the system with the following information:

- The path to the XML Attributes Description document defining the entity attributes to be used during the run
- The path to the XML Identity documents to be loaded at the start of the run (if needed)
- The path to a location where the updated XML Identity documents will be stored at the end of the run (if needed)
- A list of paths to the Source Descriptor XML documents, one Descriptor for each reference source to be processed
- The path to a location where the Link Index will be written at the end of the run

The sequence of operations controlled by the run script is shown as an interaction diagram in Figure 6.2. In the current version the system expects to read the Run Script, Attributes Description document, and Source Descriptor documents from text files. The identities and reference sources can be read from either text files or database tables.

Run Script Document Structure

The XML structure of the Run Script is shown in Figure 6.3. Not shown are the additional XML attributes for the <IdentityInput>, <IdentityOutput>, and <LinkOutput> elements that may be

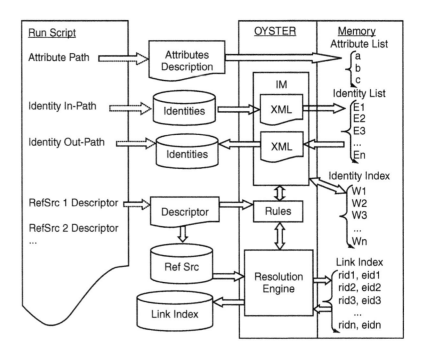

Figure 6.2: OYSTER Run Control and Data Flow

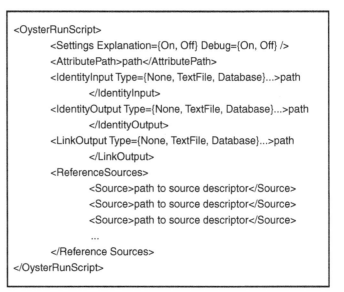

```
<OysterRunScript>
        <Settings Explanation={On, Off} Debug={On, Off} />
        <AttributePath>path</AttributePath>
        <IdentityInput Type={None, TextFile, Database}...>path
                </IdentityInput>
        <IdentityOutput Type={None, TextFile, Database}...>path
                </IdentityOutput>
        <LinkOutput Type={None, TextFile, Database}...>path
                </LinkOutput>
        <ReferenceSources>
                <Source>path to source descriptor</Source>
                <Source>path to source descriptor</Source>
                <Source>path to source descriptor</Source>

                ...
        </Reference Sources>
</OysterRunScript>
```

Figure 6.3: Run Script XML Structure

required, depending on the Type attribute—for example, user name and password values for database access. In addition to providing the file paths or database connections for the necessary files, the Run Script also controls the setting for the explanation facility and the program debug mode.

Attributes Description Document Structure

The XML structure of the Attribute Descriptions document is shown in Figure 6.4. The value of the XML attribute named "System" is a common identifier for the entity attributes defined in the document. This is necessary because the system is not entity specific; the same system could be used to process and maintain customer identities and references as well as student identities and references, each with a separate set of attributes. The value of the XML attribute named "RefID" gives the name of the reference item that will provide the reference identifier. Reference identifiers uniquely identify each reference instance in a reference source and, together with the name of the reference source, uniquely identify each reference instance in a run. Each combined source name and reference identifier becomes a key in the Link Index list and is associated with an identity identifier.

```
<OysterAttributes System="value" RefID="value">
    <Attribute Name="attrName" Algo="algoName" />
    <Attribute Name="attrName" Algo="algoName" />
    <Attribute Name="attrName" Algo="algoName" />
...
</OysterAttributes>
```

Figure 6.4: Attributes Description XML Structure

Each XML <Attribute> element in the document defines one OYSTER attribute labeled by the value of the XML "Name" attribute. These labels are used in the Source Descriptor to identify the logical items in a Reference Source that are OYSTER identity attributes. The layout for a reference may have more than one logical item labeled with the same OYSTER identity attribute type. For example, an asserted link for a customer change of address could be presented as a reference with two street number items, two street name items, and so on. In addition to the attribute name, the value of the XML attribute "Algo" specifies a predefined matching algorithm that is to be used for comparing attributes value of this type. Specifying an algorithm is optional, and if it is not given or a given name is not found, a default matching algorithm is used.

The XML structure of the Source Descriptor document is shown in Figure 6.5. The value of the XML attribute "Name" is needed so that when multiple reference sources are processed during a single run, each reference source will have a unique identifier. The reference source name together with the reference identifier uniquely identifies each reference processed during a run of the system. The value of the XML attribute "Capture" tells the system whether the reference source can be used to create and update identities. In some cases, a reference source may be processed only to identify the references without using them to update the identity set.

```
<OysterSourceDescriptor Name="sourceName" Capture={Yes, No}>
        <Source Type={FileDelim, FileFixed, Database} ...
>path</Source>
        <ReferenceItems>
                <Item Name="itemName" Attribute="attrName" ... />
                <Item Name="itemName" Attribute="attrName" ... />
            ...
        </ReferenceItems>
        <IdentityRules>
            <Rule Ident="ruleID">
                    <Term Item="itemName" MatchResult="code" />
                    <Term Item="itemName" MatchResult="code" />
                    ...
            </Rule>
            ...
        </IdentityRules>
</OysterSourceDescriptor>
```

Figure 6.5: Reference Source Descriptor XML Structure

Each item in the reference that will be used for identification must be described by both its logical name and its OYSTER attribute label. Attribute labels associated with a reference item must be defined in the OYSTER Attributes Description document. As noted earlier, different reference items could have the same attribute label.

In-Memory Structures

To avoid tying OYSTER to any particular database system or database schema, OYSTER is designed to keep a number of list structures resident in memory during a run. Keeping these lists memory resident not only avoids the requirement for an internal database, it is also necessary for efficient transitive closure and identity consolidation. The trade-off is that large applications will also require a system with a large memory space. However, this design decision was made on the premise that large internal memory is not the problem that it once was. Newer systems now accommodate large memory address spaces and the actual memory elements have become relatively inexpensive.

The three large in-memory lists are:

1. Identity List
2. Identity Index
3. Link Index

Identity List

The Identity List maintains one identity structure for each identity managed by the system. Identities are stored as XML documents that are converted into an internal memory structure at the start of a run and converted back to XML at the end. Although the in-memory representation of each identity is kept in compact data structure for efficiency, the structure can be mapped directly to its XML archival structure. The in-memory structure is based on the Compressed Tag Format (CTF) of the Compressed Document Set Architecture (CoDoSA) framework for managing unstructured data (Talburt, Nelson, 2009).

Figure 6.6 shows that each entity identity has a simple structure. It comprises a list of known values for each attribute of the identity. Because OYSTER supports the Identity Capture Model, these attributes and their values can be taken from the reference sources processed by the system. This means that an identity structure can grow in size (gain knowledge) over time. Each identity also has a special attribute, the reference identification attribute, not directly related to entity identification. The reference identification attribute saves the reference identifier value for each reference that has contributed knowledge to the identity. This indexing of references to identities is used by the explanation facility and identity management system. The reference identification attribute is called out in the Attributes Description document (Figure 6.4), where its label is defined by the value of the XML attribute "RefID."

Knowing which references have been resolved to a particular identity is important in the case of identity consolidation. When a reference resolves to two different identities, it signals the possible merging of the two identities. Assuming that the identifier of one of the identities is retained for the merged identity, it is possible to find the references that were resolved to other identities and revise the link values (entity identifiers) that they were previously assigned. If the references affected by the merger are in the run being processed, the links for those references can be adjusted dynamically in the in-memory link index. For references not in the run for which the consolidation occurs, the link revisions must be made retroactively. One way to do this is to periodically reprocess reference sources to create a new (revised) link index that can be used to update the links in the references.

```
<Identity Identifier=="identityID">
        <Attribute Name="attrName1>
                <Value>value1</Value>
                <Value>value2</Value>
                ...
        </Attribute>
        <Attribute Name="attrName2>
                <Value>value1</Value>
                <Value>value2</Value>
                ...
        </Attribute>
        ...
</Identity>
```

Figure 6.6: Entity Identity Structure in XML Format

Identity Index

The second in-memory list is the identity index. The identity index is an inverted index into the identity list. It is actually a list of lists in which the look-up key is an attribute value that returns a list of identity identifiers. The identifiers in the list represent the identities that have an attribute equal to the key value. For example, if the key value is "JOHN," it would point to every member of the identity list that has an attribute with the value "JOHN."

Although not logically necessary, the identity index is important for processing efficiency that makes the resolution process practical for large data sets. Without the index, every member of the identity list would have to be checked each time a new reference processed. The identity index is a way to implement the blocking of the identity list and reduce the number of comparison operations that must be made to a more reasonable number. For example, if an identity rule requires an exact match on last name, candidates for that identity rule can be reduced to only those identities in the list associated with a particular last name value in the identity index. If an exact match is required on another attribute, the candidate list is reduced even further by intersecting the two lists for candidates that have both values.

Where identity rules allow an approximate match, the list of candidate identities may be fairly large because some variations of attribute values may not be in the index. However, the index can learn over time. Once a reference with a variant attribute value has been resolved to a given identity through an identity rule involving an approximate match, the variant value can be captured in both the identity and identity index. Thus if the same variant were to occur in another reference, it would be found by exact match in the identity index.

Link Index

The third in-memory list is the link index. It represents the final outcome of the system's resolution decisions. It is a simple table of two columns. The first column contains the reference identifier and the second column the entity identifier. There is one row in the table for each reference input into the system during a run. In a given row, the entity identifier in the second column is the identity of the reference in the first column as resolved by the system.

In theory, every reference will have an entity identifier because it will either match an existing identity or create a new identity. However, as a practical matter there are circumstances in which the system can decide that a reference instance should not receive an entity identifier link. Two cases are when the identity capture feature is specifically turned off for a source and when the reference information is determined to have poor quality. For example, a customer reference with all missing values except a first name value of "JOHN" would not resolve to any valid customer identity under most identity rule sets. However, it would not be useful to create and manage an identity with only this value. In these cases the references are given a special link value that indicates that it does not resolve to any managed identity.

Transitive Equivalence Example

The following shows how an OYSTER run would be set up for the example reference set of five instances used in Chapter 3 to illustrate the operation of the R-Swoosh algorithm. Following the R-Swoosh example, the run does not start with an initial set of identities. Therefore the run represents a basic merge-purge operation with the exception that the system will capture and save the identities generated by the run.

Describing the Identities

Figure 6.7 shows the five-record reference source of Table 3.2 in a comma-delimited format and stored at the text file TestInput.txt. The records represent student enrollment records, and each record has the following five fields:
1. Record Identifier (labeled RefID)
2. Student First Name (labeled FirstName)
3. Student Last Name (labeled LastName)
4. Date-of-Birth (labeled DOB)
5. School Code (labeled SchCode)

Figure 6.8 shows how these attributes are defined in an OYSTER Attributes Definition script.

The Attributes Description script defines the System as "School" and the reference identifier label as "@RefID." In addition, it defines the four identity attribute labels "First," "Last," "DOB," and "SCode." Note that the Oyster identity attribute labels are independent of the column labels given in the input file. This is because one run may process several reference sources, each with different column labels for the same type of identity attribute.

In this example, the default match algorithm is to be used since the XML "Algo" attribute is not used to designate a user-defined

```
RecID, FirstName, LastName, DOB, SchCode
r1, Edgar, Jones, 20001104, G34
r2, Mary, Smith, 19990921, G55
r3, Eddie, Jones, 20001104, G34
r4, Mary, Smith, 19990921, H17
r5, Eddie, Jones, 20001104, H15
```

Figure 6.7: Example Reference Source Named TestInput.txt

```
<?xml version="1.0" encoding="UTF -8"?>
<!--Document: OysterAttributes.xml-->
<OysterAttributes System="School"
RefID="@ RefID">
    <Attribute Item="First" />
    <Attribute Item="Last" />
    <Attribute Item="DOB" />
    <Attribute Item="SCode" />
</OysterAttributes>
```

Figure 6.8: Example Attributes Description

match algorithm. User-defined match algorithms are easily created in OYSTER by extending base class OysterComparator.java as a new class with a name starting with "OysterCompare" and implementing the method

```
String: getMatchCode(String, String)
```

The OysterComparator base class automatically returns the match codes "Exact" and "Missing," If either or both strings are all blank or empty strings, it returns "Missing"; if the two strings are identical, it returns "Exact"; otherwise the comparator calls the getMatchCode() method, which, in the base class, always returns the match code "X." Extensions of this class must override getMatchCode()to implement logic for other match conditions and corresponding match codes. For example, the School system shown here could be augmented to include a user-defined comparator for the first name attribute that recognizes common nicknames. To do this, the user would have to create a new class such as OysterCompareFirst.java that extends OysterComparator.java, include a nickname look-up table, and return the match code "NickName" when the one of the first name values is found to be a nickname for the other value. It would also require changing the Attribute element in Figure 6.8 to include the XML attribute named "Algo" that identifies the Java package and class name. The result might appear as

```
<Attribute Item="First" Algo="School.OysterCompareFirst" />
```

OYSTER comes with a class OysterCompareDefault.java, which is an extension of the base comparator that returns the match code "Transpose" if two strings differ only by the reversal of one pair of adjacent characters. The default comparator also returns the match code "Close" if the normalized edit distance between the two strings is greater than 0.20. As an aid in developing custom comparator classes, OYSTER provides a number of utility classes for commonly used match conditions such as OysterUtilityEditDistance.java and OysterUtilityTranspose.java that implement the Levenshtein edit distance and adjacent transpose algorithms, respectively.

Describing Identity Rules

Table 6.1 shows the two identity (match) rules to be used for processing the reference instances shown in Figure 6.7. The entries in the cells of Table 6.1 indicate the degree of match that is required for each identity attribute. For this example, only exact matching is required, as indicated by the "Exact" match code. However, in other scenarios the rules could include other

Table 6.1: Identity Rules

Rule	First	Last	DOB	SCode
1	Exact	Exact	Exact	
2		Exact	Exact	Exact

approximate conditions, such as "Initial," to indicate that the first characters of two names are the same, or "Transpose" or "Missing," as defined previously. An empty cell means that there is no match requirement (don't care).

Figure 6.9 shows the Source Descriptor for the reference source TestInput.txt shown in Figure 6.7. It defines a source named "Test" from which identity information can be captured (Capture="Yes"). It is also described it as a delimited-field text file (Type="FileDelim") where the field-delimiting character is a comma (Char=","). The file does not use text qualification (Qual="") and the first record of the file is a nondata record with the labels of the fields (Labels="Y").

The five fields are defined in the <ReferenceItems> section. Each logical name is associated with one of the attributes defined in the Attributes Description document (Figure 6.8). Note that as in this example the logical name given in the descriptor does not have to agree with its label in the header record of the file. Items are referenced by their logical names in the <IdentityRules> section of descriptor document. The relative position (index) of the item in the record is given by the value of the XML "Pos" attribute. Here "SeqNbr" is the first item in the record (position 0), the item "Fname" is the second (position 1), and so on. The <IdentityRules> section of the descriptor document in Figure 6.9 shows how the match rules given in Table 6.1 are translated into rules.

```xml
<?xml version="1.0" encoding="UTF -8"?>
<!--Document: OysterSourceDescriptor.xml-->
<OysterSourceDescriptor Name="Test" Capture="Yes">
    <Source Type="FileDelim" Char="," Qual="" Labels="Y">
    C:\My_Code\Oyster\TestInput.txt</Source>
    <ReferenceItems>
        <Item Name="SeqNbr" Attribute="@RefID" Pos="0"/>
        <Item Name="Fname" Attribute="First" Pos="1"/>
        <Item Name="Lname" Attribute="Last" Pos="2"/>
        <Item Name="BDay" Attribute="DOB" Pos="3"/>
        <Item Name="School" Attribute="SCode" Pos="4"/>
    </ReferenceItems>
    <IdentityRules>
        <Rule Ident="1">
            <Term Item="Fname" MatchResult="Exact" />
            <Term Item="Lname" MatchResult="Exact" />
            <Term Item="BDay" MatchResult="Exact" />
        </Rule>
        <Rule Ident="2">
            <Term Item="Lname" MatchResult="Exact" />
            <Term Item="BDay" MatchResult="Exact" />
            <Term Item="School" MatchResult="Exact" />
        </Rule>
    </IdentityRules>
</OysterSourceDescriptor>
```

Figure 6.9: Example Source Descriptor

Running the Example

The final step is to create a run script that references all the necessary components—in this case, paths to the Attributes Description document shown in Figure 6.8, to the Reference Source Descriptor shown in Figure 6.9, and the locations for writing output identities and the link index. Figure 6.10 shows the run script for this example.

Running the script of Figure 6.10 creates the two identities shown in Figure 6.11. The identities in the in-memory Identity

```
<?xml version="1.0" encoding="UTF -8"?>
<!--   Document: Run Script.xml-->
<OysterRunScript>
    <Settings Explanation="Off" Debug="On" />
    <AttributePath>C:\My_Code\Oyster\OysterAttributes.xml
        </AttributePath>
    <IdentityInput Type="None" />
    <IdentityOutput Type="TextFile">C:\My_Code\Oyster\TestInput.idty
        </IdentityOutput>
    <LinkOutput Type="TextFile">C:\My_Code\Oyster\TestInput.link
        </LinkOutput>
    <ReferenceSources>
        <Source>C:\My_Code\Oyster\OysterSourceDescriptor.xml
        </Source>
    </ReferenceSources>
</OysterRunScript>
```

Figure 6.10: Script to Process Reference Source TestInput.txt

```
<Identity Identifier="E01">
  <Attribute Name="@RefID"><Value>Test.r1</Value>
   <Value>Test.r3</Value><Value>Test.r5</Value></Attribute>
  <Attribute Name="First"><Value>Edgar</Value>
   <Value>Eddie</Value></Attribute>
  <Attribute Name="Last"><Value>Jones</Value></Attribute>
  <Attribute Name="DOB"><Value>20001104</Value></Attribute>
  <Attribute Name="SCode"><Value>G34</Value>
   <Value>H15</Value></Attribute>
  </Identity>
<Identity Identifier="E02">
  <Attribute Name="@RefID"><Value>Test.r2</Value>
   <Value>Test.r4</Value></Attribute>
  <Attribute Name="First"><Value>Mary</Value></Attribute>
  <Attribute Name="Last"><Value>Smith</Value></Attribute>
  <Attribute Name="DOB"><Value>19990921</Value></Attribute>
  <Attribute Name="SCode"><Value>H17</Value>
   <Value>G55</Value></Attribute>
  </Identity>
```

Figure 6.11: Identity List in XML Format in TestInput.idty

List are translated from the compressed CTF format and written to the file "TestInput.idty" as XML documents. Note that these identities correspond to the merged records in ER(R) at the end of the R-Swoosh algorithm, as shown in Table 3.9. Each identity is a complete XML document and is written to the text file as a single paragraph.

Figure 6.12 shows the Link Index named "TestInput.link" created at the end of the run. It has one record for each reference in each source processed during the run. The first item in each record is the concatenation of the logical source name (Test) and the record identifier for each reference. The second item in each record is the identifier of the identity to which the reference corresponds.

Figure 6.13 show the contents of the in-memory Identity Index at the end of the run. This list exists only during the processing of the reference sources and is not saved as a file at the end of the run. In this simple example, each value occurs in only one identity, but for larger reference sets the same value may occur in more than one identity. For example, for a larger set of enrollment records there could be several students with the last name "Jones" or "Smith."

```
Test.r1, E01
Test.r2, E02
Test.r3, E01
Test.r4, E02
Test.r5, E01
```

Figure 6.12: Link Index File TestInput.link

```
19990921 → {E02}
20001104 → {E01}
Eddie  → {E01}
Edgar  → {E01}
G34  → {E01}
G55  → {E02}
H15  → {E01}
H17  → {E02}
Jones  → {E01}
Mary  → {E02}
Smith  → {E02}
```

Figure 6.13: Identity Index Created in Example Run

Asserted Equivalence Example

The previous example demonstrated an OYSTER run that included direct matching and transitive equivalence. The example given here shows how OYSTER supports asserted equivalence and multiple sources.

Figure 6.14 shows a simple reference source that follows the same layout as the reference source shown in Figure 6.7 of the first example. For simplicity, the rule identity rules for this simple reference source are the same as the previous example shown in Table 6.1. References are considered equivalent if they agree on First, Last, and DOB or agree on Last, DOB, and SCode.

Using these two identity rules and only the six reference instances showing in Figure 6.14, it is easy to see that OYSTER would conclude that these represent six distinct identities. Since both identity rules require agreement on last name, only two pairs satisfy this condition, pairs (1, 5) and (3, 6). Reference instances 1 and 5 also agree on DOB, but they do not agree on first name or school code. Therefore 1 and 5 are not equivalent by either identity rule. Similarly, reference instances 3 and 6 agree on last name and DOB but not on first name or school code.

```
ID, First, Last, DOB, SCode
1, Susan, Craig, 19951203, G21
2, Robert, Sims, 19940205, H15
3, Bobby, Thomas, 19940205, H15
4, Suzy, Johnson, 19951203, G21
5, Suzy, Craig, 19951203, H70
6, Russell, Thomas, 19940205, G51
```

Figure 6.14: Simple Reference Source

```
ID, First, Last, First, Last, DOB
1, Susan, Craig, Susan, Johnson, 19951203
2, Robert, Sims, Robert, Thomas, 19940205
```

Figure 6.15: Asserted Equivalences

```
<?xml version="1.0" encoding="UTF -8"?>
<!--Document: OysterSource Descriptor.xml-->
<OysterSourceDescriptor Name="Assertion" Capture="Yes">
    <Source Type="FileDelim" Char="," Qual="" Labels="Y">
    C:\My_Code\Oyster\TestInput.txt</Source>
    <ReferenceItems>
        <Item Name="SeqNbr" Attribute="@RefID" Pos="0"/>
        <Item Name="Fname1" Attribute="First" Pos="1"/>
        <Item Name="Lname1" Attribute="Last" Pos="2"/>
        <Item Name="Fname2" Attribute="First" Pos="3"/>
        <Item Name="Lname2" Attribute="Last" Pos="4"/>
        <Item Name="BDay" Attribute="DOB" Pos="5"/>
    </ReferenceItems>
    <IdentityRules>
        <Rule Ident="1">
            <Term Item="Fname1" MatchResult="Exact" />
            <Term Item="Lname1" MatchResult="Exact" />
            <Term Item="BDay" MatchResult="Exact" />
        </Rule>
        <Rule Ident="1">
            <Term Item="Fname2" MatchResult="Exact" />
            <Term Item="Lname2" MatchResult="Exact" />
            <Term Item="BDay" MatchResult="Exact" />
        </Rule>
    </IdentityRules>
</OysterSourceDescriptor>
```

Figure 6.16: Source Descriptor for Assertions

However, it turns out that there are really only three distinct identities represented in six reference instances in Figure 6.14. The reason is that there is other information about these students related to legal changes in family name. These changes represent knowledge about these entities that can be expressed as assertions.

The source descriptor for the assertion source is similar to that for the simple reference source except that it provides multiple values for the same identity attributes.

The source descriptor for the assertion source is shown in Figure 6.16. Note that the logical items Fname1 and Fname2 both share the identity attribute of First and that the logical items Lname1 and Lname2 both share the identity attribute of Last. If the assertion source is run first, the effect is to create two identities, Identity 1 for Susan Craig/Johnson and Identity 2 for Robert Sims/Thomas. When the simple reference source of Figure 6.14 is resolved:

1. The first reference for Susan Craig will resolve to Identity 1 based on the first identity rule, and the DOB and SCode values will be captured in Identity 1.

2. The second reference for Robert Sims will resolve to Identity 2 based on the first identity rule, and the DOB and Scode values will be captured in Identity 2.

3. The third reference for Bobby Thomas will resolve to Identity 2 based on the second identity rule (Last, DOB, and SCode), and the first name value of Bobby will be captured in Identity 2.

4. The fourth reference for Suzy Johnson will resolve to Identity 1 based on the second identity rule (Last, DOB, and SCode), and the first name value of Suzy will be captured in Identity 1.

5. The fifth reference for Suzy Craig will resolve to Identity 1 based on the first identity rule (First, Last, and DOB), and the new SCode value will be captured in Identity 1.

6. The sixth reference for Russell Thomas will not resolve to either Identity 1 or Identity 2 and will result in a new Identity 3.

```
<Identity Identifier="E01">
  <Attribute Name="@RefID"><Value>Assertion.1</Value>
   <Value>Simple.1</Value><Value>Simple.4</Value>
   <Value>Simple.5</Value></Attribute>
  <Attribute Name="First"><Value>Susan</Value>
   <Value>Suzy</Value></Attribute>
  <Attribute Name="Last"><Value>Craig</Value>
   <Value>Johnson</Value></Attribute>
  <Attribute Name="DOB"><Value>19951203</Value></Attribute>
  <Attribute Name="SCode"><Value>G21</Value>
   <Value>H70</Value></Attribute>
  </Identity>
<Identity Identifier="E02">
  <Attribute Name="@RefID"><Value>Assertion.2</Value>
   <Value>Simple.2</Value><Value>Simple.3</Value></Attribute>
  <Attribute Name="First"><Value>Robert</Value>
   <Value>Bobby</Value></Attribute>
  <Attribute Name="Last"><Value>Sims</Value>
   <Value>Thomas</Value></Attribute>
  <Attribute Name="DOB"><Value>19940205</Value></Attribute>
  <Attribute Name="SCode"><Value>H15</Value></Attribute>
</Identity>
<Identity Identifier="E03">
  <Attribute Name="@RefID"><Value>Simple.6</Value></Attribute>
  <Attribute Name="First"><Value>Russell</Value></Attribute>
  <Attribute Name="Last"><Value>Thomas</Value></Attribute>
  <Attribute Name="DOB"><Value>19940205</Value></Attribute>
  <Attribute Name="SCode"><Value>G51</Value></Attribute>
</Identity>
```

Figure 6.17 Final Set of Identities Created

Figure 6.17 shows the final set of three identity documents that are created by OYSTER as a result of running the assertion source in Figure 6.15 followed by the simple reference source in Figure 6.14.

Febrl: Open-Source Project

Another open-source ER project is Febrl, a Freely Extensible Biomedical Record Linkage, a project sponsored by the Australian Research Council, the NSW Department of Health, and the Australian National University (Christen, 2008). Febrl is available for free downloads on Source Forge (sourceforge.net/projects/febrl/). The code is written in Python and system provides a graphical user interface.

Like OYSTER, Febrl allows users the ability to configure a number of field comparison options but also supports options for configuring blocking schemes and record clustering. Febrl also provides functionality for assessing and cleaning reference sources. However, Febrl does not provide any support for identity management, persistent links, or asserted linking.

Summary

OYSTER is a freely available general-purpose entity resolution system that can be adapted to a wide range of applications, including instructional support. Written using the open standards of Java and XML, the system is based on the identity capture architecture and provides identity management and persistent links. A distinguishing feature of OYSTER is that it provides support for identity management and asserted linking. Appendix A provides more details on configuring OYSTER to run in various modes including merge-purge, identity capture, identity build, and identity resolution.

Review Questions

1. At the Downloads link of the ERIQ Research Center website (ualr.edu/eriq/) download and install OYSTER. Create the simple dataset shown in Figure 6.7 or a similar dataset and try to resolve it using OYSTER.
2. Try using OYSTER to resolve the Challenge Data discussed in Chapter 5. The challenge data sets and their descriptions are available from the Downloads link of the ERIQ Research Center website (ualr.edu/eriq/).
3. Propose some modifications to OYSTER that would enable some data quality standardization and data-cleaning processes that would typically be done prior to processing to be migrated directly into OYSTER.

7

TRENDS IN ENTITY RESOLUTION RESEARCH AND APPLICATIONS

Introduction

The previous chapters of this book cover the basic principles and practices of ER and IQ. They include an overview of the basic architectures and models of ER along with examples of actual ER processes. The purpose of this final chapter is to briefly describe some of the new areas of application for ER and current directions in ER research.

ER and Information Hubs

ER, particularly identity resolution, is proving to be a critical process in the movement to create systems that facilitate information sharing across entity-centric, interorganizational data stores. Ineffective interorganization information sharing is a common problem in many domains where information about a common set of entities is routinely collected and stored, such as in health care, law enforcement, public education, and the military. One of the major problems is that the organizations collecting this information evolved separately and have independently designed and built information systems with different data architectures and business rules. The result is that the exchange of information among these organizations is not very efficient and, in many cases, is largely an exchange of paper documents. Essentially a system of systems problem, it presents a number of complex technical issues and, in some cases such as health care and education, equally challenging concerns related to cultural change, privacy, legal issues, and regulatory requirements. At the same time there is a growing realization that the quality of the services delivered by these organizations is greatly improved when a complete view of the information related to a particular entity can be gathered and made available as needed.

An emerging solution to this problem is to build a single system that connects to each of the participating organizations similar to the way in which the spokes of a bicycle wheel connect to a central hub at the axle—hence the term *information hub* or *information broker* (Lawley, 2010). The adoption of the hub solution is growing in areas such as health care (eHealth, 2010), law enforcement (Nelson, Talburt, 2008), education (Holland, 2010), and the military (*Chief Information Officer*, 2009). A key element of the hub architecture is an identity resolution subsystem that maintains a master set of identities for all the entities referenced in the data stores of the participating organizations. Systems of this design represent a large-scale extension of the heterogeneous database join architecture discussed in Chapter 1, where a key function of the central hub is not only to connect to and query the other systems but also to provide an identity resolution service for the collective set of entities.

For example, in health care, the entities are primarily people in the roles of patient and health care providers, such as physicians and nurses, but can also include organizations such as hospitals and insurance providers, and items such as drugs and medical equipment. In the past, assembling a complete medical history for a patient has largely been a clerical process. It not only suffered from the fact that the records were collected by numerous independent providers, but until recently those records have been largely paper-based. The movement toward electronic medical records (EMR) is converging with the adoption of hub-based information exchange systems to create more complete and timely information products for health care providers. For example, the eHealth Initiative (eHealth, 2010) reports that there are 234 active health information exchange initiatives (HIEs) in the United States, an increase of 74 over the previous year.

Figure 7.1 shows an example of a hub system based on a layered architecture and the logical flow of how it might process a request by a physician for the medical history of a patient. The request is represented by the method "RecReq(x, y)," where a physician "x" is requesting the medical records for a patient "y." The token "y" could represent one of many possible formats for patient identification. It could include a combination name values, date of birth, gender, and patient identifiers such as insurance numbers or the patient number assigned by the physician making the request. At the services layer, the first step of the request process authenticates and validates the request. Next the patient

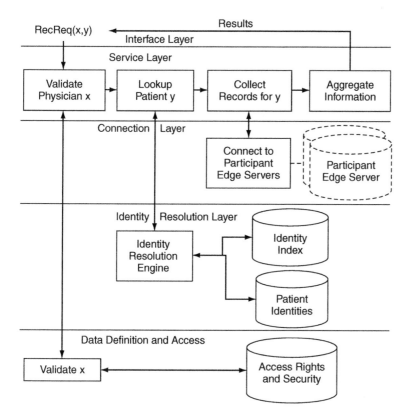

Figure 7.1: Processing a Request for Patient Records

information is passed to the identity resolution layer, where the system tries to resolve the identity of the patient against the patient identities maintained by the system. The master patient identifier is a unique, persistent identifier for each entity in the system.

If the resolution is successful, it will return a master patient identifier to be passed to the next process for collecting records at the connection layer. For security and performance reasons, the hub systems do not typically connect directly to a participant's operational system. Instead it connects to special servers, sometimes called *edge servers* (Rooney, Bauer, Scotton, 2005), maintained by each participant. These systems hold patient information that is periodically extracted from the participant's operational systems and indexed by the master patient identifier. In some hub implementations, it is the responsibility of the participant to transform the information posted on its edge server from participant's internal format into a common format used by all participants. In other implementations the data transformations are done by the hub.

For the participants to index the information posted on their edge server by master patient identifier, the hub system must also provide a link append service similar to the AbiliTec link append service described in Chapter 5 or the OYSTER link index described in Chapter 6. For the system to operate properly, each participant must periodically resolve the patient identity attributes held in its system against the master patient index in the hub in order to obtain master patient identifiers. The periodic link append operation is also necessary to update the master index information at the hub using identity capture methods as well as providing participants with the most current master patient identifiers. Schemes like these, in which a central system maintains a master index of entity identifiers as a way to link entities across disparate databases, are sometimes called *trusted broker* systems (Talburt, Morgan, Talley, Archer, 2005), "trusted" because the participants agree to allow one organization to maintain the master identity resolution service. Trusted broker systems can also be used to support anonymous ER.

Hub systems are also being used to address similar situations that occur in law enforcement. In a single region, there can be many overlapping city, county, and state enforcement jurisdictions, all collecting information on individuals with whom they have interacted. The ability to collect information about an individual's interactions across all of these agencies can be critical to investigating and preventing crime. The development of these systems, sometimes called law enforcement *fusion centers*, has been promoted in the United States by the Department of Justice and the Department of Homeland Security (Homeland Security, 2009).

Association Analysis and Social Networks

Most commercial ER systems were developed around customer contact information, which has traditionally been name, mailing address, and telephone number. With the growth of the World Wide Web and, most recently, social networks, customer contact information increasingly includes e-mail address, URL, IP address, and social network usernames and handles. Usernames and handles are aliases for the user's real name, and people often use different usernames in different networks. When users establish multiple identities in the same network for malicious purposes these are referred to as Sybil attacks (Viswanath, Post, Gummandi, Mislove, 2010). Other factors contributing to the complexity of ER in the context of the Internet are that messages and other communications tend to be less structured and more compressed and often employ slang and abbreviations.

The overall result is that direct matching tends to be less effective for linking equivalent references than in the traditional structured IT environment. For this reason much of the current research for the ER in the Web and social network focuses on determining equivalence through association analysis, as discussed in Chapter 1. Associations among references are often modeled as a network graph in which references are represented as nodes (vertices) in the graph and the edges between the nodes represent an association between the references. The benefit of using this model is that it allows researchers to draw on the existing body of knowledge on network analysis in addressing the problems related to ER in social networks.

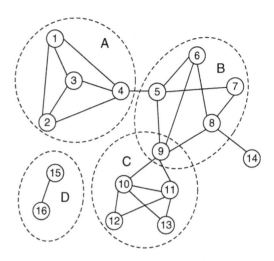

Figure 7.2: Network of Associations

Figure 7.2 shows an undirected network graph representing 23 associations among 16 references. In general, these network models try to determine equivalent references as "clusters" of nodes that share a large number of mutual associations. The problem is that in an actual application it is not always clear where one cluster ends and another begins. Figure 7.2 illustrates four situations that commonly occur. Cluster D, formed by nodes 15 and 16, is clearly not connected to any of the other nodes in the graph and is easily identified. On the other hand, even though the other 14 nodes are all interconnected, they appear to cluster into three groups, designated by the circles labeled A, B, and C. For example, the nodes in 1, 2, 3, and 4 in circle A form a closed interconnected group except for one connection between nodes 4 and 5. Cutting or removing this single connection would leave A as a separate group similar to D.

The situation with the nodes in circles B and C is somewhat different. Node 9 is connected to several nodes in each group. Xu, Yuruk, Feng, and Schweiger (2007) in their SCAN (Structural Clustering Algorithm for Networks) model identify node 9 as a "hub" node. They also term node 14 as an "outlier" because it is connected to a cluster but is not part of a cluster.

What comprises a cluster or determines equivalent references depends on the underlying model. For example, Elmaclogul, Kan, Lee, and Zhang (2007) defined Web-based linkage in terms of the commonality of "representative data"—data that is likely to be associated with a particular entity. In this model the representative data is not necessarily an identity attribute of an entity in the sense that it describes some feature of the entity, but only that it is typically found in association with that entity. For example, if an author typically writes papers with certain coauthors, the presence or absence of these coauthors can help disambiguate references to that author versus references to another similarly named author. Berkkerman and McCallum (2005) proposed a similar model for disambiguation of Web references based on a link structure model. In their model the nodes (references) are Web pages and an edge between two nodes means that "their hyperlinks share something in common."

In many models the goal of the ER algorithm is to partition the graph into disconnected subgraphs by removing a minimal number of associations (edges) in such a way that the references represented in each subgraph are equivalent. For example, in Figure 7.2 the edge between nodes 4 and 5 is a likely "cut point" in the graph that would make cluster A into its own partition class. Bilgic et al. (2006) developed an interactive tool called D-Dupe to assist in the visual analysis of these clusters. D-Dupe provides a number of visual features to assist in the analysis, such as different node shapes to highlight references of interest and different widths of edges to show the strength of the association.

In an interesting extension of the Fellegi-Sunter Model, Schweiger and Xu (2009) have proposed a method for applying network cluster analysis to traditional probabilistic matching. In their model the graph nodes represent references and the edges represent a probabilistic match between two references. Using a graph metric called *modularity*, introduced by Newman (2004), resolution decisions in their algorithm are made based on the overall weight of matches in a cluster of references rather than at the level of successive pairwise comparisons. Their work has since been extended to take into account negative (conflicting) information (Schweiger, Xu, 2010).

Network graphs are also very useful for the analysis and visualization of entity relationship analysis (ER Activity 5) such as those shown in exploration and discovery functions of the Infoglide® Identity Resolution Engine in Chapter 5. Association analysis can be thought of in terms of degrees of separation. In this terminology, zero-degree separation of references would mean that the references are equivalent. One degree of separation would be when distinct entities share a direct relationship, such as the same residential address. Two degrees of separation means that two entities both share a relationship with a third entity, but not directly with each other. For example, Agarwal, Liu, Murthy, Sen, and Wang (2009) have developed a network analysis algorithm for identifying "familiar strangers" in social networks—that is, persons who exhibit similar behaviors but who are not directly connected. In other research Agarwal, Liu, Tang, and Yu (2008) have developed an association analysis for identifying "influential bloggers" in a community of interest.

HPC in ER

The advent of low-cost, high-performance computing (HPC) and cloud computing is changing the IT landscape in many ways and is already having an impact on ER. As discussed in Chapter 5, Acxiom® Corporation was one of the first to explore the application of HPC to ER in the development of its AbiliTec® CDI technology through the use of a massively parallel grid computing system. Much of their work was done before the general availability of HPC, thus requiring their R&D teams to put almost as much effort into the development of the HPC platform, operating system, and storage network as the ER application itself. Now that HPC and Cloud Computing are readily available, they are not only increasing the performance of the basic preparation, resolution, and identity management processes (ERA2, ERA3, ERA4), they are also being brought to bear on solving some of the difficult problems related to entity reference extraction (ERA1) and entity analytics (ERA5).

Unstructured Data

Inmon and Nesavich (2008) estimate that the majority of information available in most organizations is in unstructured formats, most of it in documents that they call *unstructured textual information* (UTI). HPC is making headway in the race to unlock this reservoir of information that is largely unavailable for use in the structured environment of most organizations' IT systems. Vanover (2010) has even suggested that the processing of unstructured data is one of the main drivers for business adoption of cloud computing.

The reason that HPC is so important to processing unstructured data is that it supports data-intensive computing—that is, the ability to process very large amounts of data in or near real time. One of the side effects of data-intensive computing capability is a shift from rule-based computing models to data-driven statistical computing models (Talburt, Bell, DeClue, 2000). As an example, consider natural language translation. In any given language the number of ways in which a sentence can be constructed is virtually uncountable. Until recently the approach to managing this complexity has been to try to construct models of the language's grammar rules. In the case of translation, there must be an additional model (a meta-model) that described how the grammatical rule model of the source language is mapped in the grammatical rule model of the target language, such as English to Spanish.

However, an alternative approach to language translation that has been around for some time (Weaver, 1955) is called *statistical machine translation* (SMT). SMT is basically an application of Bayes and other probabilistic models to estimate the relative frequency with which a given phrase in the source language has been translated into the target language. Until the advent of HPC, SMT has largely been a theoretical model because it was impractical to find and count instances of previous translations on a large scale. Interestingly, Google® has done just that with its translation service. HPC has made it possible to automatically compute these statistics. The effort began in 2007 with the analysis of more than 200 billion words of parallel translations from archives of the United Nations and continues with new translations produced by both the United Nations and the European Union (Tanner, 2007).

Similar data-driven approaches are now being used to extract entity references from unstructured and semistructured information. For example, Osesina and Talburt (2010) have proposed an approach to recognizing named entity references in unstructured text by exhaustively extracting phrases from the unstructured document and assessing their similarity to statistic profiles of known references in an annotated corpus of documents of the same type, such as business news articles or customer service notes. The statistics are collected for some of the indicative properties exhibited by the entity references in the annotated corpus. These properties are both contextual, such as commonly found phrases that precede or succeed the reference, and intrinsic, such as the length and character pattern of the reference. Without HPC this kind of approach would be impractical for anything other than very small test samples.

One of the greatest advantages of data-driven statistical models over rule-based models is in how the models are updated and refined. In a data-driven model the statistical calculations remain fixed and refinements to the model come primarily from acquiring and processing more information. In rule-based models, refinements typically require continual introspection and reprogramming of the rule structure.

Large-Scale Entity Analytics

Commercial IT vendors are also exploiting the advantages of HPC. IBM has been a leader in the area of large-scale entity resolution and entity analytics. Its Entity Analytic Solutions (EAS) product "... scales to process hundreds of millions of entities ..." (IBM EAS, 2006) and was reported to be able to perform 2,000 identity resolutions/second against a 3-billion-row database describing 600 million resolved identities (Jonas, 2005). IBM is also developing the Extreme Analytics Platform (XAP) at its Almaden Research facility. The goal of XAP is to create business intelligence by processing and integrating large volumes of both structured and unstructured information (IBM Research, 2010).

XAP and other data-intensive computing platforms are taking advantage of two recently developed HPC technologies: Hadoop and MapReduce. Hadoop, sponsored by Apache, is an open-source project to develop software for reliable, scalable, distributed computing (Apache Hadoop, 2010). Hadoop comprises a collection of software modules written in Java that facilitate the development and implementation of distributed HPC systems. MapReduce, originally developed and patented by Google, is a programming model and an associated implementation for processing and generating large data sets (Dean, Ghemawat, 2010).

Integration of ER and IQ

Another area of ER research is the development methods and tools that more closely integrate ER and IQ processes. In most ER processes the IQ activities are usually part of a separate reference preparation step (ERA2) that executes prior to the actual resolution step (ERA3) similar to that shown in Figure 5.9 in Chapter 5. The coupling between the ERA2 and ERA3 processes is often simply a mapping of the sources into a fixed target layout. Although there are tools available to assist in mapping out the process, it is typically a very labor-intensive manual process. Acxiom Corporation faces this problem on a daily basis in the processing of client data and has been active in supporting research in this area through the Acxiom Laboratory for Applied Research (research.acxiom.com).

One approach to this problem is to first describe the desired ER outcome (business objective) and the reference sources available to produce the outcome. The description of the outcome and the descriptions of the sources then become the input to a system that automatically generates the item mappings, ETL flows (including data cleansing), and other ER steps necessary to produce the desired outcome. Deneke, Eno, Li, et al. (2008) proposed a declarative language called DSML (Domain-Specific Modeling Language) as means of expressing ER goals as business objectives.

In a similar vein, Gibbs (2010) has proposed the development of a declarative approach to entity resolution that has yet to be realized as an operational system. He compares the current state of ER processing as similar to way that databases were queried before the advent of standardized query language (SQL). The objective of his proposed research is to formulate a declarative language that hides the implementation of common ER operations such as matching, transitive closure, and blocking that are currently done through procedural, ETL-style processes.

Another related line of research is the problem of *layout inference*—that is, an automated process for analyzing the raw byte-content of files to determine their physical and logical structure, such as record length, field layout, and field content. In many large-scale ER operations, the preparation of input references can consume a disproportionate amount of the overall time and labor in an ER process can be expended in recreating and verifying missing or untrustworthy layout metadata. Talburt, Chiang, Howe, Wu, et al. (2008) proposed a semiotic approach to the layout inference problem that not only analyzes character patterns but also generates and analyzes semantic token patterns. Semantic patterns extend the notion of syntactic patterns that are provided by many data profiling systems.

In the rows of Table 7.1 three character strings are shown as both syntactic patterns and semantic patterns in the domain of customer contact information. A common syntactic pattern scheme is to replace each uppercase letter with a single token such as "A," lowercase letter with "a," and digits with "9." Punctuation characters and spaces are typically left embedded in the syntactic pattern.

The third column of Table 7.1 shows a method of creating a semantic pattern by replacing each token in the original string with a single character that most likely signifies its meaning. In the

Table 7.1: Comparison of Syntactic and Semantic Patterns

Value	Syntactic Pattern	Semantic Pattern	Interpretation
John R Talburt	Aaaa A Aaaaaaa	Fia	Name
C W Thompson	A A Aaaaaaaa	iiL	Name
123 N Oak St	999 A Aaa Aa	9iaS	Street Address

scheme shown here, common first-name tokens such as "John" are replaced by the single character "F," common last names by "L," and common street suffix tokens by "S." Numeric tokens are replaced by the single character "9," single letters are replaced by "i" and unrecognized alphabetic tokens by "a." Together the syntactic and semantic patterns can be used to classify each string into its most likely category in the customer contact ontology.

Again HPC has role to play. For example, suppose that an incoming file was found to have a fixed-field length record format with a record length of 200 bytes. In this case, any given field of contact information could occupy any one of 20,100 possible start and end positions in the record. Systematically testing each of these possible fields over a significant sample of records for the syntactic and semantic patterns just described can be a very computationally intensive process.

Entity-Based Data Integration

As discussed in Chapter 4, EBDI is an area in which various soft computing and machine learning techniques are being applied to create more accurate and efficient integration operators. Kooshesh, Zhou, and Talburt (2010) are currently conducting a series of experiments on the application of genetic programming to the problem of maximizing the accuracy of EBDI selection operators—in particular, how to move beyond the accuracy of naïve and naïve-voting selection schemes into the opportunity region, as shown in Figure 4.1 in Chapter 4.

Their current approach is based on defining a integration hypotheses that has the form:

$$H_t(e) = \{(C_1(e), S_1), (C_2(e), S_2), ..., (C_n(e), S_n), D\}$$

where S_j and D represent sources in an integration context, C_j represents a logical proposition related to a particular integration attribute (t), and integration entity (e) as defined in Chapter 4. For example, suppose there are four sources A, B, C, and D that provide entity references where the integration attribute (t) represents a telephone number. In this case the condition C_1 might look like:

$$C_1(e) = (A.t(e) : NE : null) : AND$$
$$: ((A.t(e) : EQ : Ct(e)) : OR : (A.t(e) : EQ : D.t(e)))$$

In this notation, A.t(e) represents the telephone number given for entity e by source A. Similarly B.t(e) represents the number given for e by B and so on. In this example C_1 would only return a true value for an entity e when the telephone number for e provided

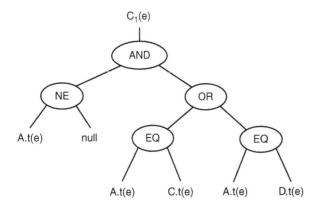

Figure 7.3: Hypothesis Condition Represented Binary Tree

by A is not missing (null) and the number provided for e by A agrees with either the number provided by C or the number provided by D. The telephone number for e provided by B does affect whether C_1 is true or false.

A hypothesis condition can be visualized as a binary tree. Figure 7.3 shows the same condition C_1 as a binary tree, where the leaves of the tree are the attribute values and the interior nodes are the logical operators.

For a given integration entity e and hypothesis H, the final selection of a value for the integration attribute t is always selected from the source preceded by the first condition in the hypothesis (from left to right) that evaluates as true. For example, if C_1 is true for entity e, the value for t is selected from source S_1; else if C_2 is true, it is selected from S_2, and so on. In the case that none of the conditions in the hypothesis is true, the final value for t is selected from D, the default source.

Hypotheses constructed in this way represent a very expressive family of selection operators. For example, it is not difficult to design a hypothesis of this format that coincides with the naïve selection operator or the naïve voting selection operator that are described in Chapter 4. It is also easy to see how these hypotheses lend themselves to a genetic programming (GP) approach. In the case where the true set of selections is known for some sample of the integration entities, the accuracy of each hypothesis can be calculated. Using accuracy as the "survival fitness" associated with each hypothesis, it becomes a simple matter to rank a given set of hypotheses from the most to the least fit with respect to their integration accuracy.

In the experiments currently being conducted at the ERIQ Research Center, the truth set and sources are synthetically generated and are represented in tabular format. Each row of the table represents an integration entity and each column one of the contributing sources for a given integration attribute. The attribute values are represented as single uppercase letters A through Z. A particular integration context is created by first selecting the number of sources (columns), including their desired accuracy and completeness, the number of values for the attribute, and the number of entities to be generated (rows). Typically half the entities are used for training and the other half are saved for testing. For example, an integration context might comprise four sources, 12 attribute values (A–L), and 2,000 rows (1,000 training and 1,000 testing).

The first step in creating such a context is to randomly generate a list of 2,000 values that represent the true values. Next each source is generated by probabilistic selection of the true values based on desired completeness and accuracy of the source. For example, if a source is intended to be 50% complete and 80% accurate, the source generator would randomly select 50% of the rows in the source to have null values, and the nonnull values would be randomly selected to agree with the true values 80% of the time.

After all the sources are generated, the next step is to randomly generate an initial generation of hypotheses within a proscribed set of limits on the number and complexity of the conditions. These initial hypotheses are the initial seed generation for an iterative process, creating a sequence of generations whereby each new generation is created from its predecessor by a process of evaluation and mutation. For example, if each generation comprises 100 hypotheses, the next generation might be created by carrying forward without change the 10 hypotheses with the highest fitness scores, then probabilistically selecting another 10 based on their relative fitness, then creating the final 80 hypotheses for the next generation by random mutation.

Hypothesis mutations fall into two primary categories: cross-over mutations that rearrange the condition-source pairs within and between hypotheses, and internal changes to a specific condition-source pair. The condition-source pairs are also called the *clauses* of the hypothesis. One example of a cross-over mutation is to randomly select two hypotheses in the current generation and, within each hypothesis, also randomly select a clause. The cross-over is to divide the two hypotheses at the selected clauses and exchange (splice) the clauses between the two hypotheses past the selected clauses. Another might be to simply randomly change the order of the clauses in a single hypothesis. The cross-over mutations change the overall structure of the hypotheses but leave each clause intact.

In addition to cross-over mutations, there are also a series of possible mutations that make changes internal to a specific clause in the hypothesis. These range from simple changes such as randomly changing the selection source of the clause or randomly changing the Boolean operator in the condition of a clause to more complex operations such as pruning a subtree of a condition and splicing it into the tree of a condition in another clause.

The following is a description of a GP experiment to optimize the integration of four synthetically generated sources with respect to the accuracy of one integration attribute. The attribute can take on any of 12 possible values, represented by the letters A through L. Each source was generated with 2,000 rows (integration entities) so that the GP algorithm could be trained on the first 1,000 rows, with the best-performing hypothesis tested on against the remaining 1,000 rows.

Table 7.2 shows the accuracy and completeness of each generated source. Due to random variation, these percentages vary slightly from the target values given to the source generator. For example, the actual targets for the first source were 85% accuracy and 50% completeness. This particular experiment simulates the situation commonly found when integrating multiple sources, namely that the sources with the higher completeness (coverage) often have lower accuracy. Table 7.2 also shows that in the best case, the integration of these four sources could have at most an accuracy of 93.1%, with almost 100% completeness. However, the naïve integration operator in the context only achieves 64% accuracy.

Table 7.3 shows the results of applying a GP algorithm to this integration context based on successive generations of 100 hypotheses each. In this algorithm, the best 10 hypothesis and a random selection of 10 other hypotheses were always carried forward into the next generation without change. The remaining 80 hypotheses in the new generation were created by a combination of cross-over and clause mutations, as previously described. For the experiment shown here, the cross-over mutation rate was set at 80% and the clause mutation rate at 50%. It is interesting to note the in the first 100 randomly generated hypotheses, the most accurate hypothesis (66.7%) was already higher than the naïve selection operator (64%). After 100 generations, the highest accuracy achieved was 81.5% on the training set and 81.8% on the test set. These values are much higher than for

Table 7.2: Synthetic Integration Context

Source	Accuracy	Completeness
1	83.1%	49.5%
2	74.2%	61.8%
3	69.1%	70.4%
4	63.2%	80.6%
Best	93.1%	99.7%
Naive	64.0%	99.7%

Table 7.3: Highest Accuracy by GP Generation

Generation	Accuracy
1	66.7%
4	66.4%
5	67.3%
8	71.4%
12	72.3%
13	72.6%
78	74.1%
84	75.1%
93	76.6%
126	78.0%
130	78.2%
131	79.0%
134	78.2%
137	79.3%
142	80.4%
149	80.7%
157	81.5%
158	80.8%
165	81.5%

the naïve selection operator but are still below the best possible accuracy of 93.1%.

Figure 7.4 shows the same information as in Table 7.3 but showing all the generations on the horizontal axis. The pattern of the experiment was a sharp increase in accuracy in the first few generations followed by longer periods punctuated with increases. More information about these and similar experiments can be found on the ERIQ Research Center website (ualr.edu/eriq).

Fundamental ER Research

There is still continuing research toward refining the basic models of ER. As noted earlier, Winkler (1988, 1989a, 1989b) and others have developed a number of refinements to the basic Fellegi-Sunter record linkage model, and Benjelloun, Garcia-Molina, et al. (2006) have extended the basic R-Swoosh algorithm to exploit the efficiencies of distributed and parallel

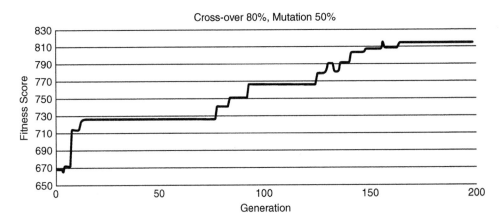

Figure 7.4: A Graph of the Results in Table 7.3

processing. Originally the calculation of the weights associated with the Fellegi-Sunter agreement patterns was done manually by validating samples of each pattern. Much of the research in probabilistic matching is directed toward developing methods and techniques to automate and optimize the pattern assessment process. In some cases these techniques have been patented for commercial applications, e.g. Automatic weight generation for probabilistic matching (Schumacher, Adams, Ellard, 2007). These automated machine learning techniques are also called unsupervised learning (Michalowski, Thakkar, Knoblock, 2004; Christen, 2007). Some of these unsupervised learning techniques have been incorporated into toolkits that support ER processes such as the FRIL (Jurczyk, Lu, Xiong, et al., 2008) and TAILOR (Elfeky, Elmagarmid, Verykio, 2002) toolkits.

Jonas (2006) has emphasized the need to develop ER systems that are sequence-neutral, as described in Chapter 3. He contends that sequence-neutral systems create an effect he calls "data find the data," meaning that each new piece of data coming into the system is dynamically related to existing information without waiting for a user query or batch process to run. Jonas (2007) also promotes the superiority of identity resolution and identity capture architectures, which he describes as record-to-set-based matching, over merge-purge-based batch architectures, which he describes as record-to-record matching. This is mainly because identity resolution systems support real-time transactional processing and the ongoing capture and retention of identity information in a process that he describes as "perpetual analytics."

The open-source ER systems OYSTER and Febrl discussed in Chapter 6 were originally developed for specific applications— education and health care, respectively. However, both are evolving into general-purpose ER systems that support ER instruction and research. In particular, the OYSTER system supports strategies for identity capture, identity management, and asserted equivalence. With the growing interest in hub architectures and information fusion centers there has been commensurate increased research around the problem of identity and identity management.

Several corporate, government, and academic organizations, such as the Center for Applied Identity Management Research (CAIMR, caimr.org), have joined together to promote research in this area. Working in collaboration with the Center for Excellence in Distributed Global Environments (EDGE, www.edge.utexas.edu) at the University of Texas at Austin, the CAIMR group is developing a comprehensive model for identity management that includes ER and identity resolution. Another effort in this direction is the Consortium for Identity Systems Research and Education (CISRE, autoid.astate.edu), hosted by the Laboratory for the Study of Automatic Identification at Arkansas State University (autoid.astate.edu/autoid/). The CISRE focus is on how automatic identification such as biometrics for humans and animals and radio frequency identification (RFID) tags for products (Moeeni, 2008) can facilitate identity management solutions in complex systems such as health care, food supply chains, and transportation logistics.

Summary

Identity resolution is proving to be a key component of the information hub architecture that is increasingly being used to harness entity-based information dispersed over different systems and organizations. HPC is having an impact on ER, making it possible to process immense numbers of records in real, or near-real, time. HPC is also opening doors to new data-intensive applications that use data-driven statistical models in lieu of traditional rule-based models. This is especially true in the area of entity reference extraction and named-entity recognition.

Fundamental research also continues around the basic activities of ER, including unsupervised learning in the optimization probabilistic matching models, the application of graph and network methods to association analysis, identity management, open-source ER systems, and tighter integration of ER and IQ activities.

Review Questions

1. Describe some of the alternatives to hub systems for managing entity-based information across multiple organizations. Discuss their relative advantages and disadvantages.
2. Describe some of the nontechnical issues (regulatory, legal, political, etc.) related to hub systems in each of the following domains: health care, law enforcement, and public education.
3. Find two applications where, as in the language translation example, a data-driven statistical approach has replaced a rule-based approach.
4. Describe the basic steps in the MapReduce algorithm.
5. Select a method for unsupervised record linkage in the published research literature and describe how it works.
6. Suggest three ways in which data quality could be more closely integrated into typical ER processes. Outline what these ideas might look like if incorporated into the OYSTER system.
7. Give a specific example of the observation by Jeff Jonas that "data finds the data."
8. Find two different definitions of identity in the philosophy and explain how these relate to ER identity. Describe how identity management from an information security perspective differs from identity management in ER.
9. Describe the basic components of the CAIMR Identity Management Model.
10. Explain how a machine learning technique other than genetic programming could be applied to the problem of maximizing the accuracy of EBDI. Describe the experiments necessary to test the approach.

Bibliography

AbiliTec. (2001). *AbiliTec customer data integration software.* http://products. enterpriseitplanet.com/dms/im/987435833.html (downloaded June 25, 2010).

AbiliTec. (2008). *Helping companies use information to improve marketing and business results.* Acxiom Corporation white paper, December 2008.

AbiliTec. (2010). *Faster, more precise customer recognition.* www.acxiom.com/ products_and_services/cdi/CDI-X/recognize/abilitec/Pages/AbiliTec.aspx (downloaded June 25, 2010).

Acxiom. (2010). *About Acxiom.* www.acxiom.com/about_us/Pages/AboutAcxiom. aspx (downloaded June 23, 2010).

Agarwal, N., Liu, H., Murthy, S., Sen, A., & Wang, X. (2009). *A social identity approach to identify familiar strangers in a social network.* Association for the advancement of Artificial Intelligence. www.aaai.org.

Agarwal, N., Liu, H., Tang, L., & Yu, P. (2008). *Identifying the influential bloggers in a community.* WSDM'08. Palo Alto, CA.

Agarwal, P., Ikeda, R., Park, H., & Widom, J. (2009). *Trio-ER: The Trio System as workbench for entity-resolution.* Stanford InfoLab Publication. ilpubs.stanford.edu.

Apache Hadoop. (2010). *Welcome to Apache Hadoop.* http://hadoop.apache.org/ Accessed 26.07.10.

Baeza-Yates, R., & Ribeiro-Neto, B. (1999). *Modern information retrieval.* Addison-Wesley.

Ballou, D., Wang, R., Pazer, H., & Tayi, G. (1998). Modeling information manufacturing systems to determine information product quality. *Management Science, 44*(4), 462–484.

Baskarada, S. (2009). *Information quality management capability maturity model.* Germany: Vieweg+Teubner.

Batini, C., & Scannapieco, M. (2006). *Data quality: Concepts, methodologies and techniques.* Berlin: Springer.

Baxter, R., Christen, P., & Churches, T. (2003). A comparison of fast blocking methods for record linkage. In *Proceedings of ACM SIGDKK'03 Workshop on Data Cleaning, Record Linkage, and Object Consolidation.*

Bekkerman, R., & McCallum, A. (2005). *Disambiguating Web appearances of people in social networks.* WWW 2005, Chiba, Japan.

Benjelloun, O., Garcia-Molina, H., Kawai, H., Larson, T. E., Menestrina, D., Thavisomboon, S., et al. (2006). *D-Swoosh: A family of algorithms for generic, distributed entity resolution.* Stanford University Technical Report. ilpubs.stanford.edu:8090/779.

Benjelloun, O., Garcia-Molina, H., Kawai, H., Larson, T. E., Menestrina, D., Su, Q., et al. (2006). *Generic entity resolution in the SERF Project.* Stanford InfoLab Technical Report.dbpubs.standford.edu/pub/2006-8.

Benjelloun, O., Garcia-Molina, H., Menestrina, D., Su, Q., Whang, S. E., Widom, J., et al. (2009). Swoosh: A generic approach to entity resolution. *The VLDB Journal, 18*(1), 255–276.

Benjelloun, O., Garcia-Molina, H., Su, Q., & Widom, J. (2005). *Swoosh: A Generic Approach to Entity Resolution.* Stanford InfoLab Technical Report. dbpubs.stanford.edu/pub/2005-5.

Bhattacharya, I., & Getoor, L. (2005). *Entity resolution in graphs.* University of Maryland Technical Report CS-TR-4758.

Bhattacharya, I., & Getoor, L. (2004). Iterative record linkage for cleaning and integration. In *Proceedings of SIGMOD Workshop on Research Issues on Data Mining and Knowledge Discovery.*

Bhattacharya, I., & Getoor, L. (2007). Collective entity resolution in relational data. *ACM Transactions on Knowledge Discovery from Data, 1*(1), 1–36.

Bilenko, M., & Mooney, R. J. (2003). On Evaluation of Training-Set Construction for Duplicate Detection. In *Proceedings: ACM SIGKDD-03 Workshop on Data Cleaning, Record Linkage, and Object Consolidation.*

Bilenko, M., & Mooney, R. J. (2002). *Learning to combine trained distance metrics for duplicate detection in databases.* Austin: University of Texas. Artificial Intelligence Laboratory Technical Report AI-02-296.

Bilgic, M., Licamele, L., Getoor, L., & Shneiderman, B. (2006). D-Dupe: An interactive tool for entity resolution in social networks. In P. C. Wong & D. Kelm (Eds.), *Proceedings of the 2006 IEEE Symposium on Visual Analytics Science and Technology.* Oct. 31–Nov. 2, 2006, Baltimore, MD.

Brackett, M. (1996). *The data warehouse challenge: Taming the chaos.* Wiley Computer Publishing.

Brizan, D. G., & Tansel, A. U. (2006). A survey of entity resolution and record linkage methodologies. *Communications of the IIMA, 6*(3), 41–50.

Chan, Y., Talburt, J., & Talley, T. (Eds.), (2010). *Data engineering: Mining, information and intelligence.* Norwell, MA: Springer.

Chen, P. (1976). The entity relationship model: Towards a unified view of data. *ACM Transactions on Database Systems, 1*(1), 9–36.

Chen, Z., Kalashnikov, D., & Mehotra, S. (2009). Exploiting context analysis for combining multiple entity resolution systems. In *Proceedings: ACM SIGMOD '09 Conference.* June 29–July 2, 2009.

Chiang, C., Talburt, J., Wu, N., Pierce, E., et al. (2008). A case study in partial parsing unstructured text. In *Fifth International Conference on Information Technology: New Generations* (pp. 447–452). Las Vegas, NV: IEEE Press.

Chief Information Officer, (2008). *Maritime domain awareness architecture management hub strategy.* Department of the Navy publication. October 2008. www.doncio.navy.mil/Download.aspx?AttachID=710 downloaded July 24, 2010.

Christen, P. (2006). *A comparison of personal name matching: Techniques and practical issues.* Technical paper TR-CS-06-02. Computer Sciences Laboratory, The Australian National University.

Christen, P. (2006). *A comparison of personal name matching: Techniques and practical issues.* Australian National University. Technical Report TR-CS-06-02.

Christen, P. (2007). A two-step classification approach to unsupervised record linkage. In *Proceedings of the Sixth Australian Data Mining Conference* (AusDM 2007). Goald Coast, Australia.

Christen, P. (2007). *Towards parameter-free blocking for scalable record linkage.* Technical paper TR-CS-07-03, Computer Sciences Laboratory, The Australian National University.

Christen, P. (2008). Febrl: A freely available record linkage system with a graphical user interface. In *Proceedings of the Australian Workshop on Health Data and Knowledge Management (HDKMF)* (Vol. 80). Conferences in Research and Practice in Information Technology (CRPIT), Wollongong, Australia. January 2008.

Codd, E. F. (1970). A relational model of data for large shared data banks. *Communications of the ACM, 13*(6), 377–387.

Crosby, P. B. (1979). *Quality is free.* McGraw-Hill.

Damerau, F. J. (1964). A technique for computer detection and correction of spelling errors. *Communications of the ACM, 7*(3), 171–176.

DataFlux. (2010). About page. www.dataflux.com/About/AboutDataFlux.aspx.

Date, C. J. (2005). *Database in depth: Relational theory for practitioners.* Sebastopol, CA: O'Reilly.

Dean, J., & Ghemawat, S. (2010). *MapReduce: Simplified data processing on large clusters.* Google Labs. http://labs.google.com/papers/mapreduce.html Accessed 26.07.10.

Deaton, R., Doan, T., & Schweiger, T. (2010). Semantic data matching: Principles and performance. In Y. Chan, J. Talburt & T. Talley (Eds.), *Data engineering: Mining, Information and Intelligence* (pp. 17–38). Springer.

Deming, W. E. (1986). *Out of the crisis.* MIT Press.

Deneke, W., Eno, J., Li, W., Thompson, C., Talburt, J., et al. (2008). Towards a domain-specific modeling language (DSML) for customer data integration (CDI). In C. Hu & D. Berleant (Eds.), *2008 Conference on Applied Research in Information Technology* (pp. 1–12). Conway, AR: University of Central Arkansas. http://research.acxiom.com/publications.html.

Doerr, M., Hunter, J., & Lagoze, C. (2003). Towards a Core Ontology for Information Integration. *Electronic Journal of Digital Information, 4*(1), Article No. 169.

Dyché, J., & Levy, E. (2006). *Customer data integration: Reaching a single version of the truth.* New York: Wiley.

EA Guide. (2001). *A practical guide to federal enterprise architecture, version 1.1.* Published by the Chief Information Officers Council, February 2001, www.gao.gov/bestpractices/bpeaguide.pdf downloaded February 18, 2010.

Eco, U. (1976). *A Theory of Semiotics.* London: Macmillan.

eHealth. (2010). *Key findings.* eHealth Initiative. www.ehealthinitiative.org/key-findings.html Accessed 09.10.10.

Elfeky, M., Elmagarmid, A., & Verykio, V. (2002). TAILOR: A record linkage tool box. In *Proceedings of the 18th International Conference on Data Engineering (ICDE'02).* San Jose, California.

Elmaclogu, E., Kan, M., Lee, D., & Zhang, Y. (2009). Web based linkage. In *WIDM'07* (pp. 121–128). Lisboa, Portugal.

English, L. P. (1999). *Improving Data Warehouse and Business Information Quality: Methods for Reducing Costs and Increasing Profits.* Wiley.

Eppler, M. J. (2006). *Managing information quality.* Springer.

(1999). *Federal enterprise architecture framework, version 1.1* Published by The Chief Information Officers Council, www.cio.gov/documents/fedarch1.pdf.

Fellegi, I. P., & Sunter, A. B. (1969). A theory for record linkage. *Journal of the American Statistical Association, 64*(328), 1183–1210.

Fisher, C., Lauria, E., Chengalur-Smith, S., & Wang, R. (2006). *Introduction to information quality.* MIT Information Quality Program Publications.

Fisher, R. A. (1925). Theory of statistical estimation. *Proceedings of the Cambridge Philosophical Society, 22,* 700–725.

Ford, C. W., Chiang, C., Wu, H., Chilka, R., & Talburt, J. (2004). Confidence on approximate query in large datasets. In *International Conference on Information Technology Coding and Computing* (pp. 480–484).

Frederich, A. (2005). *IBM DB2 anonymous resolution: knowledge discovery without knowledge disclosure. IBM White paper. May 2005.* http://faculty.washington.edu/kayee/pca/supp.pdf.

Gackowski, Z. J. (2009). Is DQ/IQ the quality of information? Two Views. In *Proceedings of the 2009 International Conference on Information Quality* (pp. 258–259) Potsdam, Germany.

Garcia-Molina, H. (2006). Pairwise entity resolution: Overview and challenges. In *Proceedings of the 15th ACM international conference on information and knowledge management.* November 5–11, 2006, Arlington, VA: ACM Publishing.

Ge, H., & Helfert, H. (2006). In J. Talburt, E. Pierce, N. Wu & T. Campbell (Eds.), *11th International Conference on Information Quality* (pp. 455–465). Cambridge, MA: MIT IQ Publishing.

Gibbs, T. H. (2010). A Declarative approach to record linkage. In Y. Chan, J. Talburt & T. Talley (Eds.), *Data engineering: Mining, Information and Intelligence* (pp. 17–38). Springer.

Gravano, L., Ipeirotis, P. G., Jagadish, H. V., Koudas, N., Muthukrishnan, S., Pietarinen, L., et al. (2001). Using q-grams in a DBMS for approximate string processing. *Bulletin of the IEEE Computer Society Technical Committee on Data Engineering, 24*(4), 28–34.

Hashemi, R., & Talburt, J. (2000). An explanation component for a dynamic non-rule based setting. In C. H. Dagli, A. L. Buczak, J. Ghosh, M. J. Embrechts, O. Ersoy & S. Kercel (Eds.), *Annie '00, Smart Engineering System Design: Neural Networks, Fuzzy Logic, Evolutionary Programming, Data Mining and Complex Systems* (pp. 103–108). New York, NY: ASME Press.

Hashemi, R., Ford, C., Vanprooyan, T., & Talburt, J. (2002). Extraction of features with unstructured representation from HTML documents. In P. Isaias (Ed.), *International Association for Development of Information Society (IADIS)* (pp. 47–53). International Conference on WWW/Internet 2002. Lisbon, Portugal.

Hashemi, R., Talburt, J., & Kooshesh, A. (2000). An explanation facility for maintenance of a very large data repository. In M. Jamshidi, P. Borne, A. Maciejewski, S. Nahavandi, R. Lumia & M. Fathi, et al. *World Automation Congress 2000, Third International Symposium on Soft Computing for Industry* (pp. 745–750). Albuquerque, NM: TSI Press.

Hernández, M. A., & Stolfo, S. J. (1995). The merge/purge problem for large databases. *ACM SIGMOD Record, 24*(2), 127–138.

Herzog, T. N., Scheuren, F. J., & Winkler, W. E. (2007). *Data quality and record linkage techniques.* New York: Springer.

Hess, K., & Talburt, J. (2007). Applying name knowledge to information quality assessments. In L. Al-Hakim (Ed.), *Challenges of managing information quality in service organizations* (pp. 99–112). Hershey, PA: Idea Group Publishing.

Holland, G., & Talburt, J. (2008). *A framework for evaluating information source interactions. In C. Hu & D. Berleant (Eds.), 2008 Conference on Applied Research in Information Technology* (pp. 13–19). Conway, AR: University of Central Arkansas. http://research.acxiom.com/publications.html.

Holland, G., & Talburt, J. (2009). An entity-based integration framework for modeling and evaluating data enhancement products. *Journal of Computing Sciences in Colleges, 24*(5), 65–73.

Holland, G., & Talburt, J. (2010). q-Gram Tetrahedral Ratio (qTR) for approximate string matching. In *2010 Conference on Applied Research in Information Technology,* Conway, AR: University of Central Arkansas.

Holland, G. (2010). *Knowledge-driven identity resolution for longitudinal education data.* Doctoral Dissertation, Little Rock: University of Central Arkansas, May 2010.

Homeland Security, (2009). *State and local fusion centers.* www.dhs.gov/files/programs/gc_1156877184684.shtm viewed July 24, 2010.

Huang, K., Lee, Y. W., & Wang, R. Y. (1999). *Quality Information and Knowledge.* Prentice Hall.

Hubert, L., & Arabie, P. (1985). Comparing partitions. *Journal of Classifications,* 193–218.

Hustadt, U. (1994). Do we need a closed-world assumption in knowledge representation? In *Proceedings of the 1st Workshop on Knowledge Representation Meets Databases* (pp. 20–22).

IAIDQ. (2010). *Certification for the information quality professional.* International Association for Information and Data Quality publication. www.iaidq.org/main/doc/iaidq_certification_fact_sheet_v3.0_web.pdf downloaded July 28, 2010.

IBM EAS. (2006). *IBM Entity Analytic Solutions V4.1.0 delivers powerful, anonymous identity recognition and relationship awareness.* IBM Software Announcement, May 23, 2006. www-01.ibm.com/common/ssi/cgi-bin/ssialias?infotype=an&subtype=ca&appname=GPA&htmlfid=897/ENUS206-117 Accessed 27.07.10.

IBM Research. (2010). *eXtreme Analytics Platform.* www.almaden.ibm.com/cs/projects/xap/ Accessed 25.07.10.

Infoglide, (2010). Corporate background page. http://infoglide.com/infoglide-corporate.htm downloaded June 21, 2010.

Inmon, W. H. (1992). *Building the Data Warehouse.* Wiley and Sons.

Inmon, W. H., & Nesavich, A. (2008). *Tapping in Unstructured Data.* Prentice Hall.

Jaro, M. A. (1989). Advances in record-linkage methodology as applied to matching the 1985 census of Tampa, Florida. *Journal of the American Statistical Association, 84*(406), 414–420.

Jonas, J. (2006). *Sequence neutrality in information systems.* Blog post, January 26, 2206. http://jeffjonas.typepad.com/jeff_jonas/2006/01/sequence_neutra.html downloaded August 15, 2010.

Jonas, J. (2007). *Entity resolution systems vs. match merge/merge purge/list de-duplication systems.* Blog post, September 25, 2007. http://jeffjonas.typepad.com/jeff_jonas/2007/09/entity-resoluti.html downloaded August 15, 2010.

Jonas, J. (2005). *Non-Obvious Relationship Awareness (NORA).* IBM Entity Analytics Solutions Presentation, Las Vegas, NV, September 15, 2005, www.cs.utsa.edu/~bylander/cs1023/SRD-IBM-Entity-Analytics-9-15-05.ppt.

Juran, J. M. (1974). *Quality Control Handbook* (3rd ed.). McGraw-Hill.

Jurczyk, P., Lu, J., Xiong, L., Cragan, J., & Correa, A. (2008). FRIL: A tool for comparative record linkage. In *Proceedings of the American Medical Informatics Association Conference (AMIA 2008).*

Kawai, H., Garcia-Molina, H., Benjelloun, O., Larson, T. E., Menestrina, D., Thavisomboon, S., et al. (2006). *Bufoosh: Buffering algorithms for generic entity resolution.* Stanford InfoLabs publication.pubs.stanford.edu.

Kawai, H., Garcia-Molina, H., Benjelloun, O., Menestrina, D., Whang, E., Gong, H., et al. (2006). *P-Swoosh: Parallel algorithm for generic entity resolution.* Stanford InfoLabs publication.ilpubs.stanford.edu.

Keizer, G. (2004). Gartner: Poor data quality dooms many IT projects. *Information Week Magazine,* May 14, 2004.

Kent, W. (2000). *Data and Reality.* Bloomington, IN: 1stBooks.

Kimball, R., Ross, M., Thornthwaite, W., Mundy, J., & Becker, B. (1998). *The Data Warehouse Lifecycle Toolkit.* Wiley.

Knorr, E., & Gruman, G. (2008). *What cloud computing really means.* InfoWorld. www.infoworld.com, April 7, 2008.

Kooshesh, A., Zhou, Y., & Talburt, J. (2010). *Application of genetic programming to entity-based data integration.* Technical Paper ERIQ-10-01, ERIQ Research Center. http://ualr.edu/eriq/projects/.

Köpcke, H., Thor, A., & Rahm, E. (2010). Evaluation of entity resolution approaches on real-world match problems. *Proceedings of the VLDB Endowment, 3*(1).

Kumar, R. (2005). *Research methodology: A step-by-step guide for beginners.* SAGE.

Landauer, T. K., Foltz, P. W., & Laham, D. (1998). Introduction to latent semantic analysis. *Discourse Processes, 25,* 259–284.

Lawley, E. (2010). *Building a health data hub.* March 29, 2010. Nashville Post online version, downloaded July 24, 2010.

Lee, Y., Pierce, E., Talburt, J., Wang, R., & Zhu, H. (2007). A curriculum for a master of science in information quality. *The Journal of Information Systems Education, 18*(2), 233–242.

Lee, Y. W., Pipino, L. L., Funk, J. D., & Wang, R. Y. (2006). *Journey to Data Quality.* Cambridge, MA: MIT Press.

Levenshtein, V. (1966). Binary codes capable of correcting deletions, insertions and reversals. *Soviet Physics - Doklady, 10*(8), 707–710.

Li, W., Bheemavaram, R., & Zhang, X. (2010). Transitive closure of data records: Application and computation. In Y. Chan, J. Talburt & T. Talley (Eds.), *Data Engineering: Mining, Information and Intelligence* (pp. 39–75). Springer.

Liberatore, P., & Schaerf, M. (1995). Arbitration: A Commutative Operator for Belief Revision. In *Proceedings of the Second World Conference on Fundamentals of Artificial Intelligence (WOCFAI '95)* (pp. 217–228).

Lim, E. P., Srivastava, J., Prabhakar, S., & Richardson, J. (1993). Entity identification in database integration. In *Ninth International Conference on Data Engineering* (pp. 294–301).

Lindsey, E. (2008). *Three-dimensional analysis: Data profiling techniques examining data content, structure, and quality.* Data Profiling LLC.

Loshin, D. (2008). *Master data management.* Knowledge Integrity, Inc.

Madnick, S., Wang, R., & Xian, X. (2004). The design and implementation of a corporate householding knowledge processor to improve data quality. *Journal of Management Information Systems, 20*(3), 41–70.

Mahesh, K. (2009). Text retrieval quality: A primer. *Oracle Technology Network,* September 4, 2009 www.oracle.com/technology/products/text/htdocs/imt_quality.htm.

Malin, B., & Sweeney, L. (2005). *ENRES: A semantic framework for entity resolution modeling. White Paper CMU-ISRI-05-134 published by the Carnegie Mellon University Institute for Software Research.*

Maydanchik, A. (2007). *Data Quality Assessment.* Technics Publications.

McBurney, V. (2010). *DataFlux still leads in the Gartner Magic Quadrant for data quality tools 2009.* Tooling around the IBM InfoSphere, Toolbox for IT Blog, http://it.toolbox.com/blogs/infosphere/dataflux-still-leads-in-the-gartner-magic-quadrant-for-data-quality-tools-2009-32223 downloaded June 17, 2010.

McGilvray, D. (2008). *Executing Data Quality Projects: Ten Steps to Quality Data and Trusted Information.* Morgan Kaufmann.

Menestrina, D., Benjelloun, O., & Garcia-Molina, H. (2006). Generic entity resolution with data confidences. *Proceedings of Clean DB.*

Menstrina, D., Whang, S. E., & Garcia-Molina, H. (2010). Evaluating entity resolution results. *Proceedings of the VLDB Endowment, 3*(1).

Michalowski, M., Thakkar, S., & Knoblock, C. (2004). Exploiting secondary sources for unsupervised record linkage. In *Proceeding of the 30th VLDB Conference,* Toronto, Canada.

Minoli, D. (2008). *Enterprise architecture A– Z: Frameworks, business process modeling, and infrastructure technology.* CRC Press.

Moeeni, F. (2008). A passive RFID location sensing. In *Proceedings of the 12th World Multi-Conference on Systemics, Cybernetics and Informatics* (vol: pp. 84–89). June 29–July 2, 2008.

Molina-Garcia, H. (2004). Entity resolution: Overview and challenges. In *Proceedings: 23rd International Conference on Conceptual Modeling* (pp. 1–2). Springer.

Monge, A. E. (2000). Matching algorithms within a duplicate detection system. *Bulletin of the IEEE Computer Society Technical Committee on Data Engineering, 23*(4), 14–20.

Monge, A. E., & Elkan, C. (1997). An efficient domain-independent algorithm for detecting approximately duplicate database records. In *Proceedings of SIGMOD Workshop on Research Issues on Data Mining and Knowledge Discovery* (pp. 23–29). .

Naumann, F. (2002). *Quality-driven query answering for integrated information systems.* Springer-Verlag.

Naumann, F., & Herschel, M. (2010). *An Introduction to Duplicate Detection.* Morgan & Claypool.

Navarro, G. (2001). A guided tour to approximate string matching. *ACM Computing Surveys, 33*(1), 31–88.

Nelson, E., & Talburt, J. (2008). *Improving the quality of law enforcement information through entity resolution. In C. Hu & D. Berleant (Eds.), 2008 Conference on Applied Research in Information Technology* (pp. 113–118). Conway, AR: University of Central Arkansas. http://research. acxiom.com/publications.html.

Newman, M. (2004). Fast algorithm for detecting community structure in networks. *Physics Review, E 69*, Art. No. 066133.

Odell, M., & Russell, R. (1918). U.S. patent number 1,261,167. Washington, D.C: U.S. Patent Office.

Olson, J. (2003). *Data quality: The accuracy dimension.* Morgan Kaufmann.

Pawlak, Z. (1984). *International Journal of Man-Machine Studies, 20*, 469–483.

Pierce, E. M. (2005). What's in your information product inventory? In P. Wang, Madnick & Fisher (Eds.), *AMIS Monograph on Information Quality* (pp. 99–114). Armonk, NY: M. E. Sharpe, Inc.

Pipino, L., Lee, Y., & Wang, R. (2002). Data quality assessment. *Communications of the ACM, 45*(2), 211–218.

Raab, D. (2010). *Reference-Based Matching: Acxiom AbiliTec and Experian Truvue.* DM News. November 2001. http://archive.raabassociatesinc.com/2001/11/ reference-based-matching-acxiom-abilitec-and-experian-truvue/ downloaded June 25, 2010.

Rand, W. M. (1971). Objective criteria for the evaluation of clustering methods. *Journal of the American Statistical Association, 66*, 846–850.

Rasmussen, R. (2000). *SAS acquires DataFlux.* Information management online, www.information-management.com/news/2329-1.html downloaded June 17, 2010.

Redman, T. C. (1998). The impact of poor data quality on the typical enterprise. *Communications of the ACM, 41*(2), 79–82.

Redman, T. C. (2008). *Data driven: Profiting from your most important business asset.* Boston, MA: Harvard Business Press.

Revesz, P. Z. (1993). On the Semantics of Theory Change: Arbitration between Old and New Information. In *Proceedings of the Twelfth ACM SIGACT-SIGMOD-SIGART Symposium on Principles of Database Systems (PODA'93)* (pp. 71–82). Washington, D.C.

Robison, L. (2010). Correcting the misconceptions about the nature of data that thwart information quality. In *MIT Information Quality Industry Symposium* (pp. 529–548). Cambridge, MA.

Rooney, S., Bauer, D., & Scotton, P. (2005). Edge server software architecture for sensor applications. In *2005 Symposium on Applications and the Internet* (pp. 64–71).

Rotman, J. J. (2005). *A first course in abstract algebra: With applications* (3rd ed.). Prentice Hall.

Schumacher, S., Adams, N. S., & Ellard, S. (2007). Automatic weight generation for probabilistic matching. *US Patent Application PCT/US2007/013049.*

Schweiger, T., & Xu, X. (2009). *Application of similarity-based clustering to entity resolution. In Proceedings of the Acxiom Conference of Applied Information Technology.* February 13, 2009, Conway, AR. http://research.acxiom.com/.

Schweiger, T., & Xu, X. (2010). *Application of similarity-based clustering to validate entity resolution.* Presentation at the 2010 MIT Information Quality Industry Symposium (IQIS). http://mitiq.mit.edu/IQIS.

Seiner, R. S. (2005). *Data steward roles and responsibilities.* TDAN.com, published July 1, 2005. www.tdan.com/view-articles/5236/ downloaded July 28, 2010.

Shankaranarayanan, G., Zaid, M., & Wang, R. (2003). Managing data quality in dynamic decision environments: An information product approach. *Journal of Database Management, 14*(4), 14–32.

Shannon, C. E. (1948). A mathematical theory of communication. *Bell System Technical Journal,* .

Sidló, C. I. (2009). Generic entity resolution in relational databases. In *Advances in databases and information systems, lecture notes in computer science* (vol: 5739). Springer.

Srinivasan, P. (1992). W. B. Frakes & R. Baeza-Yates (Eds.), *Thesaurus construction. Information Retrieval: Data Structures and Algorithms* (pp. 161–218). Upper Saddle River, NJ: Prentice Hall.

Stafford, N., Hashemi, R., & Talburt, J. (1992). A backpropagation neural network: An alternative to a rule-based expert system. In *1992 Arkansas Computer Conference* (pp. 8–11) Little Rock, AR.

Strong, D., Lee, Y. W., & Wang, R. Y. (1997). Data quality in context. *Communications of the ACM, 40*(5), 103–110.

Tachinaba, M., & Gracia-Molina, H. (2009). *Joint entity resolution.* Stanford InfoLab Publication.ilpubs.stanford.edu:8090/900/2/jointER.pdf.

Talburt, J., & Campbell, T. (2006). Designing a balanced data quality scorecard. In *2006 Information Resources Management Association International Conference* (pp. 506–508) Washington, D.C.

Talburt, J., & Chiang, C. (2009). Attributed identity resolution for fraud detection and prevention. In *2009 International Conference on Computing in Engineering, Science and Information*, Fullerton, CA: California State University.

Talburt, J., & Hashemi, R. (2008). A formal framework for defining entity-based, data source integration. In H. Arabnia & R. Hashemi (Eds.), *2008 International Conference on Information and Knowledge Engineering* (pp. 394–398). Las Vegas, NV: CSREA Press.

Talburt, J., & Holland, G. (2003). Shared system for assessing consumer occupancy and demographic accuracy. In M. Eppler & M. Helfert (Eds.), *International Conference on Information Quality* (pp. 166–177). Cambridge, MA: MIT IQ Publishing.

Talburt, J., & Mooney, D. (1989). Determination of strongly connected components in abstract thesauri by the method of quartets. In *Third Annual*

ACM/IEEE International Workshop on Applied Computing (pp. 205–209). Oklahoma State University.

Talburt, J., & Nelson, E. (2009). CoDoSA: A light-weight, XML framework for integrating unstructured textual information. In *15th Americas Conference on Information Systems*, San Francisco, CA: AIS Electronic Library aisel.asnet.org Paper 489.

Talburt, J. (2009). A new view of information quality. In *Proceedings: 2009 Database Grand Conference* (pp. 241–251) Seoul, South Korea.

Talburt, J., Bell, M., & DeClue, R. (2000). A bayesian approach to the identification of postal address lines utilizing word frequencies derived from expert coded corpora. In M. Jamshidi, P. Borne, A. Maciejewski, S. Nahavandi, R. Lumia & M. Fathi, et al (Eds). *World Automation Congress 2000, Third International Symposium on Soft Computing for Industry*. Albuquerque, NM: TSI Press.

Talburt, J., Chiang, C., Howe, M., Wu, N., et al. (2008). *A semiotic approach to file layout inference. In C. Hu & D. Berleant (Eds.), 2008 Conference on Applied Research in Information Technology* (pp. 127–133). Conway, AR: University of Central Arkansas. http://research.acxiom.com/publications.html.

Talburt, J., Kuo, E., Wang, R., & Hess, K. (2004). An Algebraic Approach to Data Quality Metrics for Customer Recognition. In *Proceeding of the 9th International Conference on Information Quality (ICIQ-2004)* (pp. 234–247). Cambridge, Massachusetts: MIT. November 5–7, 2004.

Talburt, J., Morgan, C., Talley, T., & Archer, K. (2005). Using commercial data integration technologies to improve the quality of anonymous entity resolution in the public sector. In F. Naumann, M. Gertz & S. Madnick (Eds.), *10th International Conference on Information Quality* (pp. 133–142). Cambridge, MA: MIT IQ Publishing.

Talburt, J., Wang, R., Hess, K., & Kuo, E. (2007). An algebraic approach to data quality metrics for entity resolution over large datasets. In L. Al-Hakim (Ed.), *Information Quality Management: Theory and Applications* (pp. 1–22). Hershey, PA: Idea Group Publishing.

Talburt, J., Wu, N., Pierce, E., & Hashemi, R. (2007). Entity identification using indexed entity catalogs. In H. R. Arabnia & R. R. Hashemi (Eds.), *2007 International Conference on Information and Knowledge Engineering* (pp. 338–342). Las Vegas, NV: CSREA Press.

Talburt, J., Wu, N., Pierce, E., Chiang, C., Heien, C., Gulley, E., et al. (2007). Entity identification in documents expressing shared relationships. In N. Mastorakis, S. Kartalopoulos, D. Simian, A. Varonides, V. Mladenov, Z. Bojkovic & E. Antonidakis (Eds.), *11th World Scientific and Engineering Academy and Society International Conference on SYSTEMS* (vol. 2) (pp. 223–228). Agios Nikolaos, Crete: WSEAS Press.

Talburt, J., Zhou, Y., & Shivaiah, S. (2009). SOG: A synthetic occupancy generator to support entity resolution instruction and research. In *2009 International Conference on Information Quality*. Potsdam, Germany.

Talley, T. M., Talburt, J. R., & Chan, Y. (2010). Introduction. In Y. Chan, J. Talburt & T. Talley (Eds.), *Data engineering: Mining, Information and Intelligence* (pp. 1–16). Springer.

Talley, T. M. (2010). A grid operating environment for CDI. In Y. Chan, J. Talburt & T. Talley (Eds.), *Data engineering: Mining, Information and Intelligence* (pp. 119–142). Springer.

Tanner, A. (2007). *Google seeks world of instant translations*. Reuters online March 28, 2007. www.reuters.com/article/idUSN1921881520070328.

Thomas, G. (2010). *Definitions of data governance.* www.datagovernance.com/adg_data_governance_definition.html Accessed 6.10.10.

Thuraisingham, B. (2003). *Web Data Mining and Applications in Business Intelligence and Counter-Terrorism*. CRC Press.

Ullman, J. (1989). *Principles of Database and Knowledge Base Systems* (Vol. 1). Computer Science Press.

US Census Bureau. (2010). *Population estimates*. www.census.gov/popest/states/asrh/ downloaded June 24, 2010.

Vanover, R. (2010). Private cloud storage more appealing than public? TechRepublic blogs. July, 2, 2010, http://blogs.techrepublic.com.com/networking/?p=3162.

Viswanath, B., Post, A., Gummandi, K., & Mislove, A. (2010). An analysis of social network-based Sybil defenses. In *Proceedings of ACM SIGCOMM 2010*, New Delhi, India.

Wang, R. Y. (1998). A product perspective on total data quality management. *Communications of the ACM, 41*(2), 58–65.

Wang, R. Y., & Kon, H. B. (1993). Toward Total Data Quality Management (TDQM). In R. Y. Wang (Ed.), *Information Technology in Action: Trends and Perspectives*. Englewood Cliffs, NJ: Prentice Hall.

Wang, R. Y., & Strong, D. M. (1996). Beyond accuracy: What data quality means to consumers. *Journal of Management Information Systems, 12*(4), 5–34.

Wang, R. Y., & Wand, Y. (1996). Anchoring data quality dimensions in ontological foundations. *Communications of the ACM, 39*(11), 86–95.

Wang, R. Y., Lee, Y. W., Pipino, L. L., & Strong, D. M. (1998). Manage your information as a product. *Sloan Management Review, 1998*(Summer), 95–105.

Watts, D. J., & Strogatz, S. H. (1998). Collective dynamics of small world networks. *Nature, 393*, 440.

Weaver, W. (1955). Translation. In *Machine Translation of Languages*. Cambridge, MA: MIT Press.

Welty, C., & Guarino, N. (2001). Supporting Ontological Analysis of Taxonomic Relationships. *Data and Knowledge Engineering, 39*(1), 51–74.

Whang, S. E., Benjelloun, O., & Garcia-Molina, H. (2009). Generic entity resolution with negative rules. *The VLDB Journal, 18*(6), 1261–1277.

Whang, S. E., Menestrina, D., Koutrika, G., Theobald, M., & Garcia-Molina, H. (2009). Entity resolution with iterative blocking. In *Proceeding of SIGMOD '09 Conference*. June 29–July 2, 2009. ACM Press.

Winkler, W. E. (1988). Using the EM algorithm for weight computation in the Fellegi–Sunter model of record linkage. *Journal of the American Statistical Association*, Proceedings of the Section on Survey Research Methods, 667–671.

Winkler, W. E. (1989a). Methods for adjusting for lack of independence in an application of the Fellegi-Sunter Model of record linkage. *Survey Methodology, 15*, 101–117.

Winkler, W. E. (1989b). Near automatic weight computation in the Fellegi-Sunter Model of record linkage. In *Proceedings of the Fifth Census Bureau Annual Research Conference* (pp. 145–155).

Winkler, W. E. (1999). *The state of record linkage and current research problems*. Statistics of Income Division, Internal Revenue Service Publication R99/04.

Winkler, W. E. (2006). *Overview of record linkage and current research directions*. U.S. Census Bureau, Statistical Research Division Publication No. 2006-2, 2006.

Wu, N., Talburt, J., Heien, C., Pippenger, N., Chiang, C., Pierce, E., et al. (2007). A method for entity identification in open source documents with partially redacted attributes. *The Journal of Computing Sciences in Colleges, 22*(5), 138–144.

XML, (2010). *Extensible markup language (XML)*. www.w3.org/XML/.

Xu, X., Yuruk, N., Feng, Z., & Schweiger, T. (2007). SCAN: A structural clustering algorithm for networks. In *ACM SIGKDD'07*. San Jose, CA.

Yeung, K. Y., & Ruzzo, W. L. (2001). Details of the Adjusted Rand Index and Clustering Algorithms, Supplement to the paper An Empirical Study on Principal Component Analysis for Clustering Gene Expression Data. *Bioinformatics, 17*(9), 763–774.

Yongin, Z., Qingzhong, L., & Ji, B. (2009). Enhancing collective entity resolution utilizing quasi-clique similarity. In *Proceedings of 2009 Joint Conference on Pervasive Computing*, Tamsui, Taipei.

Zachman, J. (1987). A framework for information systems architecture. *IBM Systems Journal, 26*(3), IBM Publication G321-5298.

Zhang, J., Bheemvaram, R., & Li, W. (2006). Transitive Closure of Data Records: Application and Computations. In *2006 Conference on Applied Research in Information Technology* (pp. 71–81). posted on http://research.acxiom.com/publications.html.

Glossary

Agreement Pattern – A rule that defines which corresponding identity attributes between two entity references must have values that are the same (or approximately the same) and those that can have different values.

Approximate Matching – A method or algorithm for measuring the degree of similarity between two attribute values. The term is sometimes used to describe the overall similarity between two entity references.

Approximate Semantic Matching – An approximate matching technique between two words or phrases where the degree of similarity is based on the closeness in meaning of the words.

Approximate String Matching (ASM) – A method or algorithm for measuring the degree of similarity between two character strings.

Approximate Syntatic Matching – An approximate matching technique between two character strings where the degree of similarity is based on the number and order of the characters they have in common.

ASM – See Approximate String Matching

Asserted Equivalence – One of the four methods for establishing the equivalence of two entity references in which references are declared to be equivalent based on prior knowledge that they refer to the same entity regardless of any similarity or dissimilarity between the values of their corresponding identity attributes. See also Direct Matching, Transitive Equivalence, and Association Analysis.

Association Analysis – One of the four methods for establishing the equivalence of two references based on a pattern of associations with other references. See also Direct Matching, Transitive Equivalence, and Asserted Equivalence.

Attribute – A characteristic associated with an entity that can take on a defined set of values.

Biographical Identity Attributes – Identity attributes of a person that are situational and may change over time such as name or address.

Biometric Identity Attributes – Identity attributes of a person or other living things that are intrinsic to its nature and do not change over time such as DNA markers and fingerprints.

Blocking – A technique for match prospecting based on selecting all (a block of) records that share a certain attribute value. See Match Prospecting.

Business Intelligence – A collection of data analysis methods and techniques used by businesses to improve decision making, forecasting, and operational processes in order to gain a competitive advantage in the marketplace.

Cartesian Product – A mathematical operation between two sets that forms all possible pairings of elements between the two sets.

CDI – see Customer Data Integration

Cloud Computing – A form of high-performance computing in which the user accesses the system through a network portal that hides the details of the implementation.

Cluster – see Entity Reference Cluster

Consolidation – see Entity Identity Consolidation

Consumer Household – A group of individuals, usually family units, that reside at the same address.

Co-referent Co-refer – Another term to describe entity equivalence.

Corporate Household – A group of businesses or business names (DBAs) that have common ownership

CRM – see Customer Relationship Management

Customer Data Integration (CDI) – A term used to describe an ER process in which the entities are the customers of a business.

Customer Recognition – A term used to describe an identity resolution process where the managed identities are the customers of the business or agency.

Customer Relationship Management (CRM) – A collection of policies, strategies, and processes used by a business to increase the value its customers by improving the customer's experience with the business.

Data Cleansing – Also called Data Cleaning and Data Hygiene are the processes used to standardize, enhance, correct, and otherwise transform data to improve its fitness for a particular use (data quality).

Data Governance – A defined set of policies, processes, accountabilities, and responsibilities for developing and control an organization's information assets.

Data Hygiene – see Data Cleansing

Data Mining – A collection of methods and techniques for finding non-explicit relationships in a collection of data.

Data Quality – The degree of fitness for use of data in particular application. Also the degree to which data conforms to data specifications as measured in data quality dimensions. Sometimes used interchangeably with information quality. See Information Quality

Data Quality Dimensions – Are the measurable characteristics of data. Although there is general agreement on some fundamental dimensions such as accuracy, completeness, and timeliness, many different dimensional frameworks have put forward by various researchers and practitioners, for example, the Wang-Strong DQ Framework of 16 dimensions.

Data Quality Metric – Any method for assigning a quantitative measure to either subjective or objective data quality.

Data Quality Rating – A data quality metric comprising a formula or algorithm that produces a quantitative measure of the quality of a given data configuration in a particular data quality dimension and where the rating value is on a scale from zero representing the lowest quality up to one representing the highest quality. For example a measure of completeness of an attribute (column) in a database table where the rating is defined as the ratio of non-null attribute values to the total number of rows in the table.

Data Stewardship – A key principle of data governance that views information as an asset belonging to the entire organization rather being owned or controlled by any individual or department. According to this principle, the information stakeholders are considered caretakers (stewards) of the information.

Data Warehousing – The practice of integrating all of an organization's operational data into a single repository (data warehouse) as a platform to facilitate data mining, business intelligence, and other analyses.

Decision Precision – A quality measure for decision processes such as ER, data mining, and information retrieval which measures the ratio of true positive decisions to all positive decisions (true positive plus false positive). For example if a database query to find all of the records for a particular customer returns 10 results, but only 8 of the 10 are for the customer, the precision of the query is 80% (8 out of 10)

Decision Recall – A quality measure for decision processes such as ER, data mining, and information retrieval which measures the ratio of true positive decisions to all possible true decisions (true positive plus false negatives). For example, if a database query to find all of the records for a particular customer returns 10 results and 8 are for the customer, but the customer has 12 other records in the database that were not found by the query, then the recall of the query is 40%. (8 out of 20).

Derived Link – An identifier appended to an entity reference where the value of the identifier has been created by merging or transforming the values of one or more attributes of the reference. Sometimes called a Hash Token.

Deterministic Matching – A match operation that returns a true value only when the two values being compared are exactly the same.

Direct Matching – One of the four methods for establishing the equivalence of two references based on the similarity between the values of their corresponding identity attributes. See also Transitive Equivalence, Association Analysis, and Asserted Equivalence.

Disambiguation – see Entity Reference Disambiguation

Enterprise Architecture – A formal way of representing the structure of an enterprise as a composite of several sub-components including business architecture, information architecture, solution and/or technology architecture.

Entity – A real-world person, place, or thing that has a unique identity that distinguishes it from all other entities of the same type.

Entity Analytics – see Entity Association Analysis

Entity Association Analysis – One of the five ER activities in which relationships between entities are identified and explored. Also called Entity Analytics. See also Entity Reference Extraction, Entity Reference Preparation, Entity Reference Resolution, and Entity Identity Management.

Entity Identity – A set of attribute values and distinctness rules that allow one entity to be distinguished for all other entities of the same type in a given context.

Entity Identity Consolidation – A term used in entity identity management to describe the situation where two separately managed entity identities are discovered to be equivalent. Consolidation describes the process of merging the information in the separate identity structures into a single structure. It also entails any processes or procedures for notifying system users of the change and rectifying incorrect links previously published by the system.

Entity Identity Identifier – A value that is used to represent a specific entity identity in a given context or process.

Entity Identity Management – One of the five ER activities in which the attributes that characterize an entity's identity are stored and maintained. See also Entity Reference Extraction, Entity Reference Preparation, Entity Reference Resolution, and Entity Association Analysis.

Entity Identity Split – A term used in entity identity management to describe the situation where a managed entity identity is discovered to be an amalgam of information for two or more entities. Splitting describes the process of dividing the information into separate identity structures for each of the entities. It also entails any processes or procedures for notifying system users of the change and rectifying previous published links for the identities involved.

Entity Reference – A collection of identity attribute values that describe a particular entity.

Entity Reference Cluster – In the context of entity resolution, a cluster describes a set of references that an ER process has linked together as equivalent. In the context of graph theory a cluster is a set of nodes in the graph that share a large number of edges with each other relative to other nodes in the graph.

Entity Reference Disambiguation – The decision that two entity references are not equivalent.

Entity Reference Equivalence – Two entity references are said to be equivalent if and only if they refer to the same entity.

Entity Reference Extraction – One of the five ER activities in which entity references are identified and collected from unstructured or semi-structured data. See also Entity Reference Preparation, Entity Reference Resolution, Entity Identity Management, and Entity Association Analysis.

Entity Reference Preparation – One of the five ER activities in which entity references are standardized, cleaned, enhanced, or otherwise transformed to improve the effectiveness of an ER process. See also Entity Reference Extraction, Entity Reference Resolution, Entity Identity Management, and Entity Association Analysis.

Entity Reference Resolution – One of the five ER activities in which decisions are made as to whether two entity references are equivalent or not equivalent. See also Entity Reference Extraction, Entity Reference Preparation, Entity Identity Management, and Entity Association Analysis.

Entity Resolution (ER) – A body of knowledge and practice related to the activities supporting a process to decide whether two entity references are equivalent or not equivalent.

Entity-Relation Model (ERM or E-R Model) – The most commonly used method for conceptualizing and representing a relational database schema in which the data are represented as entities that have attributes and relationships with other entities.

Equivalent Entity References – Two entity references are said to be equivalent if, and only if, they refer to the same real-world entity.

Equivalent References – see Equivalent Entity References

ER – see Entity Resolution

ERM or E-R Model – see Entity-Relation Model

ETL – see Extract, Transform, and Load

Extensible Markup Language – A standard for structured data representation developed by the World-Wide Web Organization in which data values and their metadata information are embedded in the same text document.

Extract, Transform, and Load (ETL) – A term that describes the activities used to prepare a collection of data sources for loading into a database, but also used to describe data mapping and transformation processes in general. See Entity Reference Preparation.

External View of Identity – The situation in which an observer has only partial knowledge about the identity of an entity. See Internal View of Identity.

False Negative – A term used to describe the situation where a decision process provides a negative answer when it should have provided a positive answer. For example, an entity reference resolution decision that two reference are not equivalent when in fact they are equivalent. See False Positive, True Positive, and True Negative.

False Positive – A term used to describe the situation where a decision process provides a positive answer when it should have provided a negative answer. For example, an entity reference resolution decision that two reference are equivalent when in fact they are not equivalent. See False Negative. True Positive, and True Negative

Fellegi-Sunter Record Linkage Model – A model for determining a set of agreement patterns for a direct matching ER process that will keep the false positive and false negative rates for automated equivalence decisions within pre-defined limits, and at the same time, minimize the number of equivalence decisions that must be made by inspection.

Fisher Information – A statistical approach to information theory put forward by R. A. Fisher based on measuring the variance and expectation of observed values from an information source.

Fundamental Law of ER – The principle that two entity references should be linked if and only they are equivalent.

Graph Theory – An area of mathematics concerned with the study of graphs. A graph is a mathematical structure comprising a set of vertices (or nodes) together with a function that determines whether or not two vertices are connected or not connected.

Hash Token – see Derived Link.

Heterogeneous Database Join – One of the four basic ER architectures in which a central hub is connected to multiple database tables containing entity references. User queries submitted to the central hub are automatically reformatted into a valid query to each of the database tables, the result sets are collected, resolution rules are applied, and the final result is returned to the user. See also Merge-Purge, Identity Resolution, and Identity Capture.

High-Performance Computing (HPC) – The application of large supercomputers or a large number of smaller computers working in parallel to solve computationally-intensive and data-intensive problems in a relatively short period of time.

Household or Householding – see Consumer Household or Corporate Household

HPC – See High-Performance Computing

Identity – see Entity Identity

Identity Attribute – An attribute of an entity whose values are used in establishing its identity vis-à-vis other entities of the same type. See Entity Identity.

Identity Capture – One of the four basic ER architectures in which entity references are individually resolved against the identity information extracted and saved in the processing of previous references. See also Merge-Purge, Heterogeneous Database Join, and Identity Resolution.

Identity Identifier – see Entity Identity Identifier.

Identity Management – see Entity Identity Management

Identity Resolution – One of the four basic ER architectures in which entity references are individually resolved against the identity information for a group of known entities. See also Merge-Purge, Heterogeneous Database Join, and Identity Capture.

Information Architecture – The sub-component of an enterprise architecture concerned with defining, obtaining, and managing the information needed to support the business architecture.

Information Product (IP) – Data that has been processed and organized into a form needed for a particular application.

Information Product Map (IP Map) – A systematic way to graphically represent the details associated with creating an information product by tracing the flow of individual data elements from their sources to the final product.

Information Quality (IQ) – An emerging discipline that is concerned with maximizing the value of an organization's information assets and assuring that the information products it produces meet the expectations of the customers who use them.

Information Quality Assessment (IQA) Survey – A survey instrument developed by Richard Wang and associates to obtain subjective measures of data quality from the contributors, custodians, consumers, and managers of the data.

Information Quality Gap – The situation where the characteristics of an information product that make the produce valuable to its users are not related to the data quality measurements of the data used to produce the product.

Information Theory – A formal mathematical approach to defining and quantifying information.

Internal View of Identity – The situation in which an observer has complete knowledge about the identity of an entity. See External View of Identity.

IP – see Information Product

IP Map – see Information Product Map

IQ – see Information Quality

IQA Survey – see Information Quality Assessment Survey

Knowledge-based Equivalence/Linking – Determining the equivalence to two references based on external knowledge that they are equivalent rather than indirect evidence such as matching.

Latent Semantic Analysis – A method for determining that words and phrases in a given language have equivalent or near equivalent meaning.

Levenshtein Edit Distance – An approximate string matching algorithm that determines the minimum number of character manipulations that are required to transform one character string into another character string. Typically the allowable manipulations are character replacement, character deletion, and character insertion.

Link – see Link Identifier

Link Append – The final step of an entity reference resolution process in which the input references are given link identifiers that reflect the resolution decisions. See Link Index.

Link Identifier – An attribute value added to an entity reference to represent ER decisions. If a decision is that two references are equivalent, they are given the same link identifier. References with different link identifiers are not equivalent.

Link Index – An alternative implementation of link append in which the ER process produces a cross-reference table that relates the identifier of each input references to a link identifier rather than appending the link identifier to the reference itself.

Linking – see Record Linking

Matching – An operation between two values that gives a true or false result where true indicates that the values are identical or closely related according to some rule or algorithm. In ER matching can take place between identity attributes or between entity references. See Direct Matching, Deterministic Matching, and Probabilistic Matching.

Match Prospecting – A method or technique for finding the references that are most likely to match a given reference when there are many references to chose from.

Master Data Management (MDM) – An information quality activity in which the data elements that are used by multiple systems in an organization are identified, managed, and controlled at the enterprise level.

MDM – see Master Data Management

Merge-Purge – One of the four basic ER architectures in which the entity references are standardized into a common format and run as a single batch. Direct matching and transitive equivalence are successively used to resolve the references into clusters of equivalent references. Sometimes called Record Linkage. See also Heterogeneous Database Join, Identity Resolution, and Identity Capture.

Named-Entity Recognition (NER) – A form of entity reference extraction that tries to determine the role of the entity referenced as well as extracting the reference information. For example, that in a new report XYZ Corporation is not only a reference to a business, but that it was the acquirer of another business.

NER – see Named Entity Recognition

Network Analysis – The theory and methods for examining a system of connected components such as computer networks, electrical circuits, or social networks.

Occupancy – The record of an individual, business, or household at an address and the period of time for which it was valid.

Occupancy History – A comprehensive set of occupancy records for an entity in time series order.

Persistent Entity Identity Identifier – An entity identity identifier managed in such a way that its value remains the same from one ER process to the next.

Persistent Identifier – Persistent Entity Identity Identifier

Pragmatics – The aspect of semiotics that deals with the intent of a symbolic value. For example, a date intended to designate a person's date-of-birth.

Precision – see Decision Precision

Probabilistic Matching – A match operation that returns a true value only when the two values being compared are either the same or very similar according to some rule or algorithm.

q-Gram – A sequence of characters of length q. Sometimes called n-Grams. The term also denotes a family of ASM algorithms where similarity is based on the degree to which two character strings have shared q-Grams.

Quality of Information (QoI) – A measure of the value that an information product has to the user of the information as opposed to data quality that measures the conformance of data to a certain specification,

Recall – see Decision Recall

Record De-duplication – A term commonly used to describe any ER process based on the merge-purge architecture.

Record Linkage/Linking – A term originally used to designate a specific problem of determining direct matching equivalences between two lists of references assumed to have no internal equivalences, it is now commonly used to describe any ER process based on the merge-purge architecture.

Reference – see Entity Reference

Reference Equivalence – see Entity Reference Equivalence

Role Gap Analysis – One of the analyses suggested for the Information Quality Assessment Survey that focuses on disparities between the average response of different stakeholder roles, e.g. managers versus custodians.

Root Cause Analysis – A method for tracing a problem back to where it originated.

SaaS – See Software as a Service

Semantics – The aspect of semiotics that deals with the meaning of a symbolic value. For example, a date expressed in a given format designates a particular day in history.

Semiotics – The theory of signs and symbols that comprises syntactics, semantics, and pragmatics.

Sequence Neutral ER – ER processes that yield the same resolution results regardless of the order in which the references are processed.

SERF – see Stanford Entity Resolution Framework

Shannon Entropy – A key element of the information theory put forward by Claude Shannon in which the amount of information that can be carried in a communication channel is related to the number and probability of states of the transmitted messages.

Single Point of Truth (SPOT) – see System of Record

Software as a Service (SaaS) – A form of computing in which users gain access to and execute specific software applications through a network portal.

SOR – see System of Record

Soundex – A process for creating a derived link from the character string representing the name of a person in such a way that the same link value is generated if and only if the two names sound the same, i.e. are phonetically equivalent. The Soundex link value has the form of a letter followed by three decimal digits.

Split – see Entity Identity Split

SPOT – see System of Record

Stanford Entity Resolution Framework – A formal description of the merge-purge ER architecture in terms of a match operator and a merge operator. It also sets out the conditions necessary to have a unique and finite ER outcome called Consistent ER.

Structured Information – Information that is organized in such a way that all of the attribute values describing a particular entity are presented in a consistent and predictable pattern that can be programmed into a computer, e.g. database tables, XML documents.

Surrogate Keys – A primary key for a database table where the values of the key are not related to the information in the table but only selected to guarantee that the values will all be unique, e.g. a set of sequential integer values generated by the database system.

Syntactics – The aspect of semiotics that deals with the format or structure of a symbolic value. For example, the symbol for a date has many standard and recognizable formats such as MM/DD/YYYY.

System of Record (SOR) – Also called Single Point of Truth (SPOT), is a method for addressing the data quality problems caused by having multiple, inconsistent representations of the same entity or entity attribute by designating one system as holding and maintaining the authoritative source.

TDQM – see Total Data Quality Management

Total Data Quality Management (TDQM) – An adaptation of the Total Quality Management principles, methods, and philosophy used to improve the quality of manufactured goods to the creation of information products. TDQM advocates continuous improvements by repeating a four-phase cycle of define information requirements, measure attainment of requirements, analyze low attainment, and implement improvements.

Total Quality Management (TQM) – A collections principles, methods, and philosophy that were developed to improve the quality of manufactured products. W. Edwards Deming is generally acknowledged at the founder of this movement when he published his book *Out of the Crisis* in 1982.

TQM – see Total Quality Management

Transitive Closure – The process of finding all of the references in reference source that are equivalent to a given reference by transitive equivalence.

Transitive Equivalence – One of the four methods for establishing the equivalence of two references based finding other references that form a chain of intermediate equivalent references starting with the first reference and ending with the second. See also Direct Matching, Association Analysis, and Asserted Equivalence.

True Negative – A term used to describe the situation where a decision process provides a correct negative answer. For example, an entity reference resolution decision that two reference are not equivalent when it is true that they are not equivalent. See False Positive, True Positive, and False Negative.

True Positive – A term used to describe the situation where a decision process provides a correct positive answer. For example, an entity reference resolution decision that two reference are equivalent when it is true that they are equivalent. See False Positive, True Negative, and False Negative.

Unique Reference Assumption – In the context of an ER process, it is the premise that an entity reference is always created with intentions of referring to one, and only one, entity.

Unstructured Information – Information that is not structured, e.g. free-form text, images, audio streams. See Unstructured Information.

Unstructured Textual Information (UTI) – Text-based unstructured information, e.g. business letters, contracts, medical notes.

UTI – See Unstructured Textual Information.

Wang-Strong Data Quality Dimensions – A framework of 16 data quality dimensions developed from a research study by Richard Wang and Diane Strong that includes accuracy, believability, reputation, objectivity, value-added, relevancy, timeliness, completeness, amount of data, interpretability, ease of understanding, representational consistency, conciseness of representation, manipulability, access, and security.

XML – See Extensible Markup Language.

APPENDIX A

OYSTER Configurations

As a teaching tool, OYSTER can be configured to demonstrate three of the basic ER architectures and building identities from assertion sources. These configurations are easily created by setting the appropriate parameters in the OYSTER Run Script. The base OYSTER can accept a set of input identities (optional) and one or more reference sources of different layouts where each source can be a capture source or a non-capture source. After processing the inputs, OYSTER produces a set of output identities (optional) and a link index. The configurations options are shown in Figure A.1

The merge-purge/record linking configuration shown in Figure A.2 does not involve any identity management tasks. No identities are input into the merge-purge configuration and no identities are output. However the Capture option must be set to "Yes" for each reference source processed.

The identity capture configuration of OYSTER is shown in Figure A.3. It is essentially the same as the merge-purge configuration except that the identity information discovered during the process of the reference sources is saved at the end of the run. Each identity is represented and saved as an XML document.

Identity capture can be used to build a set of identities from a set of assertions as shown in Figure A.4. Assertions represent knowledge about one or more known entity identities. The identity build step is a precursor to the identity resolution step.

The identity resolution configuration of OYSTER is shown in Figure A.5 where

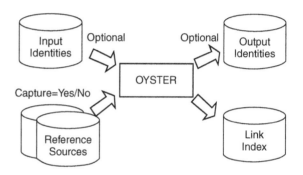

Figure A.1: OYSTER Configuration Options

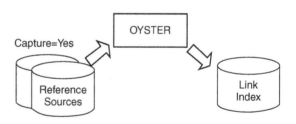

Figure A.2: OYSTER Merge-Purge Configuration

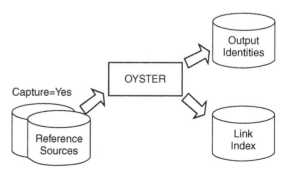

Figure A.3: OYSTER Identity Capture Configuration

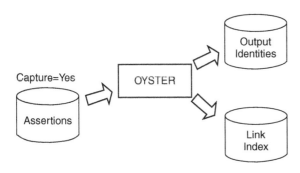

Figure A.4: OYSTER Configuration to Build Identities from Assertions

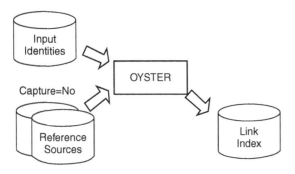

Figure A.5: OYSTER Identity Resolution Configuration

the process starts with a set of existing identities. These identities could be the result of processing assertion sources as shown in Figure A.4 or may have created through some type of GUI or editor for building identity documents.

In the identity resolution configuration, the reference sources are resolved against the input identities with capture mode off. A reference that does not resolve to any of the input identities is written to the link index with a special link value that is a string of "X" characters to indicate that identity resolution failed.

OYSTER Setup for Students

In the ER and IQ classes, each student has a virtual Windows machine on a remote server accessed through the Windows remote desktop client. Each student's machine is pre-configured so that the OYSTER.jar file and the OYSTER. bat file that calls it reside in a folder named OYSTER at the root of the machine's local drive (Z:). By convention, the Oyster Run Scripts that control each OYSTER run are also saved in the OYSTER folder.

A typical layout of the OYSTER folder for one of the student machines is shown in Figure A.6. In this example there are two Oyster Run Scripts in the folder "Test1RunScript.xml" and "Test2RunScript.xml" along with the OYSTER.jar and the OYSTER.bat file that has been highlighted. Double-clicking the Oyster batch file will start the execution of OYSTER. When OYSTER starts it will ask for the name of an Oyster Run Script which by convention it expects to find in the OYSTER folder.

OYSTER Merge-Purge Configuration

Figure A.7 shows an example of an OYSTER Run Script setup in a merge-purge or record linkage configuration as illustrated in Figure A.2 where the input is a single reference source named "Test1Source.txt".

In a merge-purge configuration the only input required is one or more reference sources with the goal of partitioning the

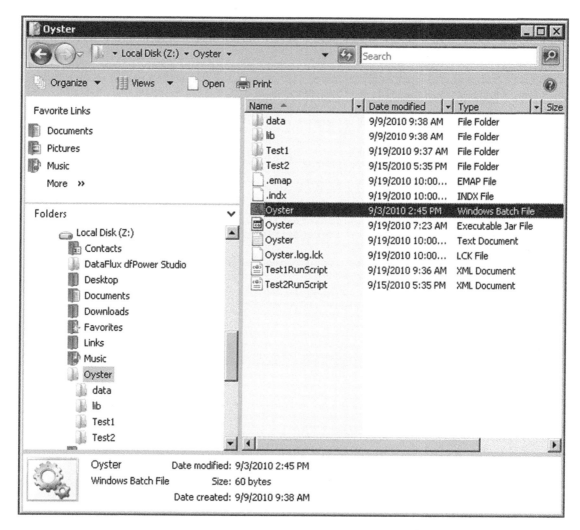

Figure A.6: OYSTER Folder on the Z: Drive

references into groups or clusters of equivalent references. Consequently there is no input or output of identity information (<IdentityInput> and <IdentityOuput> are set to "None") as merge-purge does not involve identity management. The only output from a merge-purge configuration is the Oyster Link Index file that defines the clusters by assigning each input reference a link value so that references with the same identifier value belong to same cluster.

The reference source name "Test1Source.txt" is shown in Figure A.8. For simplicity it contains only 6 entity references in the form of student enrollment records. The first item of each

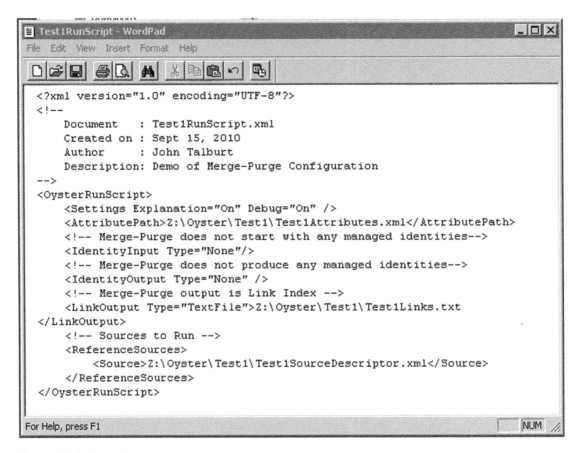

**Figure A.7: A Merge-Purge
Run Script for Test1Source.txt**

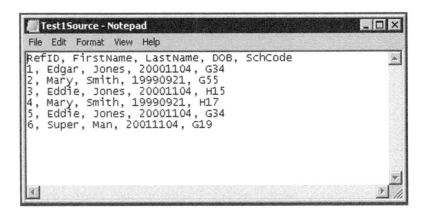

Figure A.8: Reference Source for Test 1

reference is a unique identifier for each reference, the second item is the student's first name, the third item is the last name, the fourth is an 8-digit date-of-birth in the order year, month, day, and the fifth item of each reference is an identifier assigned to the student by the school.

In this scenario there are two simple identity rules that are to be applied to this reference source. The first is that two references will be considered equivalent if they have the same first name, last name, and data-of-birth values. The second is that they will also be considered equivalent if they have the same last name, date-of-birth, and school identifier values.

The Oyster Source Descriptor in Figure A.9 reflects the layout of "Test1Source.txt" and the two identity rules as described above. In the <OyserSourceDescriptor> the reference source is given an internal name, in this case "TS1". The internal name is used to qualify the reference identifier values in the Link Index. It is also important that capture be enabled (Capture="Yes") when running a merge-purge configuration. Note that the <Source> statement of the document describes the source as a comma-delimited text file that does not use a text-qualifier character and where the first record of the file contains item labels. It also indicates that the file is located in the folder named "Test1" that is a sub-folder of the OYSTER folder. Each field of the reference source is described in an <Item> statement in the <ReferenceItems> list. Note that each <Item> statement has two names, a source-specific name "Name=" and system attribute name "Attribute=". This allows for the fact that different sources may provide different names for the same identity attribute or that one reference may contain more than one item with the same attribute.

The <IdentityRules> section defines the two rules. Note that in the rule descriptions, the items are indicated by their source name along with the type of match result that is required. In this scenario all attributes require an "Exact" match. Within a rule there is an implied AND logic that requires that all three match conditions must be met. However, between rules there is an implied OR logic that references will be considered equivalent when one or more of the rules are satisfied.

The system attribute names referenced in the <Item> statements of the Source Descriptor are defined in another XML document. Figure A.10 shows the XML Attributes script created for this scenario.

Once the Attributes Document, Source File, Source Descriptor Document, and Run Script have been created, the merge-purge scenario can be run. Figure A.11 shows the command line prompt that appears after double-clicking on the OYSTER batch file.

```
┌──────────────────────────────────────────────────────────────────────┐
│ ▣ Test1SourceDescriptor - WordPad                            _ □ ×    │
├──────────────────────────────────────────────────────────────────────┤
│ File  Edit  View  Insert  Format  Help                                │
├──────────────────────────────────────────────────────────────────────┤
│ [D][☞][🖫]  [🖨][🖎][🗚]  [✂][🖹][🖺][↰]  [🖳]                         │
├──────────────────────────────────────────────────────────────────────┤
```

```xml
<?xml version="1.0" encoding="UTF-8"?>

<!--
    Document    : TestSource1Descriptor.xml
    Created on  : Sept 15, 2010
    Author      : Yinle Zhou
    Description : Demonstrate Merge-Purge Configuration of OYSTER
       with a single reference source Test1Source.txt as input
-->

<OysterSourceDescriptor Name="TS1" Capture="Yes">
    <!-- Delimited -->
    <Source Type="FileDelim" Char="," Qual="" Labels="Y">Z:\Oyster
\Test1\Test1Source.txt</Source>
    <!-- Items in Source -->
    <ReferenceItems>
        <Item Name="RefID" Attribute="@RefID" Pos="0"/>
        <Item Name="Fname" Attribute="StudentFirstName" Pos="1"/>
        <Item Name="Lname" Attribute="StudentLastName" Pos="2"/>
        <Item Name="DOBYMD" Attribute="StudentDateOfBirth" Pos="3"/>
        <Item Name="Scode" Attribute="StudentSchoolCode" Pos="4"/>
    </ReferenceItems>
    <!-- Identity Rules -->
    <IdentityRules>
        <Rule Ident="1">
            <Term Item="Fname" MatchResult="Exact"/>
            <Term Item="Lname" MatchResult="Exact"/>
            <Term Item="DOBYMD" MatchResult="Exact"/>
        </Rule>
        <Rule Ident="2">
            <Term Item="Lname" MatchResult="Exact"/>
            <Term Item="DOBYMD" MatchResult="Exact"/>
            <Term Item="Scode" MatchResult="Exact"/>
        </Rule>
    </IdentityRules>
</OysterSourceDescriptor>
```

**Figure A.9: Source Descriptor
for Test1Source.txt**

```
Test1Attributes - WordPad                                    _ □ ×

File  Edit  View  Insert  Format  Help

  <?xml version="1.0" encoding="UTF-8"?>

  <!--
      Document    : TestAttributes.xml
      Created on  : September 15, 2010
      Author      : John Talburt
      Description : Attributes for Student Demo Examples
  -->

  <OysterAttributes System="StudentDemo">
      <Attribute Item="StudentFirstName" />
      <Attribute Item="StudentLastName"  />
      <Attribute Item="StudentDateOfBirth" />
      <Attribute Item="StudentSchoolCode" />
  </OysterAttributes>

For Help, press F1                                            NUM
```

Figure A.10: Attributes Script for the "StudentDemo" System

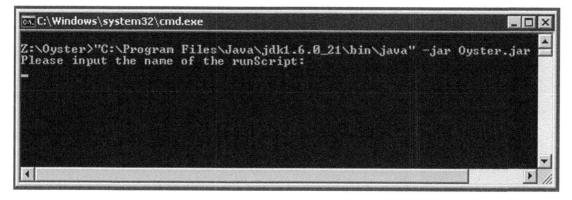

Figure A.11: Prompt for Run Script NameOnce the name of the Run Script has been entered, the program executes. Figure A.12 shows the execution of OYSTER when "Test1RunScript.xml" is entered for the Run Script name.

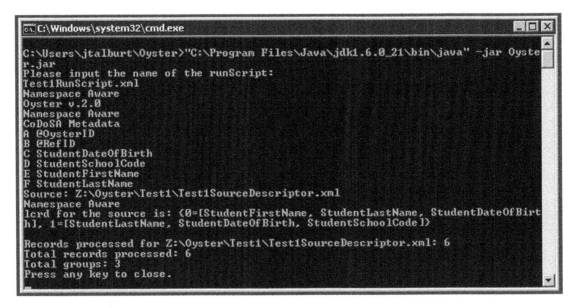

Figure A.12: OYSTER Execution of Test1RunScript. xml

If the run is successful, the Link Index "Test1Links.txt" is created in the Test1 folder as directed by Run Script. Figure A.13 shows the Test1 folder contents after the Run Script has been executed.

The Link Index created for the reference source "Test1Source. txt" is shown in Figure A.14. Note that the reference identifier is created by combining the name "TS1" given as the name of the source in the Source Descriptor (Figure A.9) with the value in the Reference ID field of the source (Figure A.8). This is necessary because OYSTER can process multiple sources in a single run some of which may duplicate the same reference identifier values. The source name from the descriptor is used to qualify the reference identifiers as a way to avoid duplicate references identifiers in the index.

The Link Index shown in Figure A.14 defines three clusters, {TS1.1, TS1.3, TS1.5}, {TS1.2, TS1.4}, and {TS1.6} with cluster identifier (link) values of 9RP2CJ61DRPJ3DQY, GCR13ZCN9TEHOBCK, and KIDHZ6U5EOX7ZD9Y, respectively. The identifier values are generated by hashing the identity structures with a 128-bit key and mapping the bit configuration into alphanumeric characters.

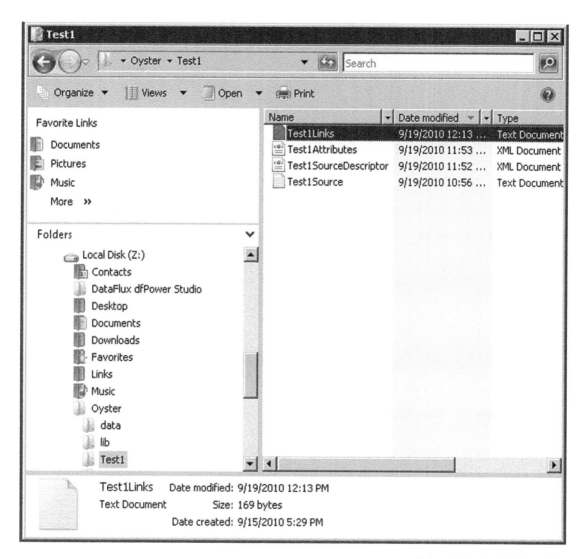

Figure A.13: Test1 Folder with Link Index

OYSTER Identity Capture Configuration

The Identity Capture Configuration for OYSTER is almost identical to the Merge-Purge configuration. The reason is that the OYSTER merge-purge process is based on capturing and creating an identity structure for each cluster of references that it links together. However like real-world merge-processes, these structures and the identity information they contain are discarded at the end of the process unless the run script directs them to be saved as shown in Figure A.15.

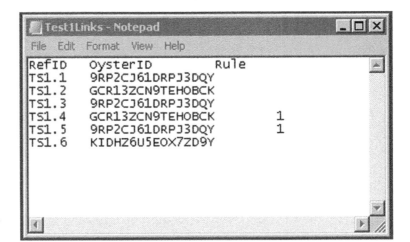

Figure A.14: The Link Index for Test1Source.txt

Figure A.15: An Identity Capture Run Script for Test1Source.txt

The file "Test2RunScript.xml" shown in Figure A.15 is a minor revision of the merge-purge run script "Test1RunScript.xml" shown in Figure A.7. It still references the same Attributes Document, Source, and Source Descriptor in folder Test 1 as in the merge-purge scenario. The primary difference is that Test2RunScript.xml specifies a path in <IdentityOutput> for the identity structures to be saved along with the Link Index in the folder Test 2.

The execution of the Run Script Test2RunScript.xml is shown in Figure A.16 and the files written to the Test2 folder are shown in Figure A.17.

The Link Index "Test2Links.txt" is identical to the Link Index produced in the previous merge-purge scenario and shown in Figure A.14. However in the Identity Capture configuration, a new file "Test2OuputIdentities.txt" is created containing the three identity structures preserving the information derived from the three clusters of references.

Figure A.16: OYSTER Execution of Test2RunScript.xml

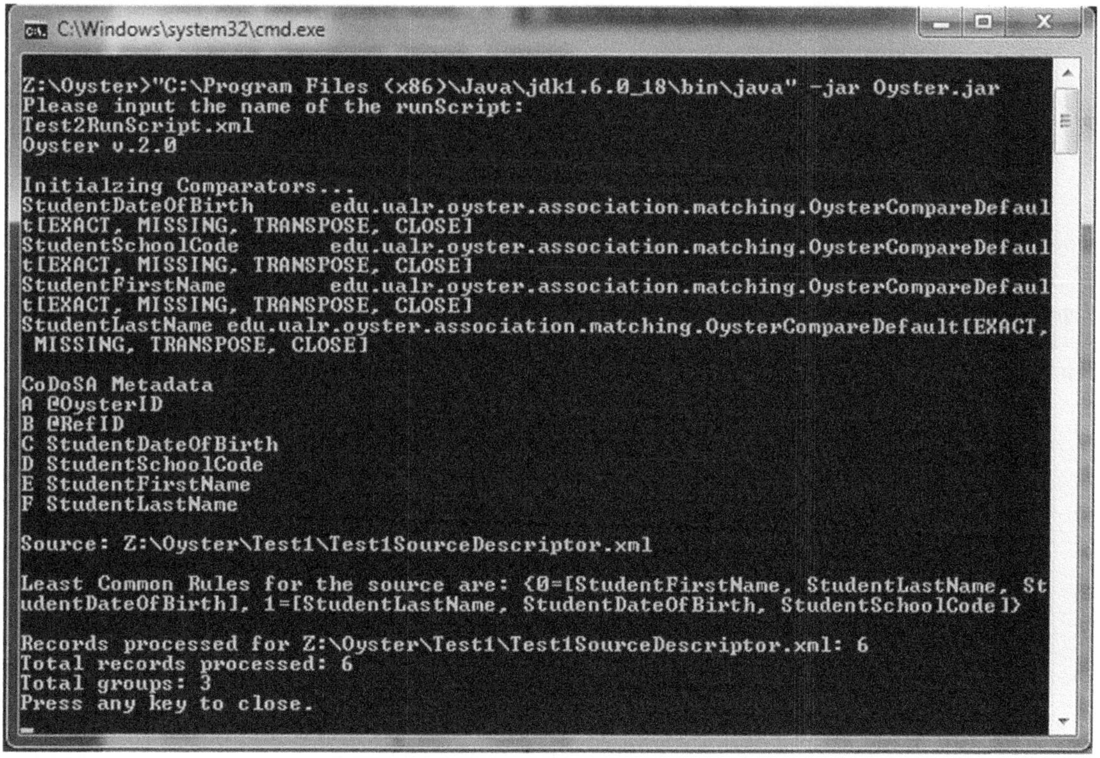

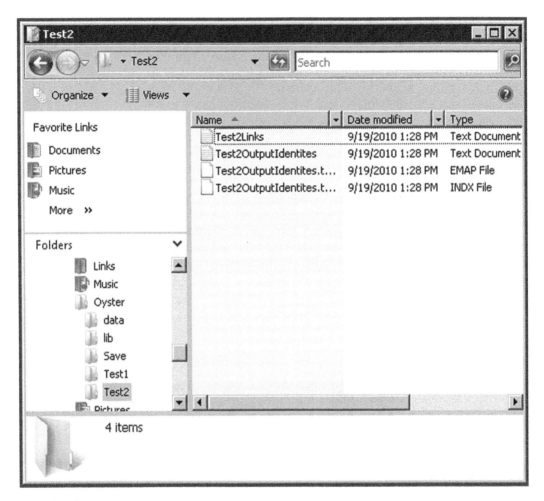

Figure A.17: Files Written to Folder Test2 in Identity Capture Configuration

By examining the identity structures created in the identity capture configuration it is easy to see how each one directly corresponds to one of the Link Index (clusters) shown in Figure A.14. The @RefID attribute shows the identifiers of the references that were used to create each identity, and conversely, the cluster identifiers in A.14 are the same as the identity identifiers in Figure A.18.

OYSTER Identity Build Configuration with Assertions

Running OYSTER in the Identity Capture Configuration allows identity information to be preserved and input into later

```
Test2OutputIdentities.txt - Notepad
File  Edit  Format  View  Help
<root>
<Identity Identifier="GCR13ZCN9TEHOBCK">
        <Attribute Name="@RefID">
                <Value>TS1.4</Value>
                <Value>TS1.2</Value>
        </Attribute>
        <Attribute Name="StudentFirstName">
                <Value>Mary</Value>
        </Attribute>
        <Attribute Name="StudentLastName">
                <Value>Smith</Value>
        </Attribute>
        <Attribute Name="StudentDateOfBirth">
                <Value>19990921</Value>
        </Attribute>
        <Attribute Name="StudentSchoolCode">
                <Value>H17</Value>
                <Value>G55</Value>
        </Attribute>
</Identity>
<Identity Identifier="9RP2CJ61DRPJ3DQY">
        <Attribute Name="@RefID">
                <Value>TS1.5</Value>
                <Value>TS1.3</Value>
                <Value>TS1.1</Value>
        </Attribute>
        <Attribute Name="StudentFirstName">
                <Value>Eddie</Value>
                <Value>Edgar</Value>
        </Attribute>
        <Attribute Name="StudentLastName">
                <Value>Jones</Value>
        </Attribute>
        <Attribute Name="StudentDateOfBirth">
                <Value>20001104</Value>
        </Attribute>
        <Attribute Name="StudentSchoolCode">
                <Value>G34</Value>
                <Value>H15</Value>
        </Attribute>
</Identity>
<Identity Identifier="KIDHZ6U5EOX7ZD9Y">
        <Attribute Name="@RefID">
                <Value>TS1.6</Value>
        </Attribute>
        <Attribute Name="StudentFirstName">
                <Value>Super</Value>
        </Attribute>
```

Figure A.18: The Identity Structures Created in Test 2

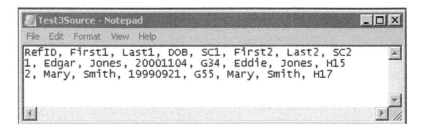

Figure A.19: Assertion Source

processes that run in the Identity Resolution Configuration. Often these identities are built from a set of assertion sources that represent knowledge about the entities.

The assertion source is shown in Figure A.19. Each assertion relates two first and second name pairs at two schools. The assertions are captured by running OYSTER in Identity Capture Configuration as shown in Figure A.20.

The resulting identities created by this run script are shown in Figure A.21.

```xml
<?xml version="1.0" encoding="UTF-8"?>
<!--
    Document    : Test3RunScript.xml
    Created on  : Sept 15, 2010
    Author      : John Talburt
    Description: Identity Build From Assertions-->

<OysterRunScript>
    <Settings Explanation="On" Debug="On" />
    <AttributePath>Z:\Oyster\Test1\Test1Attributes.xml</AttributePath>
    <!-- No input identities -->
    <IdentityInput Type="None" />
    <!-- Identity Build for Later Resolution -->
    <IdentityOutput Type="TextFile">Z:\Oyster
\Test3\Test3OutputIdentities.txt</IdentityOutput>

    <!-- Link Index is output but not used -->
    <LinkOutput Type="TextFile">Z:\Oyster\Test3\Test3Links.txt</LinkOutput>
    <!-- Sources to Run -->
    <ReferenceSources>
        <Source Capture="Yes">Z:\Oyster\Test3\Test3SourceDescriptor.xml</Source>
    </ReferenceSources>
</OysterRunScript>
```

Figure A.20: OYSTER Run Script to Build Identities from Assertion Source

```
Test3OutputIdentities - Notepad
File   Edit   Format   View   Help

<root>
<Identity Identifier="U0ZWFPVYULM7BC3X">
        <Attribute Name="@RefID">
                <Value>AS1.1</Value>
        </Attribute>
        <Attribute Name="StudentFirstName">
                <Value>Edgar</Value>
                <Value>Eddie</Value>
        </Attribute>
        <Attribute Name="StudentLastName">
                <Value>Jones</Value>
        </Attribute>
        <Attribute Name="StudentDateOfBirth">
                <Value>20001104</Value>
        </Attribute>
        <Attribute Name="StudentSchoolCode">
                <Value>G34</Value>
                <Value>H15</Value>
        </Attribute>
</Identity>
<Identity Identifier="TQP4W3QITA4QXJYM">
        <Attribute Name="@RefID">
                <Value>AS1.2</Value>
        </Attribute>
        <Attribute Name="StudentFirstName">
                <Value>Mary</Value>
        </Attribute>
        <Attribute Name="StudentLastName">
                <Value>Smith</Value>
        </Attribute>
        <Attribute Name="StudentDateOfBirth">
                <Value>19990921</Value>
        </Attribute>
        <Attribute Name="StudentSchoolCode">
                <Value>G55</Value>
                <Value>H17</Value>
        </Attribute>
</Identity>
</root>
```

Figure A.21: Identities Built from Assertion Source

OYSTER Identity Resolution Configuration

The distinguishing characteristic of the OYSTER Identity Resolution Configuration is that identity structures are input prior to processing any of the reference sources as indicated in Figure A.5. In many respects, the input identities act like a filter. A reference that does not resolve to one of the input identities does not create a new identity (when not in capture mode) and is given a special identifier value to indicate that it was not resolved.

The run script shown is Figure A. 22 resolves the set of references built in the previous step (Figure A. 21) against the set of references shown in Figure A. 23.

Figure A.22: OYSTER Run Script for Identity Resolution

Test4RunScript.xml - Notepad

File Edit Format View Help

```
<?xml version="1.0" encoding="UTF-8"?>
<!--
    Document    : Test4RunScript.xml
    Created on : Sept 15, 2010
    Author      : John Talburt
    Description: Identity Resolution Test -->

<OysterRunScript>
    <Settings Explanation="On" Debug="On" />
    <AttributePath>Z:\Oyster\Test1\Test1Attributes.xml</AttributePath>
    <!-- Input identites are output from Test3 Identity Build-->
    <IdentityInput Type="TextFile">Z:\Oyster
\Test3\Test3OutputIdentities.txt</IdentityInput>
    <!-- No identity output in identity resolution -->
    <IdentityOutput Type="None" />
    <!-- Link Index  -->
    <LinkOutput Type="TextFile">Z:\Oyster\Test4\Test4Links.txt</LinkOutput>
    <!-- Sources to Run -->
    <ReferenceSources>
        <Source>Z:\Oyster\Test4\Test4SourceDescriptor.xml</Source>
    </ReferenceSources>
</OysterRunScript>
```

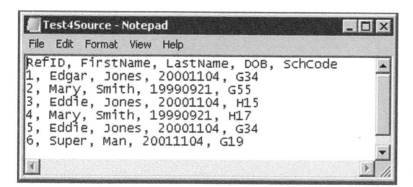

Figure A.23: References Input into Identity Resolution

The input references are the same six references to Edgar Jones, Mary Smith, and Super Man that were used in the merge-purge scenario and shown in Figure A.8. However in the identity resolution scenario, the references are run with identity capture off.

The execution of the Test4RunScript.xml as shown in Figure A.24 results in the link index shown in Figure A.25.

Figure A.24: Execution of the Identity Resolution Run Script (Test 4)

```
C:\Windows\system32\cmd.exe                                    _ □ X

C:\Users\jtalburt\Oyster>"C:\Program Files\Java\jdk1.6.0_21\bin\java" -jar Oyste
r.jar
Please input the name of the runScript:
Test3RunScript.xml
Namespace Aware
Oyster v.2.0
Namespace Aware
CoDoSA Metadata
A  @OysterID
B  @RefID
C  StudentDateOfBirth
D  StudentSchoolCode
E  StudentFirstName
F  StudentLastName
Source: Z:\Oyster\Test3\Test3SourceDescriptor.xml
Namespace Aware
lcrd for the source is: {0=[StudentFirstName, StudentLastName, StudentDateOfBirt
h, StudentSchoolCode]}

Records processed for Z:\Oyster\Test3\Test3SourceDescriptor.xml: 2
Total records processed: 2
Total groups: 2
Press any key to close.
```

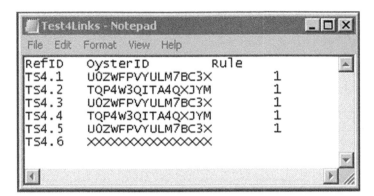

Figure A.25: Identity Resolution Link Index

Not that in the link index shown in Figure A.25 that reference 6 did not resolve to either of the two identities input into the resolution process as indicated by the link identifier value "XXXXXXXXXXXXXXXX". References 1, 3, and 5 resolved to the Edgar Jones identity and References 2 and 4 to the Mary Smith identity.

INDEX

Note: Page numbers followed by *f* indicate figures and followed by *t* indicate tables.

Printed and bound by CPI Group (UK) Ltd, Croydon, CR0 4YY

03/10/2024

01040310-0001